MISSOURI

Also in This Series

Arizona, Malcolm L. Comeaux

Colorado, Thomas Melvin Griffiths and Lynell Rubright

Hawaii, Joseph R. Morgan

Maryland, James E. DiLisio

New Jersey, Charles A. Stansfield, Jr.

Texas, Terry G. Jordan, with John L. Bean, Jr., and William M. Holmes

Wyoming, Robert Harold Brown

Forthcoming Through 1984

Alaska, Roger W. Pearson and Donald F. Lynch

Michigan, Lawrence M. Sommers

Mississippi, Jesse O. McKee

North Carolina, Ole Gade and H. Daniel Stillwell

South Carolina, Charles F. Kovacik and John J. Winberry

Utah, Clifford B. Craig

All books in this series are available in paperback and hardcover.

Geographies of the United States
Ingolf Vogeler, General Editor

Missouri: A Geography
Milton D. Rafferty

Missouri—from the gateway arch in St. Louis to the Pony Express stables in St. Joseph, from the Ozarks of the south to the rolling, corn-studded hills of the north—is the subject of this comprehensive geography. Dr. Rafferty brings together a wealth of information about Missouri's resources and people, tracing the theme of persistence versus change in the relationship between man and the land. He examines Missouri's natural setting and endowments, the imprint of its settlers, its economy, its political geography, and its four largest urban centers—St. Louis, Kansas City, Springfield, and St. Joseph. Historical background provides a context in which to understand geographic aspects of current human experience in a state that once was the starting point for a westward stream of covered wagons and now launches jetliners, that has seen both coal-burning steamboats and coal-bearing barges on its mighty rivers, and that continues to be a crossroads of East and West, North and South.

Dr. Milton D. Rafferty is professor and head of the Department of Geography and Geology at Southwest Missouri State University in Springfield. Missouri has been his particular area of study for the past fifteen years; this book incorporates much of his original research. His publications include *The Ozarks: Land and Life* and *Historical Atlas of Missouri*.

MISSOURI
A GEOGRAPHY
Milton D. Rafferty

Westview Press / Boulder, Colorado

Geographies of the United States

Portions of Chapters 1, 2, 4, and 5 in this book are adapted from the author's previous research published in *Ozarks: Land and Life* © 1980 by University of Oklahoma Press. The author is grateful for the kind permission of the press to use material from this book.

Copyright © 1983 by Westview Press, Inc.

Published in 1983 in the United States of America by
  Westview Press, Inc.
  5500 Central Avenue
  Boulder, Colorado 80301
  Frederick A. Praeger, President and Publisher

Library of Congress Cataloging in Publication Data
Rafferty, Milton D., 1932–
  Missouri, a geography.
  (Geographies of the United States)
  Includes bibliographies and index.
  1. Missouri—Description and travel. 2. Missouri—Historical geography. I. Title. II. Series.
F466.R33 1983   917.78   82-23817
ISBN 0-86531-068-8
ISBN 0-86531-435-7 (pbk.)

Printed and bound in the United States of America

CONTENTS

FIGURES

TABLES

PHOTOGRAPHS

ILLUSTRATION CREDITS

The following sources provided data for the figures indicated.

Fig. 1.1: Nevin M. Fenneman, *Physiography of Eastern United States* (New York: McGraw-Hill, 1938). **Fig. 1.2:** U.S.G.S., Topographic maps, 1/250,000 series. **Fig. 1.3:** William D. Thornbury, *Regional Geomorphology of the United States* (New York: John Wiley and Sons, 1963). **Fig. 1.4:** Missouri Geology and Land Survey Map, 1/500,000 scale, 1961. **Fig. 1.5:** James Penick, Jr., *The New Madrid Earthquake of 1811–12* (Columbia: University of Missouri Press, 1976). **Figs. 2.1, 2.2, 2.3:** U.S., Department of Agriculture, Weather Bureau, *Climatic Summary of the United States,* Sections 53–55 (Washington, D.C.: 1932). **Figs. 2.4, 2.7, 2.8:** C. L. Scrivner, J. C. Baker, and B. J. Miller, *Soils of Missouri: A Guide to Their Identification and Interpretation* (Columbia: Extension Division, University of Missouri, no date). **Figs. 2.5, 2.6:** C. L. Scrivner and James C. Baker, *Evaluating Missouri Soils,* Circular 915 (Columbia: University of Missouri, 1970). **Fig. 2.9:** U.S., Forest Service, *Geology and Landforms of Peckout Hollow* (mimeograph) (Rolla, Missouri: no date). **Figs. 2.10, 3.3:** Missouri Official Highway Map, 1981–1982. **Fig. 3.1:** Eugene Morrow Violette, *A History of Missouri* (New York: Heath and Company, 1918). **Fig. 3.2:** Daniel H. Ehrlich, "Problems Arising from Shifts of the Missouri River on the Eastern Border of Nebraska," *Nebraska History* 54, no. 3 (Fall 1973), pp. 341–363. **Fig. 3.4:** J. S. Jenner, "Areal Expansion of the City of St. Louis" (master's thesis, Washington University [St. Louis], 1939). **Fig. 3.5:** Missouri County Highway Map, St. Francois County. **Figs. 3.6, 3.7:** Norman Brown, "Missouri Land Surveys" (lecture presented at Southwest Missouri State University, Springfield, April 1980). **Figs. 4.1, 4.2:** Milton D. Rafferty, *The Ozarks: Land and Life* (Norman: University of Oklahoma Press, 1980). **Fig. 4.3:** James R. Shortridge, "The Expansion of the Settlement Frontier in Missouri," *Missouri Historical Review* 75 (October 1980), pp. 64–90. **Fig. 5.1:** Russel L. Gerlach, "Population Origins in Rural Missouri," *Missouri Historical Review* 71 (October 1976), pp. 1–21. **Figs. 5.2, 5.3, 5.4, 5.5, 5.6, 5.7, 13.2, 13.3:** U.S., Department of Commerce, Bureau of the Census, *Census of Population, 1980,* vol. 1, chapter A, part 27, "Missouri"; vol. 1, chapter B, part 27, "Missouri" (Washington, D.C.: Government Printing Office, 1982). **Fig. 5.4:** U.S., Department of the Interior, Census Office, *Census of Population, 1890* (Washington, D.C.: Government Printing Office, 1895). **Fig. 5.5:** U.S., Department of Commerce, Bureau of the Census, *Census of Population, 1940* (Washington, D.C.: Government Printing Office, 1942). **Fig. 6.1:** Hayward M. Wharton et al., *Missouri Minerals—Resources, Production, and Forecasts,* Missouri Geological Survey and Water Resources Special Publication no. 1 (Rolla, Missouri: 1969). **Figs. 7.1, 7.2, 7.3, 7.4, 7.5, 7.6, 7.8, 7.9:** Missouri Department of Agriculture, Crop and Livestock Reporting Service, *Missouri Farm Facts, 1980* (Jefferson

City; 1980). **Figs. 8.1, 9.4, 13.4:** Milton D. Rafferty, *Historical Atlas of Missouri* (Norman: University of Oklahoma Press, 1982). **Figs. 9.1, 9.2:** David Moser et al., *Missouri's Transportation System: Condition, Capacity, and Impediments to Efficiency* (Jefferson City, Mo.: Office of Administration, Division of Budget and Planning, 1976). **Fig. 9.3:** Official Map of Missouri, 1910; Rand McNally Map of Missouri, 1975; and Paul W. Gates, "The Railroads of Missouri, 1850–1870," *Missouri Historical Review* 26, (January 1932), pp. 126–141. **Figs. 11.1, 11.2, 11.3:** Missouri Office of Secretary of State, 1982. **Fig. 11.4:** Gordon D. Friedman, "Voting Trends in Missouri Primary Elections, 1908–1972" (paper presented at the annual meeting of the Missouri Political Science Association, Lake of the Ozarks, November 16, 1973). **Figs. 12.1, 12.5:** U.S., Department of Commerce, Bureau of the Census, *Major Retail Centers in Standard Metropolitan Statistical Areas, Missouri* (Washington, D.C.: U.S. Government Printing Office, 1980). **Fig. 12.2:** Robert L. Koepke, "Industry in the Saint Louis Metropolitan Area: A Guidebook for the Industrial Field Trip, St. Louis Meeting, Association of American Geographers" (mimeograph) (Edwardsville: Southern Illinois University, 1967). **Fig. 12.4:** Metropolitan Kansas City Industrial Map (Chamber of Commerce, 1970). **Fig. 12.6:** U.S.G.S., Quadrangles. **Figs. 12.7, 12.8:** Springfield Planning Department maps. **Fig. 13.1:** James E. Collier, "Geographic Regions of Missouri," *Annals of the Association of American Geographers* 45 (1955), pp. 368–392. **Figs. 13.2, 13.3:** John S. Holik, *Population Change of Missouri Towns 1890–1960* B821 (Columbia: University of Missouri, Agricultural Experiment Station, 1964).

PREFACE

Missouri: A Geography is the product of fifteen years of research and travel in the state. Much of the text is drawn from material prepared for a course on the geography of Missouri that I have taught at Southwest Missouri State University. A substantial amount of material stems from original research conducted by myself and by students for class projects and reports. Personal interviews and direct field observations, including visits to nearly all of the places I discuss, have resulted from my own desire to see and know Missouri.

The book is intended to give the reader a comprehensive overview of the physical and cultural geography of the state. I have relied on maps and photographs to present geographic information concisely and accurately. The organization, both topical and regional, is designed to serve the needs of educators, students, state officials, businesspeople and the interested public. Missouri's physical diversity, historical development, population characteristics, transportation facilities, major economic activities, political patterns, and other features are described and interpreted.

I wish to extend thanks to agencies and individuals who have helped me. State agencies that provided maps, data, photographs, and other assistance include the Missouri Department of Natural Resources, the Missouri Department of Agriculture, the Missouri Department of Conservation, and the Missouri Division of Tourism. Special thanks also go to Elias Johnson, associate professor of geography, Southwest Missouri State University, who made numerous valuable suggestions for map design, and to Debbie Dohne and Susan Lee, my coworkers in the department who assisted with typing. Finally, I wish to thank those alert students whose critical discussions in the classroom and keen observations in the field have helped me to appreciate new values in Missouri geography.

Milton D. Rafferty

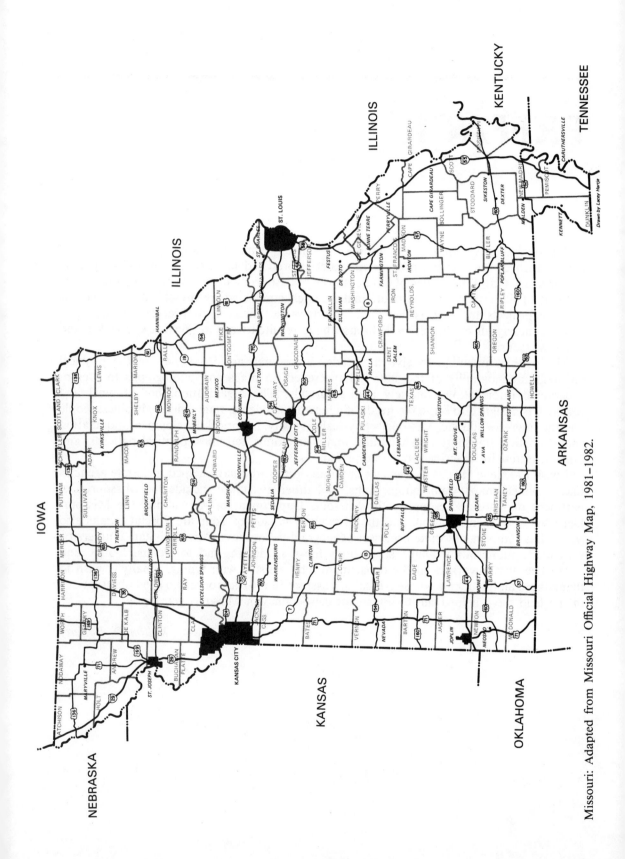

Missouri: Adapted from Missouri Official Highway Map, 1981–1982.

CHAPTER 1

GEOLOGY AND PHYSIOGRAPHY

The name *Missouri* first appeared on maps of French explorers in the 1600s. It was the name of a group of Indians living near the mouth of a river, and the French naturally gave that name to the river. From the river it was transferred later to the state through which the river ran. Even Missourians cannot agree how to pronounce Missouri. In a recent survey slightly over half the people interviewed pronounce the name "Missour-uh" whereas a little less than half pronounce it "Missour-ee." People in eastern Missouri seem to favor "Missour-ee," and western Missourians prefer "Missour-uh."

PHYSIOGRAPHY

Missouri has within its boundaries more varied natural features than those found in the states that adjoin it, except Kentucky, Tennessee, and Arkansas. These features vary not only in detail but in general character. Four of the major physiographic provinces of the United States extend into Missouri (Figure 1.1). The northern part of the state is in the Dissected Till Plains; the western section is in the Osage Cuestas Region; most of the southern part is in the Ozark Upland Region of the Interior Highlands Province; and the southeastern part (referred to as the Mississippi Alluvial Plain), including the Bootheel, is the Coastal Plain Province.

The northern, western, and southeastern parts of the state are primarily rolling or level, the southern part mainly rough. Roughness or smoothness is a function of the depth and width of valleys. The depth of a valley depends upon the elevation of the country into which it has been cut; and its width depends upon the size of the stream that has made it, the time the stream has been at work, and the relative hardness of the rocks in which it has been cut.

In the Ozarks, the valleys are cut in limestone, which is relatively hard rock, whereas in the northern part the valleys are cut in soft shale. Because the Ozark region was higher than the Dissected Till Plains Region when the streams cut their valleys, the valleys in the south are narrower and deeper than those in the north. Occasionally resistant limestone beds in the north and small areas of smooth country in the hilly region occur. The pioneers who settled the level upland tracts in the Ozarks referred to them as prairies because of the bluestem and other tall grasses that grew there. The division between the Ozark and plains regions is indistinct, but roughly it follows the Missouri River from its mouth near St. Louis to the vicinity of Miami; then it runs south to Windsor and then southwest to where the Spring River crosses

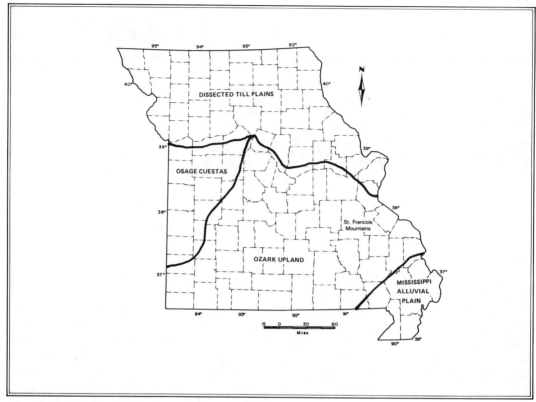

FIGURE 1.1.   Physiographic Provinces of Missouri.

the Missouri-Kansas boundary. South and east of this imperfect line are the Ozarks, north and west of it is the prairie region.

The Ozarks extend beyond Missouri into Arkansas and Oklahoma. The general structure of the region in Missouri is that of an elliptical dome, highest along the central line running from a point near Ste. Genevieve beside the Mississippi River to the state line near the southwestern corner of Stone County.

The elevation of the country around the edge of the dome-shaped Ozark Region varies from 600 ft (183 m) to 800 ft (244 m) above sea level, and the crest of the eroded dome varies from 1,400 ft (427 m) to 1,700 ft (518 m). From the line of highest elevation, the drainage runs north to the Osage, Gasconade, Missouri, and Meramec rivers and south to the White, Black, Current, and St. Francis rivers. All of the drainage streams have cut valleys. Toward

the heads of the streams that flow north, the valleys are shallow and rather wide, because the streams are small and flow a great distance before reaching large rivers. The same characteristic is true of the streams flowing southeast from the central part of Howell County. The streams flowing south from the western part of the Ozarks, however, have cut deep, narrow valleys.

The streams of the Ozarks are remarkable because they cut deeply into the plateau yet follow meandering courses. This unusual pattern may have evolved because the courses of the streams were established while they drained a low-lying plain, and the entrenchment occurred gradually as the region was uplifted over a long period of time. The districts along major streams are characterized by bold limestone bluffs, often located along the outside bends of meander loops. Not infrequently the processes of weathering and erosion have resulted in

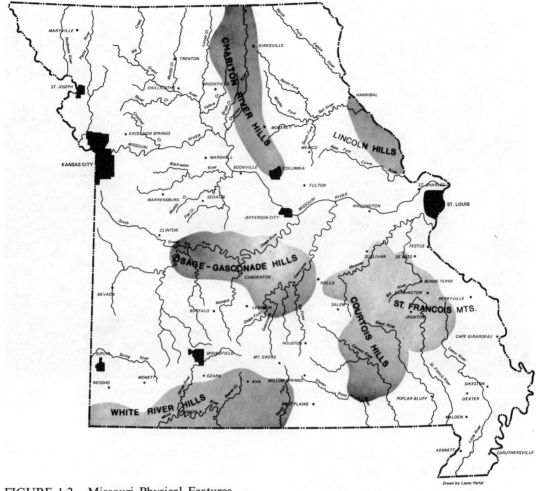

FIGURE 1.2. Missouri Physical Features.

cut-off meander loops and the isolation of hills in the center. These isolated hills are known as lost hills because they are detached from neighboring ridges or uplands. Cote Sans Dessien, located in the Missouri alluvial valley east of Jefferson City, is an example of another type of lost hill. This spectacular hill was isolated by lateral erosion of the Missouri and Maries rivers.

The limestones and dolomites of the Ozarks are subject to solution by groundwater. Over millions of years the movement of water through cracks and crevices in the rock has resulted in solution channels, caves, springs, and the development of sinkholes and solution valleys. Large collapsed sinkholes, such as Grand Gulf near Koshkonong, cone-shaped sinks as much as 80 ft (24.38 m) deep, and natural bridges are other solution features. Because water moves freely through the limestone, many of the small surface streams are dry much of the year. Many streams lose water through subsurface channels and dry up a few miles downstream from points where water is flowing freely at the surface. Such streams are referred to as losing streams or losers. A second, smaller area of mature karst landscape lies outside the Ozarks in the Lincoln Hills in Pike, Ralls, and Lincoln counties. The caves Mark Twain memorialized in *Tom Sawyer* and *Huckleberry Finn* formed in the same bedrock as the caves in southwest Missouri.

PHOTO 1.1.   Arch of Natural Bridge at Grand Gulf near Thayer. Courtesy Walker—Missouri Division of Tourism.

With the exception of the St. Francois Mountains, the central Ozarks are not as high as portions of the Springfield Plain (Springfield Plateau) and the Boston Mountain Plateau in Arkansas (approximately 2,500 ft, or 767 m). But around the central region, the countryside is somewhat rugged; the valleys are deep and narrow; and in the districts of the Courtois Hills, the Osage-Gasconade Hills, and the White River Hills, the country is completely cut by innumerable deep ravines. The Springfield Plain is less rugged and slopes west to the Osage Cuestas (plain).

The Osage Cuestas Region is lowest along its border with the Ozark Region and rises gradually west, or slightly northwest. Along the southern and southeastern borders of the Osage Cuestas Region the elevation varies from 600 ft (183 m) to 800 ft (244 m) above sea level. In the northwestern part, elevations range between 1,000 ft (304 m) and 1,100 ft (335 m). The rise occurs in a series of successively higher steps west. Each of the steps makes up a cuesta, or an asymmetric ridge with a steep east-facing slope and a more gradual western slope that follows the tilt (dip) of the rock layers. The trend of the cuestas is northeast and southwest. The most prominent of the steps is the Bethany Escarpment, which is formed by resistant Bethany Falls limestone.

The rivers of northern Missouri flow to either the Missouri or the Mississippi. Those flowing into the Missouri River have a southerly course, usually almost due south, and those flowing to the Mississippi flow to the southeast. The larger streams, such as the Nodaway, One Hundred and Two, Platte, Grand, Chariton, Des Moines, Wyaconda, Fabius, Salt, and Cuivre, have valleys as much as 5 miles (8 km) wide, with flat, meadowlike floors over which

PHOTO 1.2. Big Spring near Van Buren, Carter County. Courtesy Walker—Missouri Division of Tourism.

the stream channels meander in winding courses. Meander scars, oxbow lakes, backwater swamps and marshes, and sandbars are typical landforms found in the floodplains of these streams. The upland is undulating and rarely too steep for cultivation.

Karst Landscapes

Missouri is noted for its large areas of maturely developed karst landscape. The numerous large springs, caverns, sinkholes, solution valleys, and subsurface pinnacles and solution channels attest to the striking physiographic character of the Ozarks and the Lincoln Hills of northeastern Missouri. In these areas, all of the conditions for full development of karst features are present. First, these districts are underlain by soluble carbonate rocks, predominantly limestones. Second, the limestones and dolomites are mainly dense, jointed, and

sometimes thin bedded. Third, the valleys of the major streams are entrenched 100 ft (30.4 m) to 300 ft (91.4 m) below the upland surface, allowing adequate drainage through the subterranean channels; and, fourth, precipitation averages 41 in. (104.14 cm) per year, an amount adequate to maintain bedrock in active solution.

Although virtually all parts of the Ozarks exhibit karst landforms, their distribution is by no means uniform. The most common and most striking surface features are sinkholes and solution valleys. These features tend to be developed on broad interfluves between major rivers and creeks. Meteoric water percolates into the sinks, flows through subsurface channels frequently several miles long, and ultimately issues as springs in the banks and bluffs of streams. The sources of the largest springs, such as Big Spring and Meramec Spring, are as much as 40 miles (64.36 km) away.

PHOTO 1.3.   Fantastic Caverns near Springfield. Courtesy Walker—Missouri Division of Tourism.

Some of the most striking karst is in the Mississippian period Boone formation. The large sinkholes in the Mississippian rocks near Perryville in the eastern Ozarks, the large caves and caverns in the Springfield Plain, and the caverns of the Lincoln Hills in northeastern Missouri are notable examples of this formation.

Karst areas have a very fragile ecological system. Because sinkholes connect directly with aquifers, groundwater supplies are easily polluted. Sinks are often used as receptacles for disposal of waste and refuse. Furthermore, because water frequently travels long distances in subsurface channels, it is difficult to identify specific sources of pollution. Drainage from septic household waste-disposal systems presents an especially critical hazard in urban areas where subdivisions are extended beyond existing sewer lines and in heavily settled rural areas, such as lakeside second-home

and retirement-home developments.

Origin of the Southeast Missouri Lowlands and Ridges

In southeastern Missouri the Mississippi River has abandoned two valleys and now occupies a third. In each case a smaller stream has attracted and drawn the large stream away from part of its established course. Small tributaries of the Ohio captured the Mississippi on these two occasions. (Stream captures resulting in minor shifts in course have also occurred.) As a result of the stream capture and valley abandonment, several ridges and hills break the continuity of the alluvial valley floor. The northernmost ridge is the Commerce Hills in Scott County. West of the Commerce Hills lie Hickory Ridge and smaller upland remnants in Cape Girardeau and Scott counties, and to the southwest is Crowley's Ridge, the largest of the uplands

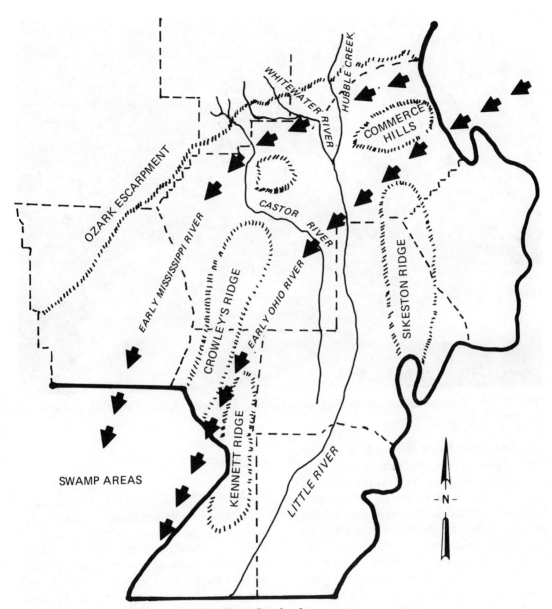

FIGURE 1.3. Landforms in the Southeast Lowlands.

in the valley. This ridge extends for about 200 miles (322 km) from Stoddard County, Missouri, to Helena, Arkansas, although it is broken by gaps at several places (Figure 1.3). Crowley's Ridge and the Commerce Hills rise as much as 200 ft (61 m) above the valley floor. The bedrock core of these uplands consists of Tertiary (Eocene) period rocks plus some small patches of Cretaceous rocks. Above the bedrock is a cover of Pliocene Lafayette gravels and loess.

The original course of the Mississippi River probably lay well to the west side of the alluvial valley, crowding the Paleozoic rocks of the Ozark Upland. Then the river, where it left the area of Paleozoic rock and entered the upper end of the alluvial valley, followed the Drum Lowland route to the west of Crowley's Ridge (Figure

PHOTO 1.4.   Johnson's Shut-ins in Reynolds County. Courtesy Walker—Missouri Division of Tourism.

1.3). The Ohio River followed the Cache Valley route across southern Illinois, and instead of joining the Mississippi near the head of the alluvial valley, as it does now, followed a route at the east side of the alluvial valley for about 400 miles (644 km) before merging with the Mississippi in middle Louisiana. Probably there were successive changes in position of the Mississippi River near the head of the alluvial valley before it established its present route through Thebes Gap and its junction with the Ohio near Cairo, Illinois. The river was diverted from its western route through the Drum Lowland to the Advance Lowland as a result of glacial outwash, which aggraded the bed, and a series of stream captures by Ohio tributaries. Most likely a further sequence of stream captures occurred, causing the Mississippi River to shift from the Advance Lowland to the Morehouse Lowland and then to the present Thebes Gap route through the Commerce Hills.

GEOLOGY

Rock Formation

Missouri rocks are mainly sedimentary, formed by the settling of masses of sediment into beds, and igneous, formed by the solidification of hot mixtures of minerals. The oldest rocks are igneous and appear at the surface in the St. Francois Mountains in southeastern Missouri. The igneous rocks are of two kinds, granites and porphyries. It may be imagined that ages ago the surface of Missouri consisted of lava with molten rock beneath. The lava probably cooled quickly and formed rhyolite porphyries, rocks consisting of large crystals embedded in a groundmass of finer crystals. Streams have cut into the resistant felsites forming steep-walled "shut-ins" in numerous locations. Johnson's Shut-ins near Lesterville are perhaps the most spectacular of these remarkable erosion features. Rhyolites of varying colors form most of the

PHOTO 1.5. Elephant Rocks near Graniteville, Iron County. Courtesy Walker—Missouri Division of Tourism.

symmetrical "knobs," or rounded mountains, of the St. Francois Mountains.

Beneath the insulating cover of rhyolites, other molten material solidified slowly to form a course-grained granite like that occurring in quarries near Graniteville. Missouri granite is composed of pink feldspar and clear, glassy quartz mineral grains. Huge blocks have weathered into spheroid shapes at various locations, notably at Elephant Rocks State Park near Graniteville.

The sedimentary rocks are of two main groups. One is limestone formed while Missouri was covered by water far from any land area. This limestone underlies 80 percent of the state south of the Missouri River and much of it north of the river. The other group of rocks was formed when Missouri was either part of a continent or covered by a shallow sea near land. Sand-

stones, shales, and certain limestones fall into this group.

Geologic History

Three of the four major time spans—the Cenozoic, Mesozoic, Paleozoic, and Precambrian (Proterozoic and Azoic) eras—are represented in Missouri along with nine of their subdivisions (periods). If all of these subdivisions were superimposed at any one place, they would make a column 3,500 ft (1,068 m) high from the top of the granites and rhyolites. The thickness of the igneous rock is unknown. The rocks of each age do not underlie the whole state, but the upfolding of beds or downcutting by streams has brought them to the surface at one place or another. The oldest rocks, in the St. Francois Mountains in Iron, Reynolds, and Madison counties, form

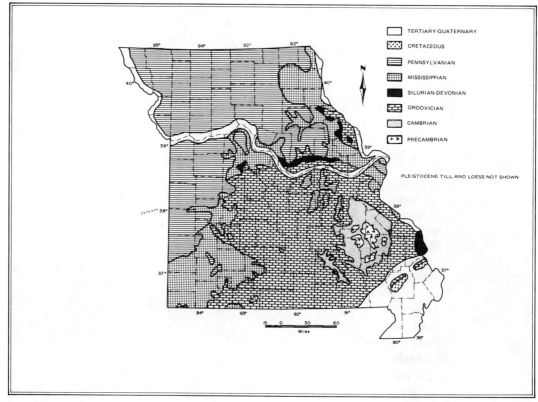

FIGURE 1.4.   Geologic Age of Bedrock.

the center of the Ozark dome and the beds that underlie large parts of Missouri, Kansas, Arkansas, Illinois, and Iowa. These rocks contain mineral resources from which these states draw much of their wealth.

For mapping purposes rocks are divided into groups, each group usually including more than one kind of rock or more than one formation. On the geologic map of Missouri (Figure 1.4), the Precambrian age granites and rhyolites, shown in a wedge pattern, are found in southern or southeastern Missouri. The main outcrops are in the St. Francois Mountains and smaller exposures in Shannon County, where the Current River has cut deeply into the overlying sedimentary rock layers. Centuries later an ocean invaded the valleys and rose high on the rounded igneous rock hills. The gravel and boulders accumulated on the low surface and were cemented to form the sandstones and conglomerates of the

Cambrian period Lamotte formation. Clay mud was washed far out to sea and upon compaction became the shale we see today. Gradually the land sank beneath the sea, and the calcium and magnesium that went into solution became limestone and dolomite (calcium-magnesium limestone) in the clear-water portion of the ocean. Bonne Terre dolomite, a gray and rather coarsely crystalline variety, was deposited in thick beds. It is comparatively free from flint (chert) and decomposes readily to a fertile and easily tilled red clay soil. Great deposits of disseminated lead, along with zinc, copper, and silver, have been found in this formation. The lead-zinc ores were mined for more than 250 years in the Old Lead Belt in St. Francois and Madison counties and are currently being mined in the New Lead Belt in western Iron and northern Reynolds counties.

Portions of the Cambrian dolomites

weathered, leaving barite, or barium sulfate (BaSO$_4$), locally known as tiff, as a concentrated ore deposit in the residual soil above the limestones. The "tiff district" of northeastern Washington County is one of the major barite-mining districts in the United States. Now the process of mining and washing barite is for the most part mechanized.

The second period of the Paleozoic era, the Ordovician, began with seas covering all of Missouri. Deposits of dolomite up to 500 ft (152 m) were laid down; then the seas retreated from most of the state, and many narrow valleys in the emerging surface eroded. The retreat of the seas was accompanied by a climatic change to very arid conditions. During the period, sand was deposited over large areas. The sandstone, called St. Peter, is loose and friable, easily quarried, and widely used in the manufacture of glass.

Following the deposition of the St. Peter sandstone, the seas advanced again and nearly the entire state was covered with dolomite (Gasconade formation), thin limestone (Kimmswick limestone), shale and sandstone (Roubidoux formation), and finally dolomite (Jefferson City dolomite). The predominant rocks of the Jefferson City formation are the thickly bedded, soft, white, noncrystalline "cotton rock" and the heavily bedded, slightly crystalline, gray limestone called spotted rock.

During the Silurian period, shallow seas covered only the southeast, northeast, and northwest extremities of Missouri. Limestones and shales accumulated to thicknesses of less than 100 ft (30 m). In the early part of the Devonian period, seas advanced over a small area near Grand Tower in Ste. Genevieve County, and in the late Devonian a narrow bay extended westward about 100 miles (160.8 km) from the mouth of the Missouri River and along the northeastern Missouri border.

After erosion in the late Devonian period, seas of the Mississippian period advanced from the east and the south, covering the state. Thick deposits of limestone were laid down, notably the St. Louis, Keokuk, and Burlington formations. These rock layers nearly encircle the Ozark Region and in Missouri form a continuous belt from Perry County to the extreme southwest. The end of the Mississippian period marked the final chapter of Missouri's marine history. The area was under the sea at various times thereafter, but for short periods only.

The later stratified rocks of Missouri are composed of land material. The first formation, a series of sand and clay beds— the Cherokee shales—was probably deposited around an Ozark island. The coal beds of practically all of central and southwestern coal-producing counties are in this formation. The total amount of coal in the state is approximately 83,000,000,000 tn (75,287,000,000 t). Limestones and shales were subsequently deposited on top of the coal-bearing formations. The Bethany Falls limestone is quarried extensively as a building stone and an ingredient in cement manufacture in the Kansas City vicinity.

In the Pennsylvanian period, fireclays formed in Missouri in two locations. The fireclays of Audrain and surrounding counties of north Missouri are sedimentary deposits of severely leached and highly purified residues from the weathering of rocks. The clay substance, much of it colloidal, was deposited in low-lying swamplands, which probably supported luxuriant growths of vegetation. Most of the deposits south of the Missouri River are in ancient sinkholes. Clay-filled sinks are strikingly exposed in the Interstate 44 road cuts near Rolla. In numerous localities iron ores are concentrated in sinkholes.

A small amount of oil and gas is present in Pennsylvanian rocks of western Missouri. There is also a small amount of heavy oil in sandstone beds in the same area, but it is not economically feasible, with present technology, to recover these resources. Major oil companies, after fairly extensive exploration, have cited few significant oil and gas possibilities in the state.

After the withdrawal of the seas from

Missouri late in the Pennsylvanian period, all of Missouri was land until late in the Mesozoic era. There is no evidence that Triassic or Jurassic seas entered Missouri, and not until the late Cretaceous period did the Gulf of Mexico extend as far north as the southeastern part of the state. Cretaceous period limestones and shales are exposed at the surface in the Commerce Hills and Crowley's Ridge in the Southeast Lowlands. Tertiary rocks—including some 400 ft (121.92 m) of marine and nonmarine sediments—were deposited when the Gulf of Mexico again entered the southeastern part of Missouri during the last phase of submergence.

After the Tertiary submergence, glaciation occurred. The first ice age (Nebraskan) advanced between 2,000,000 and 1,000,000 years ago, the second (Kansan) about 600,000 years ago, and the third (Illinoian) about 200,000 years ago. Along the Missouri River, which was the approximate southern boundary of the ice, and in a narrow belt down the Mississippi River lies a deposit of a porous, brownish clay loam, called loess. The loess, a fine material windblown from glacial outwash deposits onto the nearby bluffs, is narrowest along the elevated portion of the Missouri River between Jefferson City and Washington. It forms the basis of the most fertile large body of soil in the state. Just north of the loess belt is a belt of fine-grained, bluish clay, with occasional beds and pockets of sand. The two kinds of deposits grade indistinguishably into each other.

EARTHQUAKES

Missouri is situated in the part of North America that is generally free from serious earthquakes; nevertheless, on December 16, 1811, a quake of very high intensity occurred in the New Madrid region of southeast Missouri (Figure 1.5). Other severe quakes and minor shocks followed for several months. No deaths were known to have resulted because the area was only sparsely settled, but if a similar quake were

FIGURE 1.5.   The New Madrid Earthquake.

to occur today the loss of life and property would be great. Fissures opened in the ground, and craterlets and mounds of sand formed. The largest surface manifestation of the earthquake was the dropping of the basin, which subsequently filled with water to form Reelfoot Lake in western Tennessee, a short distance east of the Mississippi River. The lake—60 miles (96.54 km) to 70 miles (112 km) long, 3 (4.8 km) to 20 miles (32.1 km) wide, and in some places 50 ft (15.24 m) to 100 ft (30.48 m) deep—submerged the forest trees in the area. Further deep adjustments in the earth's crust have continued to take place north toward St. Louis, as indicated by the slight shocks that occasionally occur. Minor regional shocks occurred in 1967 and 1975.

CRYPTOEXPLOSIVE STRUCTURES

Six interesting geologic features occur in the Ozarks called cryptoexplosive (hidden explosive) structures. These structures, although isolated, seem to occur in a line along the same latitude, approximately 37°40′ N. Either igneous volcanic explosions or meteor impact caused them; but because some of the phenomena typical to each occurrence are not observable in each of the six structures, a controversy exists over their formation.

Sometimes meteors enter the earth's atmosphere almost simultaneously from the same orbit and, if large enough, crash to the earth's surface, forming large craters or upwarped, shattered rock structures (explosive structures). Since these meteorites can enter almost simultaneously from orbit, it is possible for large explosive structures to occur linearly. Small meteoric material has been found deposited in a linear fashion in a few other locations; thus geologists speculate that the Missouri craters are also the result of meteor impact.

SELECTED REFERENCES

Beveridge, Thomas R. *Geologic Wonders and Curiosities of Missouri.* Missouri Division of Geology and Land Survey, Educational Series, no. 4. Rolla, Mo., 1978.

Branson, Edwin Bayer. "The Geology of Missouri." *University of Missouri Studies,* vol. 19, no. 3. Columbia, 1944.

Bretz, J. Harlan. *Geomorphic History of the Ozarks of Missouri.* Missouri Geological Survey and Water Resources, 2d series, vol. 41. Rolla, Mo., 1965.

Collier, James E. "Geography of the Northern Ozark Border Region." *University of Missouri Studies,* vol. 26, no. 1. Columbia, 1953.

Cozzens, Arthur B. "The Natural Regions of the Ozark Province." Ph.D. dissertation, Washington University (St. Louis), 1937.

Dake, C. L. *The Sand and Gravel Resources of Missouri.* Missouri Bureau of Geology and Mines, 2d series, vol. 15. 1918.

Fenneman, Nevin M. *Physiography of Eastern United States.* New York: McGraw-Hill, 1938.

Flint, Timothy. *A Condensed Geography and History of the Western States or Mississippi Valley.* Vol. 2. Cincinnati: William M. Farnsworth, 1828.

Fuller, Mayron Leslie. *The New Madrid Earthquake.* U.S. Geological Survey Bulletin 494. 1912. Reprint. Cape Girardeau, Mo.: Ramfre Press, 1958.

Gist, Noel P., ed. *Missouri: Its Resources, People, and Institutions.* Columbia: Curators of the University of Missouri, 1950.

Greene, Frank, and R. M. Trowbridge. *Preglacial Drainage Pattern of Northwest Missouri.* Missouri Bureau of Geology and Mines, 58th Biannual Report, Appendix 7. Rolla, Mo., 1933–1934.

Hayes, William C., et al. *Guidebook to the Geology of the St. Francois Mountain Area.* Missouri Geological Survey and Water Resources Report of Investigations, no. 26. Rolla, Mo., 1961.

Magill, Arthur Clay. *Geography and Geology of the Southeast Missouri Lowland.* Edited by Felix Eugene Snyder. Cape Girardeau, Mo.: Ramfre Press, 1958.

Marbut, Curtis F. "The Physical Features of Missouri." *Missouri Geological Survey,* 1st series, vol. 10. Jefferson City, Mo., 1896.

Owen, Luella A. "The Loess at St. Joseph." *American Geologist,* vol. 33, pp. 223–228. 1904.

Penick, James, Jr. *The New Madrid Earthquake of 1811-12.* Columbia: University of Missouri Press, 1976.

Rafferty, Milton D. *The Ozarks: Land and Life.* Norman: University of Oklahoma Press, 1980.

Sauer, Carl O. *The Geography of the Ozark Highland of Missouri.* Geographical Society of Chicago Bulletin, no. 7. Chicago: University of Chicago Press, 1920.

Schmudde, Theodore H. "Some Aspects of Land Forms of the Lower Missouri River Floodplain." *Annals of the Association of American Geographers,* vol. 53, pp. 60–73. 1963.

Snyder, Frank G., et al. *Cryptoexplosive Structures in Missouri.* Missouri Geological Survey and Water Resources Report of Investigations, no. 30. Rolla, Mo., 1965.

Thacker, Joseph L., and Ira R. Satterfield. *Guidebook to the Geology Along Interstate 55 in Missouri.* Missouri Department of Natural Resources, Division of Geology and Land Survey Report of Investigations, no. 62. Rolla, Mo., 1977.

Thornbury, William D. *Regional Geomorphology of the United States.* New York: John Wiley and Sons, 1965.

CHAPTER 2

CLIMATE, VEGETATION, AND SOILS

WEATHER AND CLIMATE

Missouri's climate—the variable temperature, precipitation, and humidity that shape weather conditions and their long-term averages and extremes—is determined primarily by the state's mid-continent location in the middle latitudes. The altitudes and relief of the state are not sufficient to affect the climate of the region significantly.

Missouri's climate is so variable that a person living in the state only a year could not accurately estimate the weather for the next twelve months. Predicting the quality of the seasons would be similarly difficult: the experience of one summer or one winter would not give a dependable idea of general summer or of winter conditions.

Winds

The winds are largely cyclonic, and the weather variable. Missouri's temperatures are not greatly affected by the strong winter high-pressure cells of the north-central states, but in midwinter northern Missouri sometimes experiences prolonged cold spells brought on by strong continental polar air. Lesser lows and highs moving from the Great Plains Region cross the state regularly and bring changeable weather.

The prevailing wind is southerly or southeasterly. Northerly winds are frequent in northern Missouri and occur throughout the state in the winter months. In the summer, winds are stronger during the day than the night; but in the winter, winds are as common at night as during the day. At Springfield, the mean velocity is 10.1 miles (16.2 km) per hour, being highest in March (12.4 miles, or 19.9 km) and lowest in August (7.4 miles, or 11.9 km). The mean wind velocities for St. Louis and Kansas City are 9.5 miles (15.2 km) and 10.4 miles (16.7 km), respectively.

In midsummer, brisk wind from the southwest is likely to become a hot wind and may damage growing crops. For several weeks during late summer and early fall, there is little wind, the sun seems as hot as in midsummer, and the sky takes on a hazy, purplish color, especially in the late afternoon. Such weather is especially typical of southern Missouri. It is the renowned Indian summer of the Ozarks—the time of storing away crops for winter, gathering nuts and apples, and greeting tourists who come in large numbers to enjoy the Ozarks' finest season. In winter, cold brisk winds, sometimes accompanied by fine, dry snow, may blow from the north continuously for several days. At other times the brisk wind of the day quiets down with the approach of sunset, and the night is calm.

Tornadoes are an annual, usually spring and summer occurrence, invading Missouri from Oklahoma and Kansas. Therefore, the western border experiences more such storms than the rest of the state. The folk belief that tornadoes never visit the same location twice is not supported by the facts in Missouri. The vicinity of Springfield has been the site of tornadoes on at least five occasions (in 1880, 1883, 1915, 1972, and 1975). The first destroyed the town of Marshfield and resulted in at least a hundred deaths. The storm of 1972 did heavy damage in Republic and destroyed several airplanes and severely damaged buildings at the Springfield Municipal Airport. Tornadoes are more frequent from the first of April to June 30 but do occur in all months. The storm that visited the Springfield airport in 1972 was in mid-December. Both Kansas City and St. Louis have experienced damaging tornadoes on several occasions. As the cities grow in area and density, the chances of severe property destruction and multiple injuries or deaths increase greatly.

Improved tornado forecasting and storm-warning systems have done much to reduce deaths and injuries. The violent tornado that struck Neosho in April of 1975 at 5:00 P.M. caused severe property damage in residential areas and at a shopping center; but because of advanced warning there were no casualties, and the number of injuries was small.

Temperatures

The coldest month of the year in Missouri is January (see Figure 2.1). This does not necessarily mean that the temperature during January is always lower than it is during the other winter months, but an average January has a few more cold days than either an average December or an average February. January is also the month in which the temperatures in different parts of the state have the greatest disparity,

amounting to a maximum of 20°F (11°C) difference between the extreme north and south. (In April there is only 8°F [4.4°C] difference between the north and south, and in the three summer months almost none.)

Winter in Missouri usually sets in about the latter part of December and continues through January and February, with occasional cold spells in early March. Each of the winter months has twenty-two to twenty-seven days when the temperature during the warmest part of the day is at 32°F (0°C) or above and only one to three days when the temperature goes below 0°F (−18°C). In northern Missouri the cold periods last a bit longer, and in the southeast (particularly in the Bootheel) the cold weather is less severe and of shorter duration. The low temperatures of January nights average 28°F (−2.2°C) in the Bootheel, whereas the low in the north averages 16°F (−8.8°C). In both locations many nights are either much colder or much warmer. The daily maximum temperature in January varies from 48°F (8.8°C) in the southeast to 36°F (2.2°C) in the north. About three cold waves a season sweep over the state, each an average length of about three days. The average diurnal range of temperature throughout the year is 18.2°F (10°C); in winter it is 16.8°F (9.2°C), in spring 19°F (10.4°C), in summer 18.3°F (10°C), and in autumn 18.8°F (10.3°C).

Extreme temperatures of 100°F (37.7°C) or above may be expected during a Missouri summer. For the state as a whole, extremely high temperatures are likely to occur in one or two days in late June, three to five days during each of the months of July and August, and perhaps a day or two in early September. Heat waves can be protracted. During the dry summers of the 1930s, there were several periods lasting two weeks or more when temperatures exceeded 100°F (37.7°C). A number of heat-related deaths were recorded in the state during the summer of 1980, when hot, dry conditions spread across Missouri, Texas, and Oklahoma.

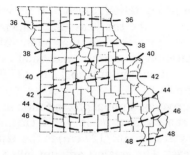

AVERAGE DAILY MAXIMUM TEMPERATURES–JANUARY

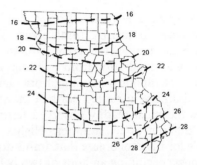

AVERAGE DAILY MINIMUM TEMPERATURES–JANUARY

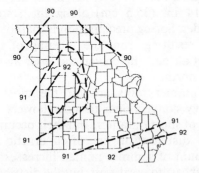

AVERAGE DAILY MAXIMUM TEMPERATURES–JULY

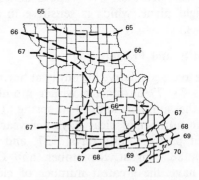

AVERAGE DAILY MINIMUM TEMPERATURES–JULY

FIGURE 2.1.   Seasonal Temperatures (F°).

Average minimum temperatures in July are in the upper sixties, except in the extreme southeast where they reach 70°F (21.1°C). The lowest average minimum of 65°F (18.3°C) occurs in the northern part of the state, but even there many summer nights are uncomfortably warm. Residents of northern Missouri refer to the hot, humid nights of July and August as corn-growing weather. Average daily maximums in July exceed 90°F (32.2°C) over most of the state with little variation. Temperatures in excess of 100°F (37.7°C) occur throughout Missouri during most summers.

Temperature ranges are at times extreme. The highest temperature ever recorded in Missouri was 118°F (47.7°C), recorded at Lamar and at Warsaw. Absolute minimum temperatures are by no means mild; Missouri's record low of −40°F (−40°C) was registered at Warsaw also on February 13, 1905. Springfield has recorded an absolute range of 135°F (74°C), with such anomalous temperatures as 74°F (23.3°C) in January and 22°F (−5.5°C) in October and April.

Temperatures in the state vary widely with the orientation of slope, nature of surface materials, relief, and presence of water. South- and west-facing slopes, which receive the greatest amount of sunlight, are subject to higher rates of evaporation. Thus ferns, most mosses, and most wild flowers do not grow on south-facing slopes, whereas the purest stands of oak and hickories do. North-facing slopes generally have much more undergrowth and ground cover. In winter, perhaps the most noticeable effect of temperature differences within a small area is the duration of snow and icicles on the north-facing slopes. The latter features, often several feet long as they hang from cliffs, may not completely melt for many days after temperatures in daytime have reached the fifties.

Temperatures in St. Louis and Kansas

City average 2°F (0.82°C) to 5°F (2°C) higher than in nearby rural areas. This increase is due to the great amount of reflection and radiation from buildings and the lack of evaporative cooling from plants.

Air drainage in rugged parts of the state creates the most readily observed temperature differences in summer. Nights are notable for the cool breeze that drains down the slopes, beginning an hour or two before sunset. Daytime temperature variations are most easily felt aloft over rugged districts in a light plane, which is sensitive to air currents.

Humidity and Precipitation

The average relative humidity at Springfield is 73; 77 during the winter months, 75 in the summer, and 70 in spring. The average number of clear days per year is 150; of partly cloudy days, 127; and of cloudy, 88. August, September, and October have the greatest number of clear days; December and January have the most cloudy days, 11 each (Figure 2.2). May has an average of 12 rainy days, whereas October has only 7. In the eastern part of Missouri and in the Bootheel, the humidity is slightly higher than in Springfield. The lowest humidity is in northwestern Missouri. On the whole, the state has abundant sunshine. With maximum frequency of rains in spring and of sunny weather in late summer, production of most crops is favorable.

Autumn in Missouri is a season of variable precipitation. When high pressure dominates the state the most pleasantly cool and clear weather may occur, but at other times fronts may produce extended periods of rain. Autumn precipitation ranges from 9 in. (22.8 cm) in the northwest to 11 in. (27.9 cm) in the southeastern part of the state.

The most pronounced precipitation gradient occurs during the winter season. Because the northwestern part of the state is more often under the influence of cold, dry Arctic air, it receives only 3 in. (7.62 cm) of precipitation, much of it snow (Figure 2.3). In the southeast the influence of Gulf air increases so that more of the precipitation is drizzle and total winter accumulation amounts to 11 in. (27.9 cm) or more.

The average annual precipitation in Missouri ranges from 34 in. (86.3 cm) in the northwest to 50 in. (127 cm) in the extreme southeast. The greatest amount falls in the spring and summer. The spring rainfall ranges from 9 in. (22.8 cm) in the northwest to 14 in. (35.5 cm) along the southern border. Spring precipitation is mainly frontal, resulting from the meeting of moist Gulf air and the cooler and drier air from the north.

Summer rains are for the most part heavy convectional thundershowers, usually of short duration, and their occurrence and distribution are often erratic. The amount of summer rainfall increases from southeast to northwest, but the distribution over the state is uneven. When dry air masses stagnate over the state, prolonged periods of time may pass without significant precipitation.

The climatic records of Kansas City are representative of the greater part of the midwestern agricultural belt. It is therefore not surprising to find that the distribution of precipitation in the Kansas City area favors plant growth; that is, it rains predominantly during nighttime hours when evaporation loss is minimal. Considering the year as a whole, 64 percent of measurable precipitation occurs between sunset and sunrise, and 77 percent occurs between 11 P.M. and 11 A.M. There is a sharp difference between the dormant, or winter, season and the vegetal, or growing, season. During the dormant season there is only a slight variation in the frequency of precipitation throughout the average twenty-four-hour day. However, during the vegetal period, with the maximum frequency at sunrise, 88 percent of the hours with measurable precipitation fall between 11 P.M. and 11 A.M.

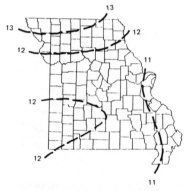

AVERAGE SUMMER PRECIPITATION

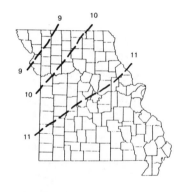

AVERAGE AUTUMN PRECIPITATION

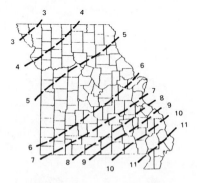

AVERAGE WINTER PRECIPITATION

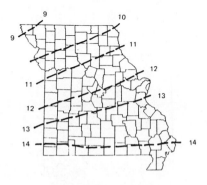

AVERAGE SPRING PRECIPITATION

FIGURE 2.2.   Seasonal Precipitation in Inches.

In Missouri the average amount of snowfall ranges from 8 in. (20.3 cm) to 23 in. (58.4 cm) a year. The average snowfall at Springfield is 15.9 in. (40.3 cm), or about 3.5 percent of total precipitation. This is less than half the snowfall of Chicago or New York. Snowfalls normally amount to less than 5 in. (12.7 cm), but very heavy snows of 20 in. (50.8 cm) or more are not unknown. In the Ozarks and the Southeast Lowlands, snowfalls are usually only 2 in. (5.08 cm) to 3 in. (7.62 cm), and they seldom remain on the ground more than a day or two. Nevertheless, because state and county highway crews are poorly equipped to handle heavy snow, roads are sometimes difficult to travel. Steep grades and packed snow may keep rural roads impassable or dangerous for days after the main highways are clear of snow. Schools in the region usually allow for two to five "snow days" in their schedules; that is, days they close due to hazardous driving conditions.

The latitude position of the Ozarks favors sleet storms and freezing rain. Freezing rain does considerable damage to trees and wires and makes travel treacherous for a day or two. In November 1848, a "big sleet" in the western Ozarks was extraordinarily destructive to trees and to livestock, which could not forage. In December 1972, a heavy, freezing rain in the same section brought down power lines and left farms and communities without electrical power for several days. National Guard units with portable electrical generators were dispatched to dairy farms so that the dairy stock could be milked. Hail is most frequent in western Missouri, but the

AVERAGE ANNUAL SNOWFALL

AVERAGE DATE OF FIRST SNOWFALL

AVERAGE YEARLY NUMBER OF DAYS WITH SNOWFALL

AVERAGE DATE OF LAST SNOWFALL

FIGURE 2.3.   Snowfall.

region as a whole normally receives fifteen to twenty damaging hailstorms in the period from May to September.

The dry season usually sets in about the latter part of June or the first part of July and lasts forty to sixty days. During this period widespread rains of more than 1 in. (2.54 cm) are not common, and the greater part of the rainfall comes in showers.

Droughts cover a larger area, last longer, and do more damage in Missouri than periods of excessive rain. They affect both uplands and river bottomland, farm and village alike. Springs stop flowing, reservoirs empty, and field crops suffer permanent injury. Severe droughts occurred in 1881, 1911, 1913, 1914, 1935, 1936, 1955, 1956, 1975, and 1980.

Flash floods, though less prolonged and less destructive, are frequent in Missouri, damaging property and farmland. Because

of steep slopes, runoff from heavy downpours, associated with squall lines, fronts, and isolated thunderstorms, can rapidly reach flood stage. It is recorded that the Big Piney River, in May 1892, rose 30 ft (9.1 m) from 4:00 P.M. to 12:00 midnight. The Current River during this same month rose 27 ft (8.2 m) in about the same time, sending torrents of water down small valleys that had been without the semblance of a stream a few hours before. Chert, washed from hillsides, covered acres of bottomland along the Finley River and blocked roads in Stone County for days, reaching the second strand of wire on fences in some places. The Missouri and Mississippi rivers both are subject to widespread flooding. The famous Missouri River flood of 1950 destroyed the Kansas City stockyards and flooded nearly all of the industrial river bottomland. The record flood of

PHOTO 2.1. Winter Scene near Jefferson City. Courtesy Walker—Missouri Division of Tourism.

1972 on the Mississippi River brought the water more than 40 ft (12.19 m) above flood stage at Cape Girardeau.

The most remarkable of all intense small area rainfalls occurred at Holt, Missouri, on June 22, 1947. The point rainfall value (the amount of rainfall at one given area for one given period of time) of 12 in. (30.4 cm) in 42 minutes is a world record.

Early morning fog is common in the valleys in the hill and mountain districts due to the drainage of cool air into the valleys overnight. The fog ordinarily dissipates by mid-morning as temperatures climb in the valleys. Heavy fogs often hover over the large water bodies such as Lake of the Ozarks, Pomme de Terre, Table Rock, and Bull Shoals. The larger river valleys are also frequently blanketed by fogs in the early morning hours. In the hill districts, a bluish haze is characteristic in panoramic views even in fair weather.

The average length of the growing season for the state as a whole is nearly six months. The likelihood of unseasonable frost depends much more on topographic location than on latitude. As a rule frosts occur in the valleys, especially the larger valleys in the hill regions, several weeks earlier in fall and later in spring than they do on the uplands. The margins of the uplands have the best air drainage and are least subject to frosts.

In general, the climate of the Missouri region, which has escaped severe drought in most years, is characteristically continental. It is humid, temperate, pleasant and healthful, and well suited to the cultivation of a large variety of crops.

SOIL CHARACTERISTICS AND TYPES

To the pioneers who settled Missouri, the single most important factor contributing to the region's economic development was the quality of soil resources. Today, after more than a century of agricultural settlement, the well-being and prosperity of the people depend on the continued use

of the soil. Nevertheless, of the three groups of renewable natural resources—soils, plants, animals—soils are perhaps generally understood the least.

Soil Composition

Soil is a complex material. It is composed of weathered rock material, decayed and partially decayed organic matter (humus), air, and water in various forms. The soils of Missouri have great diversity both in physical properties and in levels of fertility. The variations are due to the several factors that affect soil formation—including "parent" or geological material from which the soils are derived—climate, topography, drainage, natural vegetation, and the length of time the soils have weathered. The physical features that give diversity to soils include color, depth of topsoil, texture, subsoil, subsoil pans, tilth (structure), and underlying material. Each of these features is of great significance in identifying soils and also in interpreting their fertility levels. Soil profiles, or the succession of layers of horizons in the soil, indicate much diversity in Missouri soils.

The chief parent materials of Missouri soils are loess, glacial till, limestone and dolomitic limestone, shales, and alluvial deposits. Sandstone and granite are of minor importance.

During the glacial period, the northern half of Missouri (and a large part of the surrounding states) was completely covered by a mantle of windblown loess. As shown on the map of parent materials (Figure 2.4), the loess occurs along the Missouri and Mississippi rivers, particularly in the northwestern part of the state, where it is 75 ft (22.8 m) or more in depth. It is easily identified by its distinctive yellow buff color, uniform texture, and ability to stand in vertical cuts. Along the two rivers it is known as bluff soil. Just as in other areas of the world where loess occurs—notably China and the Ukraine of the Soviet Union—it forms very productive agricultural soils that are persistently fertile under long and intensive use. Some of the most

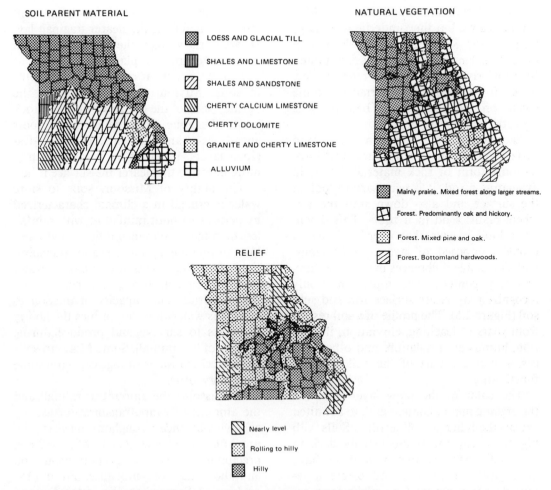

FIGURE 2.4.   Relief, Soil Parent Material, and Natural Vegetation.

productive agricultural counties of Missouri are in the northwest and west-central Missouri loess belt.

The tills deposited by the glaciers consist of clays, sands, and gravels, which form loam and clay loam soils. Till soils are exposed on sloping land in the loess regions and over extensive areas drained by the Grand and Chariton rivers.

The soils of the prairie region are largely formed from weathered shales and, to a lesser extent, sandstones. Because the shales and sandstones are in alternating layers, the texture of the soils varies from place to place.

Most of the soils of the Ozarks were formed by decay of local rock formations.

On uplands and gentle slopes, the surface materials are derived primarily from the underlying rock, and contacts of rock formations are often marked by sharp differences in soils. On steep slopes, the more resistant beds of rock dominate the soils as they do the topography. Cherty limestones, because of their resistance, frequently occupy summit elevations, and weathered chert mantles the lower slopes. In many instances, chert comprises 50 percent or more of the soil. Certain limestones are chert free and produce fertile soils. Notable examples are the limestone soils of the Springfield Plain and the red limestone soils in Madison and St. Francois counties.

Alluvial soils are found along all Missouri streams, but they underlie truly large areas in the Southeast Lowlands and in the bottomlands along the Mississippi and Missouri rivers. These soils range widely in age, from the oldest on terraces to quite recent on the floodplain. Their physical properties also vary greatly.

Each soil occupies a certain area of land surface and depth, usually extending down to some form of rock material. Thus, in evaluating a soil, it is necessary to look at the surface and also down into the soil where plants send their roots. This downward look reveals that every soil has a profile composed of layers, or horizons, with detectable differences in color, texture, and clay content. The most commonly recognized layers are surface soil and subsoil (Figure 2.5). The profile of a soil results from years of leaching, eluviation, illuviation, humus accumulation, and other processes that are part of the soil system's functioning.

The color of the plow layer indicates the organic matter content and, to a limited extent, the inherent soil fertility. Soils with high organic content are usually dark in color, release more nitrogen for plants, have better tilth (tillability), and create a favorable environment for soil bacteria action.

The size and proportion of soil particles in the surface layers give a soil its characteristic texture. Texture of the surface soil affects moisture intake, moisture-holding capacity, aeration, the ability to hold or release nutrients, susceptibility to erosion, and tilth. The primary particle sizes used to describe texture are sand size (greater than .05 mm in diameter), silt size (.05 to .002 mm diameter), and clay size (less than .002 mm diameter).

Fragipan layers occur mostly in the lower subsoil. They result from accumulation of minerals (iron, magnesium, calcium) and cementation of chert and other rock fragments. Their high density, relative to overlying soil horizons, restricts movement of air and water in the soil and, with their

acid condition, severely limits plant root growth. Therefore, the nearer fragipan layers are to the surface, the more detrimental they are to growing plants.

Bedrock occurs at rather shallow depths in some Missouri soils, such as in the "glade" soils of the Ozark Region. Bedrock limits the zone from which plant roots absorb water and nutrients. Thus, like fragipan layers, its effect on plant growth is more negative the nearer the surface it lies.

The ability of Missouri soils to store water is crucial in a climate characterized by periods without rainfall or with rainfall less than the evapotranspiration (total water loss through evaporation and transpiration). Growing plants use available water stored in the soil during such periods and the soil dries. The capacity of the soil to store this water thus determines the ability of plants to survive and produce during periods of low rainfall. Some Missouri soils have excellent water storage capacity; some have very little.

In Missouri the amount of rainfall and the amount of evapotranspiration usually achieve a balance throughout the year (Figure 2.6). From September to May or June, precipitation exceeds evapotranspiration and the soils store moisture. From May or June to September, the water demand is greater than the expected rainfall. During this period the available water stored in the soil is consumed.

Texture greatly affects the amount of water retained in soils. Sands have very low available-water-storage capacity. Special soil horizons such as fragipan horizons, rocky or gravelly layers, and bedrock limit available-water capacity. Such layers may restrict root development and growth as well.

Soil chemistry, in combination with the air and water relationships in the soil, largely determines the productive capacity of soil. The chemistry of the upper 7 in. (18 cm) of soil is especially critical. The relative amounts and balance of minerals such as phosphate (P_2O_5), potassium (K), magnesium (Mg), and calcium determine

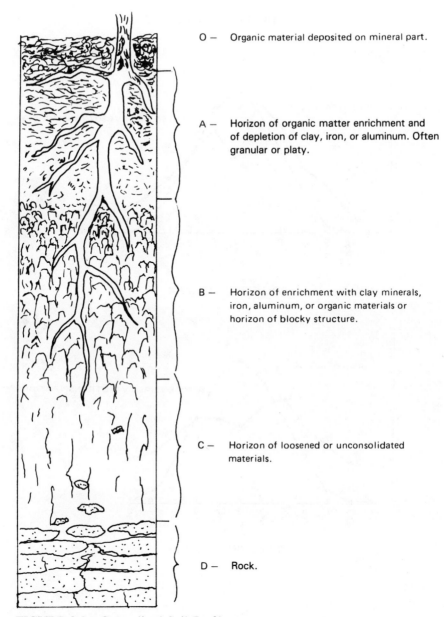

O — Organic material deposited on mineral part.

A — Horizon of organic matter enrichment and of depletion of clay, iron, or aluminum. Often granular or platy.

B — Horizon of enrichment with clay minerals, iron, aluminum, or organic materials or horizon of blocky structure.

C — Horizon of loosened or unconsolidated materials.

D — Rock.

FIGURE 2.5.   Generalized Soil Profile.

a soil's capability to support plant growth. The relative acidity of soils is important in plant growth. Most Missouri soils are slightly acidic and must be limed for optimum production.

Major Soil Landscapes

There are seven major soil landscapes in Missouri (Figure 2.7). These soil regions are closely related to the distribution of the soil-forming material, the pattern of vegetation, general topography, and the amount of precipitation.

The northern Missouri loess and loess-till soils are derived from loess and glacial till (Figure 2.8). Typically, the loess soils are on the upland flats, whereas the loess-till soils occupy the slopes. These soils

26

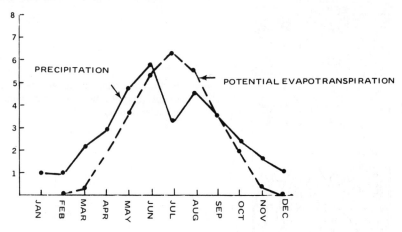

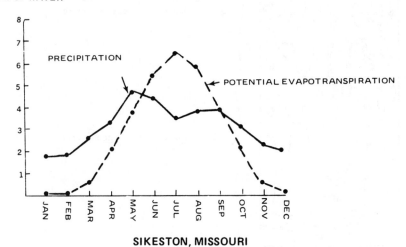

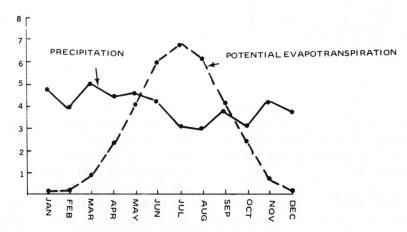

FIGURE 2.6. Water Balance at Selected Locations.

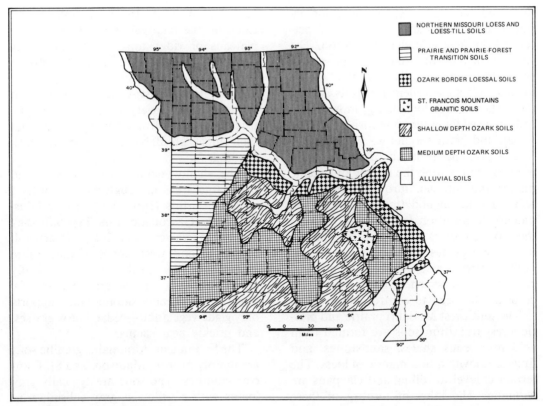

FIGURE 2.7. Major Soil Areas.

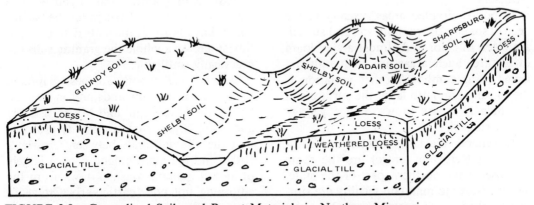

FIGURE 2.8. Generalized Soils and Parent Materials in Northern Missouri.

generally have dark colors, except where erosion has removed the topsoil, and silty textures varying from clay loams to loams. Their textures, aided by rolling surfaces, have made them subject to rapid and destructive erosion; and because of their intensive use over more than 100 years, these soils are the most severely eroded in the state. Gullies formed are usually deep with perpendicular walls. Cuts 15 ft (4.5 m) to 30 ft (9.1 m) deep are common near the rivers and are sometimes made in one season.

Practically all of the northern Missouri

loess and loess-till soils are used for agricultural purposes and over 50 to 75 percent of the area is under cultivation. The staple crops of the state can be grown successfully on the soils, and most of the upland soils are excellent for fruits. Where the surface is not too rolling, most of the soils are used for cultivating corn, soybeans, wheat, and grain sorghums.

The principal problem of soil management is maintaining the supply of organic matter and nitrogen through proper systems of rotation and (manure and green manure) fertilization. In northeast Missouri the productivity is somewhat less and the use of phosphates produces good results. Gully control is also a problem. Terracing, grassed waterways, check dams, and cover crops are all used to control soil erosion.

The southwest Missouri prairie and prairie-forest transition soils are formed from acid micaceous shales, sandstones, and limestones with a thin mantle of loess. The terrain is level to rolling and claypans are common. The inherent fertility of these soils is only moderate, but most of them respond readily to treatment with chemical fertilizers.

In poorly drained areas, usually at the head of shallow draws, both soil and subsoil are black in color and almost a clay loam in texture. Such areas are frequently referred to as gumbo. Another variation is the so-called mulatto land, the surface soil of which is a dark brown with a yellow-brown subsoil.

In general, the farm practices of cultivation and erosion control are the same as those in the northern part of the state. The measures to maintain fertility are similar to those used in northern Missouri except that the requirements for lime are somewhat higher.

The Ozark border loessal soils are silty, brown loams. The depth of the soil and the content of organic matter vary considerably. Except for steep slopes, practically all of the land is under cultivation and has been for nearly 150 years. As a result, some areas are severely eroded.

The medium-depth Ozark soils are located on the relatively smooth, stone-free plateaus or ridge tops, most extensively along the Ozark divide. They are gray to red loams underlain by yellow to dark red subsoils. In the past, these soils were used to produce a variety of crops including truck crops and fruits, but it is clear that their most profitable use is in livestock farming.

The shallow-depth Ozark soils extend over large areas of rough and stony land in the Courtois Hills, White River Hills, and Osage-Gasconade Hills. Typically they are gray to red, very stony loams. In general, the south and west slopes contain more stones than the north slopes. Practically all of these soils are timbered (Figure 2.9). Some of the steeply sloping land supports only glade vegetation—cedar, hardy grasses, and prickly pear cactus.

The St. Francois Mountains granitic soils are mainly in Iron, Madison, and St. Francois counties. The soils are typically gray loams with a yellowish-gray subsoil, containing considerable sand, stones, and boulders. The underlying rocks are igneous, consisting of granites and rhyolites. The whole area is forested except for the basins, which have fairly fertile soils derived from limestone. As a whole the granitic soils are practically untillable.

Alluvial valley soils are best exhibited in the Southeast Lowlands and in the valleys of the Mississippi and Missouri rivers and their larger tributaries. It is probable that the alluvial lands between Crowley's Ridge and the main upland consist largely of loessal material washed down from the adjoining uplands (particularly Crowley's Ridge). Thus they are more homogeneous in source than are the alluvial lands east of the ridge. The similarity of the alluvial soils along the streams within Crowley's Ridge to those of the main body of alluvial lands west of the ridge is almost conclusive evidence that those soils are primarily of local origin.

A large belt of sandy soils lies near the Mississippi, and another of heavy clayey

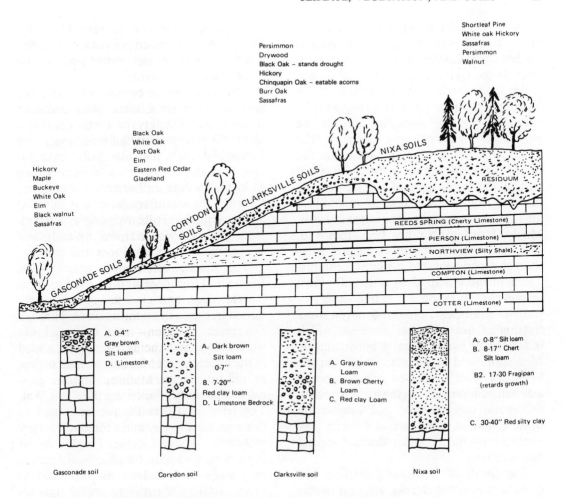

FIGURE 2.9. Generalized Soils and Natural Vegetation in the Ozarks.

soils lies in the old river channel, which extends through the interior of the area east of Crowley's Ridge from near Cape Girardeau to the Arkansas state line. The sand ridge in Dunklin and Stoddard counties and Sikestone Ridge in Scott and New Madrid counties are both second bottoms representing old riverbanks. Their sandy and gravelly texture is the result of erosion and deposition from channel changes similar to those now occurring along the present banks of the Mississippi.

The lowland soils are extremely variable. It is difficult to find even a 10-acre (4-hectare) field of the same character throughout. Sandy spots or streaks occur commonly in the prevailingly heavier soils, whereas the generally sandy areas are intersected by swales of lower-lying land of heavier character. The lower and heavier soils are used extensively to grow soybeans; the better drained sandy areas have long been recognized as cotton land.

In general, the alluvial soils of the Southeast Lowlands and the bottomlands bordering Missouri's largest rivers are fertile, heavily cultivated, and productive; however, they have poor drainage and are subject to severe flooding.

NATURAL VEGETATION

At the time of white settlement, probably more than 60 percent of Missouri was forested. With the exception of occasional prairie ridges, the entire Ozark Region and the Southeast Lowlands were covered with trees. In the Ozark Region the alluvial and valley lands along streams as well as the rougher parts of the upland had fairly heavy vegetation. On the smoother uplands the growth was scattered and open so that bluestem grass grew abundantly. In the prairie regions in the northern and western part of the state, belts of timber varying in width from a few rods to 10 miles (16.1 km) or more bordered all the larger streams. Much of this timber has been removed, and it is only on the more rugged areas that any considerable amount remains. Tracts of more than .5 sq mile (1.29 km²) in one concentration are extraordinary.

In the southeastern lowland, only a small fraction of heavy timber remains, which is located in swampy tracts bordering the Mississippi and St. Francis rivers. On the low-lying, poorly drained areas, cypress, ash, and gum prevail. On the higher ground, elm, gum, hickory, oak, and catalpa are most abundant. Post oak and white oak predominate on the better-drained second bottoms.

Two-thirds of Missouri's existing forested land is in the Ozarks, where it occurs in both large blocks and woodlots in the more level areas. Outside the Ozarks timberland is confined to the steep slopes along streams and to small farm woodlots.

Most of the forested land is privately owned and the average size of a landholding is small. There are some large private holdings of forestland in the Ozarks, but their proportion of total forestland is small. Mark Twain National Forest contains approximately 8 percent of the forested area.

Reports of pioneers and the field notes of the surveyors who carried out the first land surveys in the Ozarks indicate that the trees on uplands were often stunted. Hard-cemented fragipan layers under level upland tracts may have retarded penetration of tree roots and caused slower tree growth. Many forested tracts had a parklike appearance and young trees and brush were

not as widespread as at present. Flat ridge tops, commonly called post-oak flats, today constitute some of the poorer lands of the Ozark Region.

Although small prairies, such as "the barrens" in Perry County, were common in the eastern Ozarks, the western part was about 50 percent parklike grasslands. The Springfield Plain had especially luxuriant bluestem grasses, reported to have grown as high as a man on horseback. In Greene County, for example, land was divided almost equally between prairie and woodland; the prairies occupied uplands and timber covered valley floors and slopes.

The practice of burning prairies that Indian and European hunters used to drive buffalo, deer, and elk may also have retarded tree growth on the uplands. Through this practice, sprouts and tree seedlings were killed, and the grasslands expanded at the expense of the forests. Yet, according to old-time settlers, many prairies grew over with timber following the Civil War. The term *bald* that the pioneers used to describe these grassy areas often refers now to heavily wooded knobs. Finally, it has been suggested that edaphic (soil) factors may have been at least as important as fire in limiting tree growth on the uplands in some locations.

Settlers continued the practice of burning for many years to provide grazing for their stock. With further settlement and with fencing, the forest began to take over the burned-over tracts. Pastures are still maintained with fire at present, even though "brush hogging" of persimmon sprouts, scrub cedar, and other "increasers" is the more common method of controlling the growth of undesirable plants.

Small grassy areas—balds, or knobs—occur on hilltops where there is a deficiency of soil and groundwater. These areas, which typically have red cedar (juniper), prickly pear, and scrubby oaks interspersed, are known as glades when they occur on hillsides or over extensive areas (see Figure 2.4, p. 23). Cedar trees that line fence rows in the vicinity of the glades are less likely

PHOTO 2.2. Mingo Wildlife Refuge near Puxico, Stoddard County. Courtesy Walker—Missouri Division of Tourism.

to have been planted by industrious farmers than by birds having fed on juniper seeds. The glade lands, most widely distributed in the White River Hills, also occur along the Gasconade, Niangua, and some other north-flowing streams where the Jefferson City dolomite outcrops. Thin soils and southern exposures account for the combination of dry conditions and peculiar vegetation. Glades also occur in the vicinity of the St. Francois Mountains where the Potosi formation provides similar conditions.

The Ozarks are one of the northernmost regions for the growth of southern pine. Extensive forests of shortleaf pine were found in early years on the piny forks of the Gasconade and in Ozark, Douglas, Reynolds, Carter, and Washington counties in Missouri. These forests were also found in the White River country of Missouri and northern Arkansas.

Among the hardwoods there is sharp contrast between upland and lowland types. The upland forests are comprised almost exclusively of oaks, generally 90 percent or more of the total timber. White oak, post oak, black oak, and blackjack are the main varieties. On the ridges, black oak and white oak are common; on the hillsides, post oak and blackjack do well. Chinquapin oak, like the softwood cedar, is a bluff tree. Hickories and walnut grow on better upland soils.

Neither the blackjack nor post oak is of any particular value except for fuel, although the post oak, where large enough, is used as tie timber. These trees, especially the second growth, are usually dense and bushy. In recent years, as energy prices have increased, the value of Missouri's forest as home heating fuel has increased. At the present rate of consumption, Missouri forests and woodlots produce about

PHOTO 2.3. Cedar Bald on Thin Soils in Taney County. Photograph by the Author.

twice as many cords of firewood as are cut.

In the valleys, there is a greater variety of species because of better soil and water conditions, and individual trees grow much larger. Sycamore occupies stream-bank locations, often forming a canopy that nearly covers small streams. Originally, cottonwood, maples, black walnut, butternut, hackberry, tulip, and bur oak were most abundant and are very abundant still. In the southeastern Ozarks, bordering the Mississippi embayment, cypress, gums, and birch are also present.

The understory of Missouri's forests has great variety. Flowering redbuds and dogwoods are harbingers of spring while blackberries, currants, dewberries, and huckleberries are gathered in season.

In the western Ozarks, the Osage orange, also known as bois d'arc ("bo-dark"), bow wood, or hedge, has become widespread in pastures and in fence rows. It is hardy, thorny, and resistant to drought. Posts made from bois d'arc are nearly indestructible. In early days the seed of the Osage orange was shipped from east Texas, Oklahoma, and western Missouri to the treeless plains in Oklahoma and Kansas, where it was planted to form fences. The seed brought as much as $40 a bushel in the 1870s.

Today the state is approximately 34.5 percent forested. The percentage of land in forests corresponds rather closely to the landform divisions of the state. Northern and western Missouri counties are all less than 20 percent forested. Because these areas are well suited to crop production, a large share of the land is under cultivation. The counties of the Southeast Lowlands are similarly lacking in forest cover.

The Ozark Region is heavily forested, especially in the interior portions. Most of the interior Ozark counties are over 60 percent forested, whereas Reynolds, Shannon, and Carter counties are more than

80 percent forested. In recent years counties in the northern and western plains have shown moderate gains in woodlot acreage. Throughout the Ozarks the amount of land in forests has remained fairly stable, but the general condition of the timber has deteriorated in many areas. Many of the heavily forested counties, such as Washington, Iron, Reynolds, Madison, Wayne, Shannon, and Carter, report only a small income for the large amount of forested land.

The prairies, even more than the forests, have been modified by humans. Most of the prairies, consisting of bluestems and other tall grasses, were plowed in the latter half of the nineteenth century, when agriculture became more intensive. In the Ozarks Kentucky bluegrass replaced the bluestems, and it now grows wild wherever soil conditions are good. Most pastures presently are of highly mixed varieties of fescue, which has been planted throughout the Ozarks in recent years. Fescue has revitalized the range-cattle industry of the Ozarks by providing hardy forage that persists in cold weather.

Some 15 million acres (6,075,000 ha) of tallgrass prairie stretched across northern and western Missouri when the state was a hunting ground for the Osage, Missouri, Otoe, Kansas, Iowa, and various other wandering Indian tribes. There were large prairies in the western Ozarks and occasional prairie openings in the forest as far east as land now part of Perry and Cape Girardeau counties. The large grassland areas or prairies in the Ozark forest typically occupied upland tracts between major streams.

European settlers discovered that land capable of growing big bluestem and Indian grass 7 ft (2.15 m) tall was also capable of growing crops. Plows bit into the tough sod and the rich, black soil rolled up, moist and inviting. In the span of a hundred years—from 1820 to about 1920—the natural prairies were converted to cropland. The 15 million acres (6,075,000 ha) of prairie now are less than 75,000 (30,375

ha)—or half of 1 percent of what existed when the first white settlers arrived.

Unfortunately, economic considerations will probably force most of the few privately owned acres of prairie remaining into cultivation. High grain prices are an almost irresistable incentive to convert tall-grass prairie to cropland.

Some individuals have a love for the prairie that transcends the desire to make money, however. A 270-acre (109-hectare) prairie near King City, one of the very few remaining native prairies in north Missouri, has been owned by the same family since 1868. It is part of the Spiking brothers' 1,200-acre (486-hectare) livestock farm. The owners are renovating some of their other pasturelands with native grass, which is nutritional and hardy although far more expensive than the introduced grass. The Eugene Poirot farm near Golden City also successfully manages native prairie for modern beef-cattle production.

Several tracts of prairie have been put in public trust by three agencies—the Missouri Conservation Commission, the Nature Conservancy, and the Missouri Prairie Foundation. The largest is Taberville Prairie, a 1,360-acre (551-hectare) tract in St. Clair County. Nearly as large is the 1,115-acre (452-hectare) Osage Prairie in Vernon County.

WATER RESOURCES

The earth's supply of water constantly circulates in a natural process of evaporation, precipitation, and transportation. This process is known among hydrologists as the *hydrologic cycle.* An understanding of the basic pattern of this cycle is fundamental, for through some modification or control of it, human beings are able to utilize water to their advantage.

Water, after falling as precipitation, completes its natural cycle back to atmospheric moisture by one of three routes: (1) reevaporation from the surface; (2) infiltration and subsequent reappearance as groundwater, capillary moisture, or plant-tran-

PHOTO 2.4. Finley Falls on Finley Creek, Christian County. Photo by the Author.

spired vapor; or (3) direct overland flow into streams, where it either evaporates in transit or is carried to large lakes and the ocean from which evaporation continually takes place. The total amount of moisture in the earth's atmosphere has been estimated to remain the same at all times, whereas the amount at any given locality fluctuates. Only a relatively minute quantity of water is formed or destroyed by natural processes of growth and decay.

Water is one of Missouri's most valuable resources. The state's great agricultural economy, its industries, cities, and inland navigation all require great quantities of water to function. Every 1 lb (.45 kg) of grain produced requires 1,000 lb (454 kg) of water. An average rainfall of 40 in. (101.6 cm) spreads 4,500 tn (4,081 t) of water over each acre (.405 ha) or 3 million tn (2,721,000 t) over each square mile (2.59 km²) of area every year.

As the population and consequently the use of water have increased, interest has grown in the state's water resources. The sources available determine the kind of water supply developed for purposes other than hydroelectric power. If surface water and groundwater are both available, the costs of obtaining and treating water from each source are compared. Major rivers are the primary source of the large quantities of water nearby big cities and their industries require. North of the Missouri River, where the development of groundwater supplies is difficult and minimum flows of streams are insufficient to meet demand, reservoirs store the drainage for small areas. During extended dry periods, some of these supplies are inadequate, and water must be hauled to supply the emergency domestic needs of small towns and farms.

The average runoff from streams in the state varies from 4 in. (10.1 cm) in the northwest to 22 in. (55.8 cm) in the southeast. Runoff for selected locations is as follows:

City	Average Runoff
Maryville	5 in. (12.7 cm)
Kansas City	6 in. (15.2 cm)
Kirksville	6 in. (15.2 cm)
Sedalia	10 in. (25.4 cm)
Jefferson City	10 in. (25.4 cm)
St. Louis	10 in. (25.4 cm)
Springfield	12 in. (30.4 cm)
Poplar Bluff	18 in. (45.7 cm)
Kennett	22 in. (55.8 cm)

All of Missouri is drained either directly or indirectly by the Mississippi and Missouri rivers. Distinctive low-flow regimens (the volume of water after a prolonged dry period) exist in each of Missouri's major landform provinces. In the plains, the low-flow potential of the streams is small because of the low storage capacity of the shales and clays of the area. In the Ozarks, where the base flow is largely from springs, the base flows are the highest in the state. In the Southeast Lowlands, large amounts of surface water are available without storage, and the region ranks second to the Ozarks in terms of available surface water. The yield of streams during long periods of low precipitation is larger south of the Missouri River than in the glaciated areas of northern Missouri. The rock formations underlying the Ozarks contribute more water to sustain the low flow of streams than do those underlying the glaciated region.

The rivers of northern Missouri flow to either the Missouri or the Mississippi (Figure 2.10). Those flowing to the Missouri have a southerly course, usually almost due south, whereas those flowing to the Mississippi flow southeast. The larger streams, such as the Nodaway, One Hundred and Two, Platte, Grand, Chariton, Des Moines, Wyaconda, Fabius, Salt, and Cuivre, have valleys as much as 5 miles (8 km) wide, with flat, meadowlike floors over which the stream channels meander in winding courses. Meander scars, oxbow lakes, backwater swamps and marshes, and sandbars are typical floodplain landforms.

The Ozark dome forms the major drainage divide in Missouri midway between the Missouri River and the southern boundary of the state. The two major streams flowing north to the Missouri River are the Osage and the Gasconade. Major streams flowing south to the White River include the James, North Fork, Eleven Point, Current, and Black rivers. The largest streams flowing to the Mississippi are the Meramec, which enters the larger stream just south of St. Louis, and the St. Francis, which flows southward out of Missouri to join the Mississippi many miles to the south near Helena, Arkansas.

All of Missouri's large lakes are artificially made. The first, Lake Taneycomo, was formed when the Powersite Dam was constructed on the White River by the Ozark Power and Water Company in 1912. Power transmission lines were extended from the dam to Springfield and to the cities and mines in the Tri-State Mining

FIGURE 2.10.   Rivers and Lakes.

District. The second major impoundment, Lake of the Ozarks, was much larger. It was formed when Bagnell Dam was completed in 1931. The dam and power plant built by Union Electric and Power Company supplied electrical power to St. Louis and to the towns and mines in the Old Lead Belt in St. Francois County.

Beginning with the construction of Clearwater Lake on Black River in 1948, the U.S. Army Corps of Engineers assumed the role of dam builder in Missouri. During the 1950s and 1960s, several large reservoirs were completed: Bull Shoals, Table Rock, Wappapello, Pomme de Terre, Stockton, and Thomas Hill. The largest and most expensive impoundment, Harry S. Truman Reservoir, began filling in early 1978 when the dam on the Osage River was closed. Smithville Lake on the Little Platte River, Long Branch Lake on the Little Chariton River, Blue Springs Lake on the east fork of the Little Blue River, Longview Lake on the west fork of the Little Blue River, and Clarence Cannon Reservoir on the Salt River are scheduled for completion early in the 1980s. Work on the proposed Meramec Dam on the Meramec River has been delayed because of objections from environmentalist groups and local landowners.

The importance of groundwater in the development of the state is indicated by the number of communities obtaining water supplies from this source. About 60 percent of the public water systems of Missouri depend on groundwater as the primary supply. If a good supply of groundwater is present, it is generally more economical for the small community to use wells instead of surface supplies, avoiding the need for a filtration plant.

Groundwater sources, aside from springs and mines, are either shallow wells or deep

PHOTO 2.5. Bagnell Dam and Lake of the Ozarks. Courtesy Walker—Missouri Division of Tourism.

wells. The term *deep well* refers to wells 100 ft (30.4 m) or more in depth. These sources occur throughout most of the geologic formations, filling voids below the water table in the zone of saturation. The availability of the water depends upon the depth of highly porous saturation formations known as aquifers.

The groundwaters of Missouri are divided into four provinces. The groundwaters of northwest Missouri come from glacial sands and gravels. These aquifers usually yield sufficient water for farms and small villages. Wells drilled in a belt extending from the northeastern part of Missouri to south of Kansas City yield fresh water to a depth of 500 ft (152 m); at greater depths they often yield salty or sulfurous water, depending on location. Wells in the alluvial valleys of the Mississippi and Missouri rivers and the Southeast Lowlands have a nearly unlimited supply of water, producing up to 1,000 gal (3,785 l) per minute. Wells drilled into several formations in the Ozarks have fairly large capacities. In the vicinity of Joplin, a few industries and communities rely on water from wells drilled into abandoned zinc and lead mines that have filled with groundwater.

Springs are an important water resource in Missouri, particularly in the Ozarks, where some of the world's largest are located. Only a minor part of the discharge of Missouri springs is used directly for municipal and domestic water supplies, for medicinal purposes, and for commercial fisheries. Springs contribute indirectly to the economy, however, by sustaining the flow of streams and by serving as scenic and recreational attractions.

Most Ozark springs are outlets for subterranean streams, which intersect surface streams as the latter deepen their valleys. The interconnected solution channels, some of which are caves in various stages of formation, are spring supply systems, filled or partly filled with water. The springs, located at many points along the streams, add much to the scenic beauty.

There are fifteen springs in the Missouri Ozarks that have an average daily flow (ADF) in excess of 24 million gal (90,840,000 l). The four largest springs have average daily flows of 100 million gal (378,500,000 l) or more. The largest is Big Spring (276 million gal ADF) (1,044,660,000 l), followed by Greer Spring (214 million gal ADF) (809,990,000 l), Double Spring (100 million gal ADF) (378,000,000 l), and Bennett Spring (100 million gal ADF) (378,000,000 l).

Pollution of surface water and groundwater endangers aquatic life and can contaminate the water supplies of Missouri's cities, towns, and farms. The most common sources of pollution of Missouri streams are large spills of toxic materials due to truck wrecks, pipeline breaks, or train derailments. Other sources include intentional or inevitable discharges of pollutants—municipal sewage waste-water-treatment effluents, leachate from solid-waste landfills, and industrial, mining, and agricultural effluents or drainage.

Leaks from oil-storage tanks, especially at service stations, also have generated many pollution reports. Several instances of spring and groundwater contamination in southwest Missouri have been traced to leaks in underground oil-storage tanks.

Mining activities have created a greater threat to aquatic life than any other type of Missouri industry over the past few years. Mine water discharged from abandoned coal strip mines, underground shafts, ore washing and milling operations, or ore smelters sometimes contains high levels of dissolved metals that are toxic to fish and other aquatic life. Gravel removal from streambeds is another mining activity that has caused considerable concern in recent years, particularly among fishermen and floaters.

In the karst areas of Missouri, notably in the Ozarks, the hazards of groundwater pollution are especially critical. The collapse of a sinkhole under the West Plains sewage lagoon in 1979 caused severe pollution of water wells throughout several dozen square miles of south-central Missouri and north-central Arkansas.

SELECTED REFERENCES

Baver, L. D. *Soil Erosion in Missouri.* University of Missouri Agricultural Experiment Station, bulletin 349. Columbia, 1935.

Bratton, Samuel T. "Climate." Chapter 1 in *Missouri: Its Resources, People, and Institutions,* edited by Noel P. Gist, pp. 11–16. Columbia: Curators of the University of Missouri, 1950.

Britton, Wiley. *Pioneer Life in Southwest Missouri.* Kansas City: Smith Grieves Co., 1929.

Christian County: Its First Hundred Years. Ozark, Mo.: Christian County Centennial, 1959.

Cole, Lela. "The Early Tie Industry Along the Niangua River." *Missouri Historical Review,* vol. 48, pp. 264–272. Fall 1953.

Ferguson, Judy. *The Boom Town of West Eminence and Its Lumbering Days.* Rolla, Mo.: Rolla Printing Co., 1969.

Ganser, David A. *Timber Resources of the Missouri Prairie Region.* Bulletin B797. Columbia: University of Missouri, July 1963.

_____. *Timber Resources of Missouri's Southwestern Ozarks.* Bulletin B845. Columbia: University of Missouri, January 1966.

_____. *Timber Resources of Missouri's River Border Region.* Bulletin B846. Columbia: University of Missouri, 1966.

_____. *Timber Resources of Missouri's Northwestern Ozarks.* Bulletin B847. Columbia: University of Missouri, 1966.

Garland, John H., ed. *The North American Midwest: A Regional Geography.* New York: John Wiley and Sons, 1955.

Hull, Clifton E. *Shortline Railroads of Arkansas.* Norman: University of Oklahoma Press, 1969.

Ingenthron, Elmo. *The Land of Taney.* Point Lookout, Mo.: School of the Ozarks Press, 1974.

Lott, George A. "The World Record 42-Minute Holt, Missouri Rainstorm." *Monthly Weather Review,* vol. 82, no. 2, pp. 50–59. February 1954.

Marbut, Curtis F. *Soil Reconnaissance of the Ozark Region of Missouri and Arkansas.* Bureau of Soils, Field Operations of the Bureau of Soils. Washington, D.C.: U.S. Department of Agriculture, 1911.

Martin, James W., and Jerry J. Presley. "Ozark Land and Lumber Company: Organization and Operations." Unpublished manuscript. Columbia: School of Forestry, University of Missouri, 1958.

Miller, M. F., and H. H. Krusekopt. *The Soils of Missouri.* University of Missouri Agricultural Experiment Station, bulletin 153. Columbia, March 1918.

Myers, J. K., and R. C. Smith. *Wood Products and Missouri's Forests.* Missouri Economic Study, no. 6. Columbia: University of Missouri School of Business and Public Administration Research Center, 1965.

Rafferty, Milton D. "Persistence Versus Change in Land Use and Landscape in the Springfield, Missouri, Vicinity of the Ozarks." Ph.D. dissertation, University of Nebraska, 1970.

_____. *The Ozarks: Land and Life.* Norman: University of Oklahoma Press, 1980.

_____. *Historical Atlas of Missouri.* Norman: University of Oklahoma Press, 1982.

Sauer, Carl O. *The Geography of the Ozark Highland of Missouri.* Geographical Society of Chicago Bulletin, no. 7. Chicago: University of Chicago Press, 1920.

Schoolcraft, Henry Rowe. *Journal of a Tour into the Interior of Missouri and Arkansas in 1818 and 1819.* 1821. Reprinted in *Schoolcraft in the Ozarks,* edited by Hugh Park. Van Buren, Ark.: Press-Argus, 1955.

Scrivner, C. L., and James C. Baker. *Evaluating Missouri Soils.* Circular 915. Columbia: University of Missouri, 1970.

Scrivner, C. L., J. C. Baker, and B. J. Miller. *Soils of Missouri: A Guide to Their Identification and Interpretation.* Columbia: Extension Division, University of Missouri, no date.

Schroeder, Walter A. *Presettlement Prairie of Missouri,* Natural History Series, no. 2. Jefferson City, Mo.: Missouri Department of Conservation, 1981.

Steyermark, Julian A. *Vegetational History of the Ozark Forest.* University of Missouri Studies, vol. 31. Columbia, 1959.

_____. *Flora of Missouri.* Ames: Iowa State University Press, 1963.

Westveld, R. H. "Forests," Chapter 7 in *Missouri: Its Resources, People, and Institutions,* edited by Noel P. Gist, pp. 151–189, Columbia: Curators of the University of Missouri, 1950.

CHAPTER 3

BOUNDARIES AND LAND SURVEYS

The boundaries of Missouri, as originally proposed, were to include the territory situated between parallels 36°30′ N latitude and 40° N latitude, with the Mississippi River as a boundary on the east and the Osage boundary on the west. The Osage boundary was a line extending from Fort Osage north and south about 24 miles (38.6 km) east of the mouth of the Kansas River. If Congress had adopted this first proposal, the geographical appearance of the state would have been as shown in Figure 3.1.

The proposed boundaries were not satisfactory to many of the residents, and petitions were circulated to make the Missouri River the northern boundary, extending the new state to the west. Some of the people of the settlements situated south of parallel 36°30′ N also objected to being left out of the new state. One of the settlements so excluded was Little Prairie, now Caruthersville, situated about 30 miles (48.3 km) south of New Madrid and adjacent plantations. The settlements on the Black and White rivers were also excluded, and at that early day they were important. Pressure brought by groups in these settlements caused the territorial legislature to propose more extensive boundaries for the new state,

beginning at a point in the main channel of the Mississippi River at the 36th degree of north latitude and running in a direct line to the mouth of Black River, a branch of White River, thence in the middle of the main channel of the White River to where the parallel of thirty-six degrees and thirty minutes, north latitude, crosses the same; thence with that parallel of latitude due west to a point from which a due north line will cross the Missouri River at the mouth of Wolf River; thence due north to a point west of the mouth of Rock River; thence due east to the main channel of the Mississippi, opposite the mouth of Rock River, and thence down the Mississippi, in the middle of the main channel thereof, to the place of beginning.[1]

If this boundary proposal had been adopted, about three tiers of counties now on the southern side of Iowa and about two tiers of counties in eastern Kansas, as well as a large part of northeastern Oklahoma, would have been included within the state of Missouri.

The second proposal for enlarged boundaries was defeated in Congress mainly because eastern legislators refused to support the creation of a very large state with poorly defined boundaries. The boundaries of the state were at last fixed so as to extend south to parallel 36° N, then west to the St. Francis River, then following the middle of the main channel of the St. Francis to parallel 36°30′, and then west on this par-

PHOTO 3.1.   Historic Fort Osage near Sibley, Jackson County. Courtesy Walker—Missouri Division of Tourism.

allel to a point where a north-south meridian line would intersect the mouth of the Kansas River. This moved the boundary west about four townships from that of the Osage boundary in the first proposal. In the north the boundary line was delimited where the parallel of latitude (40°36′50″), which passed through the rapids of the Des Moines River, would intersect this meridian line. These boundaries were legally adopted under the Act of 1820, the Missouri Compromise.

At statehood the Bootheel region was added to Missouri, primarily because of the work and influence of J. Hardeman Walker, a wealthy and influential plantation owner in the vicinity of Little Prairie (Caruthersville). As soon as the original boundary proposal was made known, Walker began a vigorous and persistent campaign to include the country south of New Madrid and Little Prairie.

In 1837 the state was still further en-

larged by the annexation of the so-called Platte Purchase. This territory is about 3,000 sq miles (7,770 km^2) situated east of the Missouri River and west of the original meridian line, which ran north from the mouth of the Kansas River. Out of it have come the counties of Platte, Buchanan, Andrew, Holt, Atchison, and Nodaway.

The territory was annexed primarily as a result of the trouble between the settlers and the Sauk, Fox, and Potawatomie Indians, who occupied the area as hunting ground. As usual, the frontier people were the aggressors, entering the Indian country to hunt and to settle. When the Potawatomies offered to sell their land, the route lay open to settlers to acquire it for the state of Missouri. Senator Thomas Hart Benton introduced legislation in Congress to purchase the territory in 1836, and in October 1837 the Missouri legislature accepted the additional land.

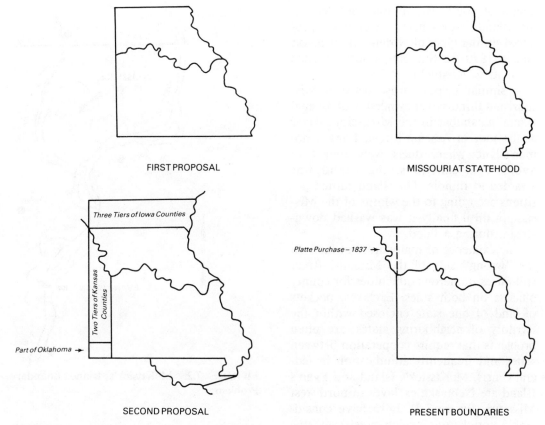

FIRST PROPOSAL

MISSOURI AT STATEHOOD

Three Tiers of Iowa Counties

Two Tiers of Kansas Counties

Part of Oklahoma →

Platte Purchase – 1837 →

SECOND PROPOSAL

PRESENT BOUNDARIES

FIGURE 3.1. Missouri Boundary Proposals.

BOUNDARY DISPUTES AND ADJUSTMENTS

The northern boundary line between Missouri and Iowa was once a matter of dispute. The Act of 1820, which defined the boundaries of Missouri, provided that this line, known as the Indian boundary line, should run east from a point where the meridian line running north from the mouth of the Kansas River intersected the parallel of latitude passing through the rapids of the Des Moines River. In 1837, however, a new line, known as Brown's Line, was surveyed to the Des Moines rapids in the Mississippi River. The confusion apparently stemmed from the language in the Act of 1820, which could be interpreted to be either "the rapids in the Des Moines River" or "the Des Moines rapids in the Mississippi River." The ter-

ritory in question amounted to 2,600 sq miles (6,734 km²).

The controversy, which included some arrests for failure to pay taxes and the ordering up of militia, culminated in a suit in the U.S. Supreme Court between the states of Missouri and Iowa. In 1849, the Court decided on the original boundary, or the Indian boundary line.

Another controversy, of less territorial importance, arose between Missouri and Kentucky concerning Wolf Island (Mississippi County), some 15,000 acres in area, in the Mississippi River. The question was whether this land, once an island but now attached to Missouri, was on the east or west side of the main channel of the Mississippi. Missouri contended, through maps, that the main river channel ran east of the island, that it was originally surveyed as part of Missouri, and that one of the circuit judges of southeast Missouri resided on the island. Nevertheless, Kentucky produced similar types of evidence in its favor, and in 1870 the Supreme Court awarded the land to Kentucky.

A similar dispute arose between Missouri and Illinois over ownership of Arsenal Island, a sandbar in the Mississippi River at the foot of Arsenal Street. Long a no-man's-land where duels were fought to avoid legal sanctions, the island was awarded to Illinois. The island shifted positions according to the whims of the Mississippi until finally it was washed downstream during a flood.

The existence of many areas of land on the "wrong" side of the Missouri River still raises numerous difficulties for county officials on both sides. Exclaves, pockets of land of one state enclosed within the territory of neighboring states, are often problems that require cooperation between states and frequently adjudication in federal courts. McKissick's Island and Evan's Island are Nebraska exclaves in northwest Missouri (Figure 3.2). Both have considerable populations, which must cross the territory of at least one neighboring state to reach the main part of their own state. No bridge crosses the Missouri at either point. McKissick's Island is in the unusual situation of being largely dependent for its nonadministrative services on a town—Hamburg, Iowa—two state boundaries away. No longer an island in the strict sense, McKissick's Island is joined to the mainland on the northwestern side. The Nishnabotna River separates the island from the mainland to the south and east.

Several developments have recently raised some questions as to the future of settlement on McKissick's Island. Until 1966 the island's children attended a small school that also served as the polling place of the area. In that year the building was torn down, and McKissick's Island was incorporated into the voting district of Auburn—the Nemaha County seat— and into the school district of Peru, Nebraska. Until the change in districting, property

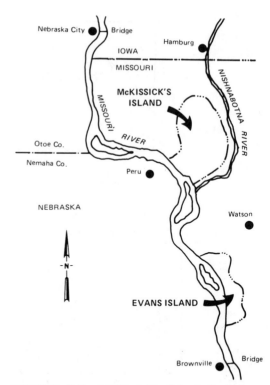

FIGURE 3.2. McKissick's Island Boundary Problem.

taxes on McKissick's Island were lower than in surrounding areas of Atchison County, Missouri, but now they are higher, which causes irritation to some property owners.

If the area were annexed to Missouri, the bridge over the Nishnabotna River would undoubtedly be replaced. Sentiment among farmers in the adjacent parts of Atchison County appears to be moving in favor of annexation for several reasons. The issues of taxation and law enforcement are commonly cited, as well as the fact that the island is now protected against flooding by the Missouri levee district. Population on the island has declined in recent years and only half of the sixteen families present in 1955 remains. If the area were completely depopulated, the pressure for annexation to Missouri could intensify, for the farmland is very fertile and valuable.

Perhaps the most unusual boundary ab-

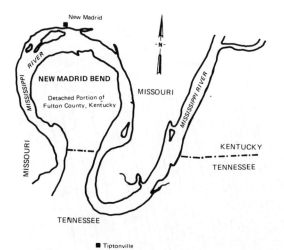

FIGURE 3.3.   New Madrid Bend.

erration is in southeastern Missouri where the New Madrid Bend of the Mississippi River forms a 40-mile-long (64.5-kilometer-long) loop around an enclave of Kentucky territory (Figure 3.3). This bit of mixed-up geography results from an 1859 survey of the Kentucky-Tennessee boundary. Commissioners from both states were appointed to delimit the boundary, generally following a line fixed by the state of Virginia years before. It was further agreed that west of the Tennessee River, the line would follow parallel 36°30′ N latitude to the west bank of the Mississippi River. The problem for the commissioners was to determine which west bank should be used, since the river crossed the proposed boundary line at three locations. The boundary between Kentucky and Tennessee was extended to the west bank of the westernmost channel of the Mississippi River.

The result was New Madrid Bend, a 7,000-acre (2,835-hectare) parcel of Kentucky land intruding into Missouri and separated from the remainder of Kentucky by 50 miles (80.45 km) of Tennessee territory. New Madrid Bend is less than half a mile (.805 km) in width at the neck of the bottle, but it is more than 40 miles (64.36 km) around the perimeter. The 150 residents of New Madrid Bend are Ken-

tuckians by warrant of their votes and the taxes they pay, but they go to church and school in Tennessee. They must travel over about 50 miles (80.45 km) of Tennessee highways to get to their own county-seat community of Hickman, Kentucky. Law enforcement and courts also are 50 miles (80.45 km) distant. If Tennessee owned the land, law and justice would be closer at hand at Tiptonville, Tennessee.

The land is some of the richest gumbo in the United States, with prime yields of cotton, soybeans, and wheat. Although it is seldom up for sale, it would fetch $2,000 or more per acre (.405 ha) in today's market. A narrow blacktop road leads into the area from Tiptonville, Tennessee. There are no bridges over the Mississippi within the bend. The only way out is through Tennessee.

LAND SURVEYS

Missouri, the "Show-Me State," became part of the United States with the signing of the Louisiana Purchase on April 30, 1803. After Congress approved the purchase in October, many explorers were sent into the vast, new territory to gather information. The French and Spanish, however, were the first to explore and settle this land west of the Mississippi River.

The French entered the area in the early 1700s looking for silver. Failing to find any, they explored the region and later traded with the Indians. In the process, the French discovered lead in the east-central Ozarks and immediately began mining operations, settling mainly along the rivers. In subdividing the land, the French used the long-lot system. Their unit of area was the arpent, equal to approximately two-thirds of an acre (.27 ha). Strips of land ran at right angles to the river giving a maximum number of people access to transportation (Figure 3.4). This system also provided each settler with land for crops, an area on the hillside with trees, and a homesite out of the floodplain. Besides giving these advantages, long-lot farms

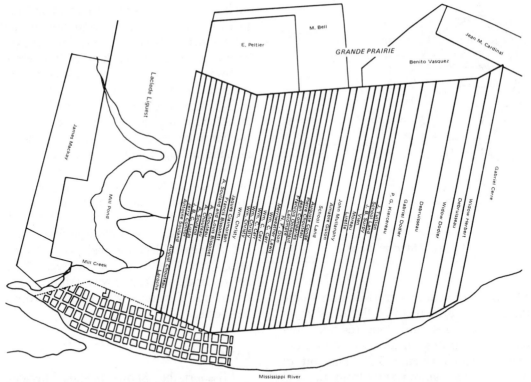

FIGURE 3.4.   The French Long-Lot Land Survey in Downtown St. Louis.

were economical; a road built along the end of the lots could serve more people per mile (1.609 km) than other survey systems. Once outside the river bottoms, however, the long-lot system was of little advantage over other systems. Only a few tracts of Missouri land were actually surveyed under this system.

Following the Seven Years' War, the French at Fontainebleau (1762) ceded to Spain the lands west of the Mississippi. To attract more settlers, both to maintain control and to mine the lead deposits in the Ozark hills, the Spanish Crown made land grants, charging only surveying and land registration fees. A farm of 800 acres (324 ha) cost approximately $41 filing fees plus the surveyor fees. A "settle-now, pay-later" policy developed. The grants, which constituted the best land in the region, were irregular-shaped parcels with no orientation to any reference points or to each other (Figure 3.5). Later, when the U.S.

Land Survey was established, these Spanish grants were confirmed (often after litigation), surveyed, and assigned a U.S. land survey number.

By far the most important system used in Missouri has been the rectangular land survey. The land is divided into tracts called congressional or land survey townships, each 36 sq miles (93.2 km²), 6 miles (9.654 km) per side. The boundaries are based on principal meridians running north-south with true east-west baselines emanating from them. Ranges, aligned east-west, are ordered in sequence from Range 1 east and Range 1 west. Townships run north-south from the baselines and are ordered in sequence from Township 1 north and Township 1 south. Thus, any particular township can be located by the township and range numbers (e.g., Township 3 north, Range 4 east).

The first step in surveying the state of Missouri was to establish a principal me-

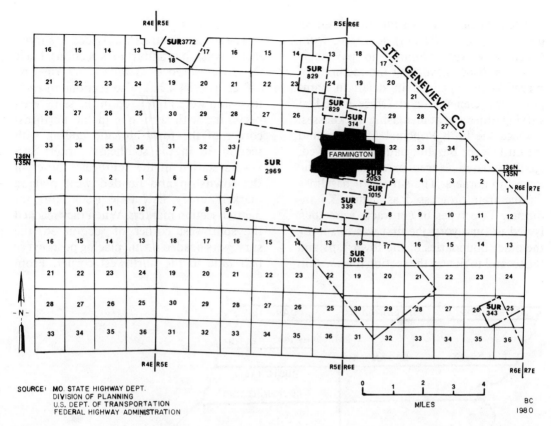

FIGURE 3.5.   Spanish Land Grants and the U.S. Land Survey in Southern St. Francois County.

ridian—the Fifth Principal Meridian. The origin of this meridian is the midpoint of the Arkansas River where it flows into the Mississippi River (Figure 3.6). Prospect K. Robbins, deputy surveyor, was issued a contract on October 9, 1815, to survey from the point in Arkansas River north to the south bank of the Missouri River, a distance of 317 miles, 35 chains, 76 links (510 km). The survey took two months and one day. This meridian was eventually extended into Iowa.

The survey of the Little Rock Baseline was begun by a second party on the same day. The line was to run from the midpoint of the St. Francis River where the river intersects the Mississippi and be surveyed due west from this point. A contract was issued to Joseph C. Brown, deputy surveyor, to survey from this midpoint to the western Arkansas border.

FIGURE 3.6.   Origins of the U.S. Land Survey in Missouri.

The surveyors in Missouri were paid $3 for each mile (1.609 km) surveyed, from which they were required to pay their expenses. Rules governing the methods of survey were explained in detail in pamphlets the General Land Office issued at varying times and at increasing thicknesses.

Once the Fifth Principal Meridian and the Little Rock Baseline had been surveyed, auxillary baselines were extended from the township corners. The survey of baselines for the state progressed as Figure 3.7 indicates. Two types of contracts were then issued to surveyors: the first was to survey the outer boundaries of the townships and the second to survey the section lines within the townships.

The second contract was issued to survey each township into thirty-six sections. Each section enclosed 1 sq mile (2.59 km²) or 640 acres (184.4 ha). The sections in each township were numbered in the same way, beginning with section 1 in the northeast corner of the township and ending with section 36 in the southeast corner. Surveyors started in the southeast corner of the township and headed west placing markers every half mile (.804 km) for quarter-section markers. When they reached the southwest corner of section 36, the surveyors headed north, placing posts every half mile to the northwest corner. From

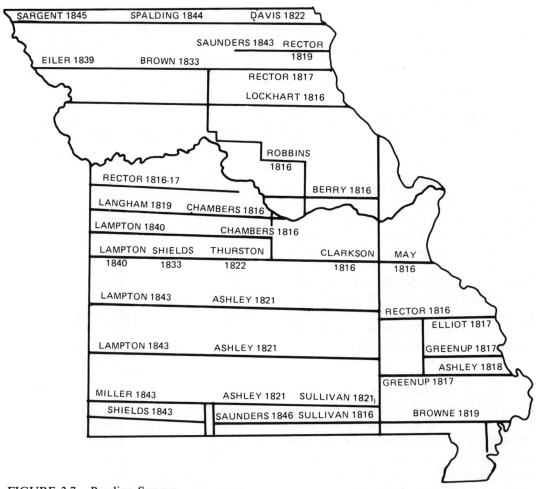

FIGURE 3.7.   Baseline Surveys.

there, they surveyed east, placing posts every half mile until they reached the northeast corner of section 36. Then they back surveyed to the northwest corner and headed north to the northwest corner of section 25; from there they surveyed east to the northeast corner. This procedure was continued until they reached the northeast corner of the township. From there the surveyors returned to the southwest corner of section 36 and headed west, repeating the procedure with this column of townships.

In this manner all of the township boundaries of Missouri were surveyed. Surveyors were required to keep extensive field notes on the area they covered. Posts were placed as markers along the way, and trees were blazed as reference points back to the posts. By 1850 the state was completely surveyed except for a swampy area in the Bootheel.

Land offices were then set up in Boonville, Ironton, Springfield, and other locations to issue titles to incoming settlers. All of the offices were closed in 1893.

Because of adverse conditions and the inexperience (or simply ineptitude) of the surveyors, many mistakes were made in the original surveys. In Missouri the original meridian Prospect Robbins surveyed was inaccurate and later surveys had to be adjusted. Robbins was trained in survey work in New England where it was the custom to add an extra chain (66 ft) (19.8 m) every mile (1.60 km) "for good measure" or to "correct for hilly terrain." Later surveys were conducted without the good-measure factor resulting in the need for a corrective tier of sections in Township 29 north. These sections, the north tier of Township 29 north, are approximately 2.5 miles (4.02 km) north-south and 1 mile (1.6 km) east-west. They are subdivided into normal 160-acre (64.8-hectare) southwest and southeast quarter sections and oversized northwest and northeast "quarters," which are then subdivided by platting.

NOTES

1. Louis Houck, *A History of Missouri,* vol. 1 (Chicago: R. R. Donnelley and Sons, 1908), p. 5.

SELECTED REFERENCES

Brown, Norman. "Missouri Land Surveys." Lecture presented at Southwest Missouri State University, Springfield, April 1980.

Conrad, Howard L. *Encylopedia of the History of Missouri.* Vol. 1. New York: Southern History Company, pp. 338–343. 1901.

Ehrlich, Daniel H. "Problems Arising from Shifts of the Missouri River on the Eastern Border of Nebraska." *Nebraska History,* vol. 54, no. 3, pp. 341–363. Fall, 1973.

Greenhood, David. *Mapping.* Chicago: University of Chicago Press, 1964.

Haskell, Henry C., and Richard B. Fowler. "The Attempted Annexation of Kansas City to the State of Kansas." *Missouri Historical Review,* vol. 44, pp. 221–224. April 1950.

Mann, Clair V. "How Shall We Preserve the Federal Land Survey Within Missouri?" *Surveying and Mapping,* vol. 26, pp. 85–94.

McClure, Clarence H., and Marguerite Potter. *Missouri, Its Geography, History, and Government.* New York: Laidlow Brothers, 1940, pp. 54–58, 93–94.

McKee, Howard I. "The Platte Purchase." *Missouri Historical Review,* vol. 32, pp. 129–147.

Meyer, Duane G. *The Heritage of Missouri: A History.* St. Louis: State Publishing Company, 1963, pp. 5, 180–185.

Robins, Ruby Matson. "Americans in the Valley, Part III." *Missouri Historical Review,* vol. 45, pp. 275–279. April 1951.

Sherman, C. E. *Original Ohio Land Subdivisions.* Columbus, Ohio: Ohio State Reformatory Press, 1925.

Shoemaker, Floyd Calvin. *Missouri and Missourians.* Vol. 1. Chicago: Lewis Publishing Company, 1943, pp. 5, 59–64, 172–176, 442, 445.

Stevens, Walter B. *Missouri, The Center State.* Vol. 2. Chicago: S. J. Clarke Publishing Co., 1915, pp. 763–766.

Thomas, John L. "Mo.-Iowa Boundary Dispute." *Missouri Historical Review,* vol. B, pp. 259–274. July 1908.

Thrower, Norman J. W. *Maps and Man.* Englewood Cliffs, N.J.: Prentice-Hall, 1972.

Trexler, Harrison A. "Missouri in the Old Geographies." *Missouri Historical Review,* vol. 32, pp. 148–155. January 1938.

Violette, Eugene Morrow. *A History of Missouri.* New York: Heath and Company, 1918.

Wood, W. Raymond. "William Clark's Mapping in Missouri." *Missouri Historical Review,* vol. 76, pp. 241–252. April 1982.

CHAPTER 4

SETTLEMENT

Missouri is unique among the states of the Union. Broadly speaking, other states are northern or southern, eastern or western, whereas Missouri is both western and southern with many characteristics of the north. Other regions have their distinctive attributes; Missouri to a large degree unites the features of all.

The peculiar development of the state is due in large part to its control of the Missouri River. Missouri early became the natural gateway to the west and southwest and the natural meeting place of the two great streams of emigration from the east. The population of the state is of varied origin, drawn from different areas of the east and from many European countries. The variety of natural resources makes Missouri economically one of the most self-sufficient states.

There were three phases in the settlement of Missouri. The first phase, from the early 1700s to 1860s, was the development of pioneer-frontier settlement, which spread from the Mississippi and Missouri rivers to the lead mines in the eastern Ozarks, then along the major tributaries, and finally over the whole state including the upland prairies. The French were in the vanguard; Americans of mainly Scotch-Irish descent from the upper-south hill country followed later.

The second settlement phase was part of the post–Civil War national development referred to as the Reconstruction or New South. During this phase, from about 1870 to 1900, the railroads spread rapidly, bringing elements of modernity with them. Many of the New South immigrants were from the northern states; and with northern capital, commercial agriculture, mining, and manufacturing developed quickly.

The third stage of occupancy, which may be called the resettlement phase, began with the events surrounding World War I and has proceeded to the present. During this period, the population of the state has grown, particularly in the large urban centers like St. Louis and Kansas City, and farm population has decreased. Recently, the settlement frontier has been the urban fringe—the counties on the periphery of the large cities—and the attractive recreational areas of the Ozarks. At the same time, the core areas of Missouri's largest cities have declined in population. The propensity for mobility among the American people continues to the present as they seek new opportunities in response to changing economic and social conditions. These processes of change have helped to reshape the geography of Missouri for the past sixty years.

THE FRENCH

The present territory of Missouri was originally part of the French province of Louisiana, but prior to the cession of the western bank of the Mississippi to Spain in 1762, most of the area was unexplored and unoccupied by Europeans. The first immigrant groups who did explore and settle in Missouri were French. They entered the Mississippi valley from their settlements on the Great Lakes and, in their quest for furs and minerals, systematically ranged the rivers of the interior lowlands of the United States. The Mississippi River was the main link between the major French settlements on the Great Lakes and in lower Louisiana. The eastern Ozarks were strategically located in the midsection, where the great east-west navigable rivers—the Ohio and Missouri—entered the Mississippi. It is not surprising that the French early established settlements along this section of the Mississippi, which linked the upper Mississippi, Wisconsin, Illinois, Missouri, Ohio, and Arkansas rivers. Following the famous voyage of Jacques Marquette and Louis Joliet in 1673, the French made numerous expeditions. In 1699, they established a mission settlement at the Indian village of Kaskaskia, on the Illinois side of the Mississippi across from Ste. Genevieve (Figure 4.1). Soon after, they also founded Cahokia and Fort Chartres on the fertile Illinois bottoms. The process of settlement followed a familiar sequence—the missionaries first, then the fur traders, soldiers, and farmers in that order. The French eked out a living by combining fur trading, boating, and a casual form of agriculture. Because of fertile soils and favorable growing conditions, a surplus of grain was available to ship to New Orleans in exchange for manufactured goods.

The French soon learned about the mineral wealth in the hill country to the west, probably through their contacts with the Indians. As early as 1700, the French knew of the lead deposits on the Meramec, and in 1702 Pierre d'Iberville asked for patents to work the mines.

Salt springs on Saline Creek, below Ste. Genevieve, were known even before Kaskaskia was settled. These springs and the lead ore attracted permanent settlement to the west bank of the Mississippi. In 1704, Governor Sieur Bienville reported that French were settled west of the river. This first official documentation of white settlement in the Ozarks was three-quarters of a century before the U.S. Republic was born.

Prodded by the stories of great hoards of silver and gold seized by the Spanish in Peru and Mexico and inflamed by discoveries of lead, which often occurs with silver, the French hoped to find a great bonanza. As might be expected, silver finds were soon reported, and investors were quick to underwrite prospecting and mining ventures. In 1717, the Company of the West assumed control of Louisiana and by 1719 had established exploratory mining on the Meramec. Failing to find silver, the smelter apparently "salted" the mine with a few ounces of silver. The legend of silver mines was thus established.

The first large-scale effort to explore and exploit minerals was the expedition of Sieur Renault, who in 1720 entered the lead diggings in what are now Washington and St. Francois counties reportedly with "two hundred artificers and miners provided with tools"[1] and slaves for working the mines. The expedition uncovered rich deposits of lead at the junction of the Big and Meramec rivers. In 1723, Renault received the site as a land grant, the first on record in upper Louisiana.

Although Renault's companions discovered several rich deposits of lead, they did not find precious metals. In 1723, lead was discovered at Mine La Motte, a few miles north of the present site of Fredericktown. The mines at Fourche à Renault were opened in 1724-1725, and the Old Mines north of Potosi were discovered in 1725.

As mining gradually expanded, the French established permanent residences on the west bank of the river. The site of the original settlement, about 1735, was on the Mississippi floodplain in the "Big Field," below the present site of Ste. Genevieve and across the river from Kaskaskia. After 1763, when the lands east of the river were deeded to Protestant England, many French families moved to Ste. Genevieve to be under a Catholic government. By

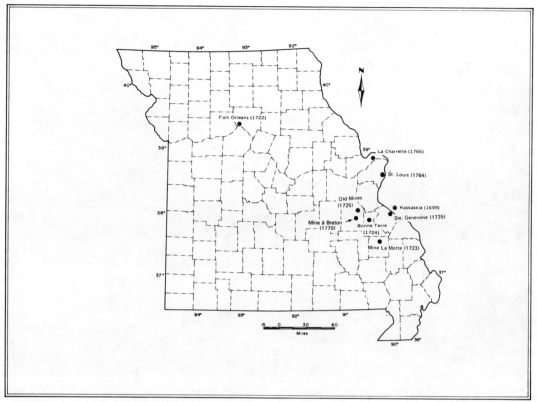

FIGURE 4.1.   Important French Settlements.

1769 the population of Ste. Genevieve and vicinity was estimated at about 600, which was more than the St. Louis area at that time. The Indian raids during the French and Indian War and General George Rogers Clark's capture of Kaskaskia during the American Revolution brought additional immigration to the west bank.

The site of Ste. Genevieve was subject to flooding and in 1785, "l'année des grandes eaux," the town was virtually destroyed. Residents of the old town and many residents of the towns on the Illinois side moved to the new-founded town at the bottom of a hill to the north. In 1787 the new U.S. government passed the ordinances that prohibited slavery in the Northwest Territory, prompting a number of wealthy slave owners to move to the Ste. Genevieve settlement.

By the end of the French period, about 1800, the French population lived pri-

marily in Ste. Genevieve and New Bourbon, a town about 1 mile (1.6 km) downriver, and in scattered temporary settlements at Mine à Breton (Potosi), Old Mines, Mine La Motte, and St. Michaels (Fredericktown). In addition, there were small settlements, which consisted of only a few families, at Cape Girardeau and on the Meramec.

The French settlers were engaged in one or more of four occupations: salt making, mining, agriculture, and trade with the Indians. Salt, made by evaporating weak brine from springs on Saline Creek below Ste. Genevieve, not only supplied the needs of the French settlers, but also was an important item of commerce. The digging and smelting of lead were conducted in the area now within Washington and St. Francois counties. Mining began in the fall after the harvests were in and lasted until the onset of winter, a period of time when

PHOTO 4.1. Bolduc House at Ste. Genevieve Built by French Settlers After the Flood, Circa 1785. Courtesy Walker—Missouri Division of Tourism.

the pits were driest. The galena ore was dug entirely from residual clays with wooden shovels and was heaped on piles of burning logs to be melted down. At first the lead was fashioned into the shape of a collar and draped across the neck of a horse. Later two-wheeled carts were used to transport the lead to the docks at Ste. Genevieve. The Big Field and Grand Park, an upland, were used for farming staple crops, wheat and corn; and in spite of constant threat of flood and a somewhat casual approach to cultivation, enough wheat was grown to supply local needs and to ship surpluses to New Orleans. The Big Field, the favored location, was divided into lots and distributed among the heads of household. Grand Park was a communal pasture for the livestock. Trade in grain, salt, and furs provided livelihood for many settlers.

The French pursued the fur trade into the Missouri valley, and in 1722, Fort Orleans was built near Brunswick for the purpose of controlling the nearby Indians. Since the fur traders frequently moved about, often living with the Indians, only a few permanent settlements were established in this area. St. Charles and a small village (the La Charrette settlement) at the mouth of La Charrette Creek in what is now Warren County were the only settlements on the Missouri at the time of the Lewis and Clark expedition in 1804. These settlements were a collection of small cabins and huts. Unlike the French at Ste. Genevieve, the voyageurs of the Missouri River frequently intermarried with the Indians.

The founding of St. Louis was a major landmark in the settlement of Missouri for it quickly grew into the most important town west of the Mississippi River. Eventually it became the largest city of Missouri and one of the great cities of the United

States. The first house in St. Louis was erected by Pierre Laclede Liguest, of the firm of Maxent, Laclede, and Company, merchants of New Orleans, who held a license for the fur trade on the Missouri River. After a winter at Fort Chartres, Laclede established his trading post in St. Louis in February 1764. The situation, near the mouths of the Missouri and Illinois rivers, was ideal for control of the fur trade of the upper Mississippi basin. The site, a natural landing on an outcrop of limestone on the first high ground south of the mouth of the Missouri, was free from flood and malaria.

In 1765 an English garrison arrived at Fort Chartres precipitating an exodus of the French from the east bottomlands of the Mississippi. In three years St. Louis was a thriving town of over 500 inhabitants, already rivaling Ste. Genevieve as the largest settlement in the valley north of New Orleans.

After the Spanish took formal possession in 1770, that portion of Louisiana north of the Arkansas River, known at the time as the Illinois country, was ruled by a succession of Spanish lieutenant governors at St. Louis. Each governed with absolute power, receiving orders only from New Orleans; controlled the troops and militia; and acted as chief justice under a code that did not recognize trial by jury or law by popular assembly. The transfer of allegiance, however, did little to disturb the cultural continuity of the area. The governors adopted the customs of the people and maintained French as the official language, even of official documents.

There was a steady growth in population, at first of French from Canada, Kaskaskia, and New Orleans and after 1790 of Americans from Kentucky. Thirteen years later, at the time of the Louisiana Purchase, the population of the district was over 7,000. Commandants, subordinate to the governor, were stationed at towns strung out along the Mississippi south of the mouth of the Missouri—New Madrid, Ste. Genevieve, New Bourbon, St. Charles, and St.

Andrews. New Madrid and Cape Girardeau contained a large number of Kentuckians, but the majority of the newcomers settled on detached farms along the creeks between St. Louis and Ste. Genevieve and around St. Charles. The settlement of the entire area, governed by Spanish, largely comprised French and Americans.

The country was largely agricultural, and with few exceptions there was little distinction of rank or wealth among the French. The richer men were merchants who sent the products of the colony to New Orleans or Montreal and sold manufactured goods. The younger men spent winters with professional trappers on the upper Missouri or Mississippi collecting furs, which were still one of the staple exports. Furs, lead, salt, and wheat were transported downriver. In the long and tedious return voyage against the current, the boats were laden with the few articles the colonists required, such as sugar, spices, and manufactured goods. Artisans were few and barely competent, so that all the implements except the rudest were imported. Even the spinning wheel was a rarity among the French, and butter was a special luxury. The Americans were more enterprising, but there was surprisingly little cultural exchange between the two groups.

The intellectual life was limited. There were no schools, and illiteracy was prevalent. The few books to be found were mainly in the libraries of priests. The religion was by law Roman Catholic, but Protestant Americans were not molested as long as they worshipped quietly. Political life was nonexistent; neither town meetings nor elections were held. Taxation was light, land was freely granted for nominal fees, and on the whole the Spanish governors were lenient and tolerant. There was rude abundance, a gentle, easygoing people, and a general absence of unrest.

THE AMERICANS

The Louisiana Purchase of 1803 was consequent to the great westward migration and colonization in the United States. There were four great routes from the Atlantic to the Ohio, all through accessible river valleys. The northern and easiest passage via the Mohawk River valley, later the route of the Erie Canal and now of the New York Turnpike, was barred by the Iroquois Indians until about 1800. The earlier pioneers thus crossed Pennsylvania to Pittsburgh or followed the Potomac or the Yadkin into the Shenandoah valley, crossing the ridges of the Appalachians through several passes, of which the Cumberland Gap was most famous. The settlers planned to reach either the Ohio, the Tennessee, or the Cumberland. The wanderings of Daniel Boone in eastern Kentucky in 1769–1771 mark the beginning of migration. A constantly increasing stream of settlers from the back country of Virginia and the Carolinas followed behind him.

Probably the first American settlement in trans-Mississippi territory was Colonel George Morgan's colony at New Madrid in 1788. Because Spain feared British attack on its far-flung empire, Spanish officials welcomed American immigrants and offered attractive, gratuitous grants of land. In return, the Americans, accustomed to loose government on the frontier, were willing to transfer their allegiance to the Spanish king. Those settlers who moved down the Ohio River were quick to take up lands along the eastern Ozark border, in part because of the French traders' widespread accounts of lead mines and fertile soils. In addition, the prairie regions to the north were considered less well suited to agriculture. Slave owners were attracted to the fertile and temperate Missouri River bottoms where they could reproduce the plantation system based on hemp and tobacco. The trans-Mississippi lands were cheaper, could be acquired in smaller tracts, and the titles were more secure than in Kentucky, where they were often contested.

Americans began to enter the region in large numbers in 1787. At that time Spain, then owner of the Louisiana Territory and anxious for settlers, initiated its policy of issuing land grants and other concessions in exchange for a loyalty oath. The prohibition of slavery in the Northwest Territory in 1787 added a second impetus for Missouri settlement for southern Americans; the Louisiana Purchase of 1803 provided a third (Figure 4.2). Americans already outnumbered Frenchmen by 1800, when Missouri's total population probably reached about 7,000. The figure rose rapidly under American ownership to 19,783 in 1810 and 66,586 in 1820. From 1796 to 1803, the Spanish were overwhelmed with petitions for land grants. The Spanish grants, as they are still called, form a mosaic of irregular tracts, (usually rectangular in shape, but only occasionally oriented in cardinal directions) in the Fredericktown soils, the Hagerstown loess, and alluvial soils primarily. The better lands of the Mississippi and Missouri river borders and the St. Francois Mountains were the first to be settled. Many of the Spanish grants were fraudulent and were subjected to title investigations for many decades. The act of 1815 that allowed settlers to relocate lands damaged or lost in the New Madrid earthquakes of 1811-1812 exposed a great many contested titles in the Missouri valley. Perhaps even more rapid settlement would have occurred if land titles had been more secure and the price of land ($1.25 per acre) lower.

The first immigrants were southern, the majority from Tennessee and Kentucky, accompanied by frontiersmen from North Carolina, Virginia, and Pennsylvania. Most were poor yeoman farmers, Scotch-Irish by descent, restless enterprising adventurers cut in the mold of Daniel Boone and Kit Carson. A wealthier group, mainly slave owners from the same districts in the South, occupied the better river bottoms where slaves could be used to clear timber and plant fields of hemp, tobacco, and corn. A third group consisted of settlers with some capital to invest in commerce or in the manufacture of commodities needed on the frontier. Very often this group be-

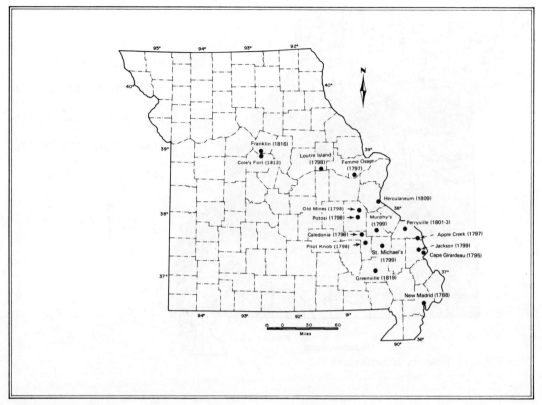

FIGURE 4.2.   Pioneer American Settlements.

came the leaders of communities and the initiators of change.

GEOGRAPHY OF SETTLEMENT

The Mississippi River Border

Initially settlement was by and large detached farms or small hamlets along rivers and creeks. Uplands were usually settled later because of water scarcity and generally poorer soils. Very soon there was an inhabited strip along the Mississippi and inland to the lead mines. Another strip of settlement followed the Missouri River. A close examination of the Mississippi and Missouri valley settlements, as they exist today, reveals that many are not properly riverine, but rather are located 10 miles (16.2 km) or so inland. New London and Bowling Green in the upper Mississippi valley fit this pattern as do Apple Creek

and Jackson in the Cape Girardeau vicinity and Columbia and Loutre Lick (Danville) near the Missouri River. Health considerations, land quality, and transportation routes were important in determining the locations of the settlements. Many observers at the time reported on the malarial conditions (fevers) found in the major river bottoms and some asserted that settlements failed for health reasons (Figure 4.3).

If settlers avoided some fertile river bottoms for health reasons, the next best place to establish a farming community was a few miles inland, away from the rough bluff lands. The upland loess soils along the river borders were proclaimed to be equal or superior to any of the same type east of the Mississippi River. Good transportation accompanied good soils in many cases, because travelers, as well as farmers, were naturally attracted to the level uplands. The old El Camino Real

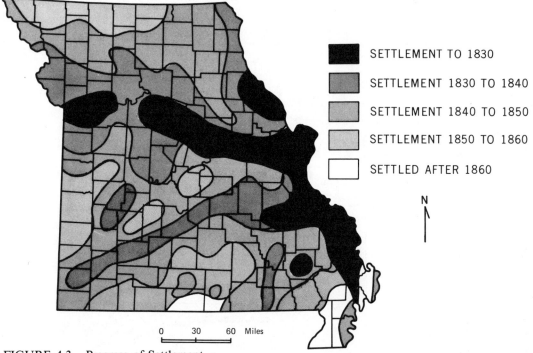

SETTLEMENT TO 1830

SETTLEMENT 1830 TO 1840

SETTLEMENT 1840 TO 1850

SETTLEMENT 1850 TO 1860

SETTLED AFTER 1860

N

0   30   60   Miles

FIGURE 4.3.   Progress of Settlement.

(King's Highway), laid out in 1789, followed the upland for most of its route
from St. Louis to New Madrid, although
it touched the Mississippi at Ste. Genevieve
and other key towns.

One of the first American settlements
was at Cape Girardeau. Farmers cleared
land on a creek south of the present-day
site in 1795, on the Whitewater River in
1796, and on bottomland along nearby
Hubble Creek in 1797. By 1799 settlers
began to occupy the upland soils in the
Ozarks northwest of Cape Girardeau (see
Figure 4.2, p. 55). Both the loess and
weathered limestone (Hagerstown) soils
proved to be well suited to corn and wheat,
the staple pioneer crops. Mill sites were
plentiful, soils were fertile, and the settlements were linked to the outside world
via the Mississippi River. As a result, settlement progressed rapidly, and by 1821
the district had a population of 7,852.

Cape Girardeau, the river port and first
town to be established, had 300 inhabitants
by 1811. Its growth, however, was eclipsed
by the founding of Jackson in the midst
of the fertile upland soil districts. Jackson
is still the county seat even though Cape
Girardeau, after challenges to land titles
were cleared, became the largest city of the
county.

Settlement along the eastern border progressed at about the same time as in the
Cape Girardeau district and in the same
sequence. Well-drained bottomlands were
settled first, and nearby fertile uplands were
explored for later settlement. In Perry
County, Pennsylvanians entered the Bois
Brule bottoms of the Mississippi in 1787,
and ten years later other Americans occupied the bottoms along Brazeau and
Apple creeks. A large group of Kentuckians
penetrated the upland prairie or "barrens"
of Perry County in the period from 1801
to 1803. Perryville, founded in 1822, became the largest city of the barrens, whereas
St. Mary's became the chief river port for
the district and for Mine La Motte.

The St. Francois Mountains

Americans settled at Ste. Genevieve primarily to engage in business and commerce, particularly in connection with the lead mines to the west. However, large numbers of Americans were attracted to the lead district in St. Francois and Washington counties. Moses Austin, an entrepreneur and metallurgist, secured 1 square league (1,796 ha) of land at Mine à Breton (Potosi) in 1798, and in 1799 a settlement was established. Families that accompanied Austin settled near the mines and on fertile farmlands in the Belleview Valley. Several new discoveries of lead were made in St. Francois County at Mines à Joe (Desloge), à Lanye, à Maneto, and à la Plate. These mines, all situated on Big River, formed the beginnings of what was to become the fabulous Old Lead Belt, which produced lead and zinc ores until 1973. Numerous other mines were opened in Washington County. Henry Rowe Schoolcraft, the noted naturalist and adventurer who traveled through the Ozarks in 1818 and 1819, listed forty-five mines in the district, of which twenty-five were in the vicinity of Potosi.[2]

The few sections of the St. Francois region suitable for agriculture were discovered and settled by 1810. The quality of the soils in the limestone basins was appreciated widely, and both the Belleview Valley and Murphy's (Farmington) were settled by 1798. The Arcadia Valley, St. Michael's (Fredericktown), and other pockets of alluvial and limestone soils were settled at about the same time. A few widely scattered farms were located farther north on the Meramec and on Plattin and Joachim creeks.

An examination of topographic maps shows that better soils and mineral lands were claimed under Spanish grants prior to the Louisiana Purchase, in the eastern Ozark counties of Cape Girardeau, Perry, Ste. Genevieve, St. Francois, Washington, Madison, and Jefferson. These grants are especially numerous near Jackson, Perryville, Ste. Genevieve, Farmington (Murphy's), Potosi (Mine à Breton), Fredericktown (St. Michael's), Greenville, and along the Joachim and Plattin valleys in Jefferson County.

The Missouri River Border

That the Missouri River was on the main route to the west and nearly as accessible as the Mississippi River Border is borne out by the fact that several American settlements were in existence there prior to 1800. Kentuckians, notably Daniel Boone and his followers, inhabited St. Charles and southern Warren County only a few miles above the mouth of the Missouri. Boone, in 1797, settled on the bottoms of Femme Osage Creek in Warren County, and others soon followed suit on Tuque, Charrette, and Lost creeks. Apparently the settlers preferred the tributary valleys, which had fertile soils, good springs, and easy access to the Missouri River as well as protection from its devastating floods. The Loutre Island settlement (1798) on the Missouri floodplain in Montgomery County was established on a high tract of alluvium that was insular during floods.

The Boon's Lick country in Cooper and Howard counties was first settled in 1810, although Boone had boiled salt at springs in the area as early as 1807. News of the country's timber, grass, good water, good bottomland, extensive areas of loess soils (the first deep loess region upstream from St. Charles), and numerous salt springs spread quickly. The earliest settlements were at Heath's Creek salt springs on the Lamine River in Cooper County and near New Franklin in Howard County. Although immigrants of diverse circumstances and origins came to the Boon's Lick country, the region was especially attractive to southern slave owners.

The Boon's Lick Trail, extending from St. Charles to Franklin, in Howard County, paralleled the Missouri on its northern side. Colonel Benjamin Cooper had blazed the initial trace in 1810, and by 1822 significant settlements had begun to grow up along it. The Boon's Lick region became the largest and most famous settlement outlier in Missouri history. Perhaps the magic of the Boone name, in addition to the area's geographic advantages, attracted many.

Boonville (Cole's Fort), a harbor and trading town for the western Ozarks, was established in 1812 on the south bank of the river where it makes a rectangular bend to the north. In 1816 the town of Franklin was laid out near the present site of New Franklin across the river from Boonville. A profitable land office was established there. Many other towns were soon established in the country between Boon's Lick and the Loutre Island settlement. Bottomland could be purchased at $1 to $5 an acre, and the influx of immigrants encouraged entrepreneurs to establish towns at strategic locations. The town of Gasconade was founded at the mouth of the Gasconade River as a prospective site for the state capital.

Town promoters sold lots for the Osage City settlement at the mouth of the Osage River. Newport occupied a similar location at the mouth of Boeuf Creek. The bustling towns of Pittsburgh, Cincinnati, and St. Louis excited visions of wealth and economic prosperity in the minds of nearly every settler. A host of towns—Pinckney, Thorntonsburg, Missouriton, Rocke au Pierce, and Columbia—were founded on the river floodplain at landings. Malaria and flood, however, took their toll, and only the bluff towns, Boonville and Jefferson City, survived long enough to prosper.

The Springfield Plain

Settlement of the Springfield Plain lagged behind that of the Mississippi and Missouri river borders. Its few navigable streams, the Osage, White, and Neosho, were far from the main routes of commerce, and transportation was dangerous and only seasonable. The rugged hills of the interior discouraged overland travel as well. The vast mineral wealth of the Joplin area, which attracted many settlers, was not discovered until later.

The earliest settlement of record on the plain was at Delaware Town southwest of Springfield in Christian County where Wilson's Creek joins the James River. From their homes on the Muskingum River in Ohio, the settlers of Delaware Town followed a circuitous route first down the Ohio, then south on the Mississippi, and finally up the Arkansas, White, and James rivers. The region had an excellent reputation for game and was known in Tennessee, the origin of most of the early immigrants, as the country of the six bulls (corrupted from *boils,* or springs).

By 1830 the Osage River had become a route of navigation, and Warsaw a major port for the disembarkment of immigrants and later for the region's trade. Although keelboats could reach Osceola during spring and fall, Warsaw remained the main port on the river and second in importance only to Springfield among the towns in southwest Missouri. Overland roads also left the Missouri River at Boonville and Jefferson City.

Other overland routes from the Mississippi River crossed the interior Ozarks following upland divides. The most important route was the Springfield Road from St. Louis, which connected Rolla, Lebanon, Marshfield, Springfield, Mt. Vernon, and Neosho. This route was later followed closely by the Atlantic and Pacific Railroad (Burlington Northern), U.S. 66, and most recently by Interstate 44. A branch of the route, beginning at Ste. Genevieve and passing through Caledonia and Steelville, joined the main trail near St. James.

Because of relatively easy access, the pioneers of the Springfield Plain were preponderantly from Tennessee and then from Kentucky. Like those who settled the Mississippi and Missouri river borders, they were farmers and adventurers—albeit there were fewer slaveholders among them—and followed the same practices in selecting sites for homes. The first to enter the region chose bottomlands near springs and timber.

Those who followed settled in the fertile upland prairies and still succeeding immigrants located on less choice tracts.

The settlement of Springfield, the self-styled "Queen City" of the Ozark region, was typical. John Polk Campbell, a Tennesseean, visited the site in 1829 and found good soils in the Kickapoo Prairie and in the small bottoms along Jordan Creek (a tributary of Wilson's Creek), where abundant, good water issued from springs. The following year he returned with his family and friends and erected several cabins close by a sinkhole spring, or natural well, under the north-facing valley slope.

Some of the counties on the western border between Kansas City and Joplin were settled late because of political strife between Missouri and the free state of Kansas during the 1850s. Bands of free-state sympathizers from Kansas raided farms and towns in Missouri, partly in retaliation for raids Missourians conducted in Kansas in search of escaped slaves.

The Interior Ozarks

The progress of settlement in the interior Ozarks was slow. Isolated and impoverished, the region served as a barrier that deflected immigration north and south. By 1811, however, settlers had penetrated nearly every fertile valley in the St. Francois Mountains to the margins of the Courtois Hills. After the border regions of the Ozarks were well settled, they began to enter the interior. The valleys were narrow and offered limited possibilities for agriculture; therefore, settlement came late to the Courtois and Osage-Gasconade hills and even later to the wilderness on the Arkansas-Missouri border.

The central Ozarks offered few prizes to ambitious investors. Geographically isolated from the rest of the state, the people developed a distinctive culture that remains to this day. Many of the counties are the bulwarks of the Republican party in Missouri and Arkansas. Only in recent years, as schools have improved, and radio and television have become nearly universal, has this region reflected state and national trends.

Schoolcraft observed settlements, undoubtedly temporary, on the upper Gasconade in 1818–1819.[3] Saltpeter caves were worked in the same area at about the same time. In 1826 Thomas Massey opened the Maramec ore bank and in 1829 founded the Maramec Iron Works. By 1835 there were fifty families at the settlement. Several other iron furnaces were established in Crawford and Dent counties.

From 1817 to 1825, land bounties, in lieu of wages, granted to soldiers of the Revolutionary War and the War of 1812 stimulated population growth in the Ozarks. In addition, surveys of the preemption lands were begun in 1819, ushering in an era of speculation with the preemption acts (beginning in 1820). However, because of the availability of superior lands in other districts, these laws did not greatly influence land purchases in the interior Ozarks.

Agricultural settlement developed first in the valleys of the larger and more accessible rivers and then around progressively smaller and more isolated streams. By 1825 there were settlements at Wayne County on the St. Francis River, in Ripley County on the Current River, in Oregon County on the Eleven Point River, and along the Osage, Gasconade, and Meramec rivers on the north slope of the Ozark dome.

The minimum price of $1.25 an acre (.405 ha) for public lands was considered too high for the uplands in the interior. After the Graduation Act of 1854, land entries were greatly stimulated. By 1858, 1,890,000 acres (765,450 ha) were sold, of which 1,140,304 (461,823 ha) brought $0.125 per acre and 227,940,000 acres (92,315,700 ha) $0.25 an acre (.405 ha). Because speculators purchased much of the land, the increase in population was not proportionate to the amount of land sold.

The region suffered heavily during the Civil War due to the fact that the settlements were weak and isolated and the wild broken hills offered protection to lawless bands. The population of many of the present counties bordering the Missouri-Arkansas boundary decreased substantially as residents moved out of the wilderness to more protected areas near military posts.

Northern Missouri

An overwhelming dominance of Southerners among Missouri's early settlers contributed to the scarcity of settlers north of St. Charles. Even as late as 1850, people from the South constituted 66 percent of all Missourians, over 90 percent if foreign-born immigrants are excluded. The Missouri valley offered a closer climate parallel with Kentucky and Tennessee than did the upper Mississippi valley. Also, in the early 1800s, raids by the Sac and Fox Indians in the Cuivre River country probably discouraged settlement. Although these raids were minor, fear of a major attack continued until 1815.

The Cuivre River skirmishes along with the events leading to the annexation of the Platte Purchase lands, in the northwest part of the state, are the only major instances in Missouri where Indian occupancy slowed the advances of American settlers on the frontier. The major tribe in the state, the Osage, had ceded most of their lands in 1808, retaining only a strip south of the Missouri River and west of Fort Osage in present-day Jackson County. The tribe ceded even this 23-mile-wide (36.8-kilometer) strip in 1825, before whites exerted severe pressure to occupy it. The federal government moved a Delaware Indian group, including a few members of several other eastern tribes, to southwestern Missouri along the James River in the early 1820s. This action may have deterred a few settlers, but by 1830 this tribe too had been removed.

As settlement progressed west along the Missouri River, pioneers moved into the larger tributary valleys where they selected homesites. The conditions of soil and terrain in the valleys of the Chariton, Grand, Platte, and other rivers were similar to those in the Mississippi and Missouri val-

leys. By 1830 settlements had spread along the Mississippi to the northern border of Missouri and up most of the larger tributaries of the Mississippi and Missouri. Settlers took advantage of the better-drained soils and the most advantageous mill sites. Settlements at Canton and La Grange in Lewis County were founded in 1819. Macon, later the seat of the county of the same name, was founded in 1827. Fulton, in Calloway County, was settled in 1825. Many of the other larger trade centers of northern Missouri were founded in the 1830s and 1840s. Among these were Plattsburg (1833), Gallatin (1837), Trenton (1837), Mexico (1837), Kirksville (1841), Bethany (1842), and Maryville (1845).

Most of the towns founded in northern Missouri were located away from the major streams. Although health and flooding remained important concerns, many of these new towns were established for political reasons, as government seats for newly formed counties. Troy and Benton exemplify this pattern along the Mississippi border as do Independence, Richmond, and Fulton along the Missouri. Transportation limitations dictated the situation. Given the existing bridge technology, a county could not span the larger rivers; yet its seat of government required a central location to serve the predominantly rural population. Many local rivalries arose between the older, river town of a county and its inland, government center. Glasgow and Fayette, in Howard County, serve as a classic example of this.

Settlers avoided the region now known as Chariton and Carroll counties in part because its location did not promote a profitable trade. Towns there faced competition from established urban centers both in the Boon's Lick and on the western border. The area also lacked good roads. The principal road of the upper Missouri valley, a continuation of the Boon's Lick Trail, passed to the south side of the Missouri River at Arrow Rock to avoid the large northern bend of the river at that point. Potential settlers were further discouraged by absentee ownership of many tracts. After the War of 1812, the federal government established twenty-four townships in present-day Chariton, Carroll, Randolph, and Macon counties as a military reserve for veterans. Speculation in the military land scrip led to substantial numbers of absentee owners, who were difficult for potential purchasers to find.

The Platte Purchase in 1837 encouraged expansion on the Missouri upstream from Independence. Weston soon emerged as the center of this region, carrying on a profitable trade with Fort Leavenworth and various Indian groups just across the Missouri River. Caldwell County was organized in 1836, partly because its isolation would provide safety for the Mormons, a beleaguered people previously expelled from Jackson and Clay counties. Some 3,000 moved to the county in 1838 and began construction of a temple. Very soon opposition grew, and in 1839 the Mormons fled Missouri entirely.

There is little evidence that the prairie environment of northern Missouri delayed settlement. It appears that the earliest north Missouri settlers—highly dispersed, poor in technology, and necessarily self-sufficient—located in the familiar and diverse natural environment of the stream valleys. As population density increased to the point that towns and county governments could be established, urban issues such as centrality and trade access determined the location of settlements. More purely agricultural factors, including the timber-prairie question, became secondary. Probably the completion of the federal land surveys and the associated land advertisements were of prime importance in stimulating land sales in a given section. As county governments were organized, the county seats, which were usually centrally located, served as local settlement magnets—for example, Maryville, Bethany, Princeton, Trenton, Milan, and Kirksville. The largest and flattest area of prairie in northern Missouri, and in the state—the Grand Prairie in

Audrain, Ralls, and Monroe counties—was settled in the 1840s.

The Southeast Lowlands

By all geographic criteria, physical and cultural, the Southeast Lowlands are Missouri's most unique region. Certainly the history of settlement and the geographic patterns in the cultural landscape set it apart from Missouri's other regions.

The earliest settlements in the Southeast Lowlands were at New Madrid and Cape Girardeau. New Madrid is located at the southern end of the fertile, well-drained Sikeston Ridge where it meets the Mississippi River. French voyageurs traveling on the river discovered the area was not covered by swamps. North from New Madrid along the ridge, a great Indian trail and warpath led to the Scott County Hills and farther on to the Missouri and its tributaries. On Sikeston Ridge, the works of the Mound Builders were then visible at many sites, and the location of the town was reportedly once an aboriginal encampment. The bend of the river where the town of New Madrid is now situated became known as L'Anse à la Graise, "cove of fat," or "grease." The name is said to be derived from the fact that great quantities of bear meat were stored there for the use of military forces and French and Spanish travelers.

At first New Madrid was a trading post for bartering with Indians; but as population grew, settlers pushed northward along the ridge, opening up plantations and farms that added to the trade at the riverfront settlement. All traffic to New Orleans and to the eastern settlements was by water, and the only way by which the river could be reached was down the ridge to New Madrid. The swamps of the Charleston Lowland (Tywappity Bottoms) were barriers to any movement east to the river. Wheat was the chief crop grown on the ridge, and in later years wheat grown on the northern end of the ridge was hauled along a road at the base of the Scott County Hills (Commerce Hills) to the river at

Commerce where another trading post was established. Flour mills were built and Commerce became a major trading center for the northern part of Sikeston Ridge as New Madrid was for the southern part.

Cape Girardeau was established by a French trader named Sieur Jean Pierre Girardot to trade with the Indians in the Ozark highland. Girardot's post was on the cape or upland extending to the river just north of the present city. For many years Cape Girardeau was a settlement of minor economic importance, later maintained primarily by the Spanish as a military post to control the Indians.

In the early 1800s settlers began to locate northward on Crowley's Ridge and the terraces along its western flank. The main access to the river followed a route north to the foot of the Ozark Escarpment, then eastward at the foot of the escarpment to Cape Girardeau. Travel east from the Crowley's Ridge settlement was blocked by the swamps of the Morehouse Lowland. The commerce to "Cape" was so substantial that it was not unusual to see 100 wagonloads at a time unloading corn, cotton, and other products of the region at the levee during the months of September and October. The products of the Ozark Region west of the Advance Lowland also were transported to the levee at Cape Girardeau. By handling the commerce of two areas, Cape Girardeau soon outstripped Commerce and New Madrid as the major trade center along 300 miles (482.7 km) of the Mississippi.

The King's Highway was opened in 1789 to link New Madrid, Cape Girardeau, and Ste. Genevieve with St. Louis. Primarily a military road, it was used little for commerce because water transportation of goods was so much cheaper.

Local trading points grew up along Sikeston Ridge, Crowley's Ridge and its foreland terrace, and along the foot of the Ozark Escarpment. At these places people bought supplies and sold their products, which were then assembled for shipment to New Madrid, Commerce, and Cape Girardeau.

Because of poor roads and transportation facilities, the maximum distance people could travel to a trading center and return home in a single day was about 8 miles (12.87 km). Therefore, towns sprung up about 12 miles (19 km) to 16 miles (26 km) apart along the north-south ridges and terraces.

Railroad transportation changed the flow of commerce and the fortune of settlements in the Southeast Lowlands. The rail line that was to link Cairo with Poplar Bluff was started before the Civil War and completed in 1867. Sikeston was founded where the railroad crossed Sikeston Ridge, and Dexter was laid out on the crossing of Crowley's Ridge. Since the cost of transportation by rail was much less than by horse-drawn vehicles, the direction of the flow of commerce on Sikeston Ridge gradually reversed: now the flow from both parts was toward the center to the railroad at Sikeston. Likewise, the products that had formerly moved up Crowley's Ridge to Cape Girardeau from as far south as Arkansas were intercepted at the railroad at Dexter.

The lowlands of the Charleston, Morehouse, and Advance basins were marshes covered with water most of the year. In this wetland grew cypress, tupelo, and other swamp trees. Huge oaks grew on the better-drained terraces and sand ridges. The building of railroads made possible the establishment of numerous sawmills along the tracks and the movement of the lumber to market. Bernie, Grayridge, Gideon, Morehouse, Miner's Switch, Bertrand, Kennett, Wyatt, and many other towns were thus established as sawmill camps.

In the last decade of the nineteenth century, Louis Houck began his extensive railroad building in southeast Missouri. Lines were built southwest from Cape Girardeau along the Ozark Escarpment to Hoxie, Arkansas. A branch line extended south along Crowley's Ridge; and another branch was extended south to Commerce, then west along the settlements at the base of the Scott County Hills before turning south through the swamps to Kennett. The effect of these rail lines was to capture the traditional wagon routes and to tap new trade areas diverting goods to Cape Girardeau and eventually to St. Louis.

DRAINAGE AND DEVELOPMENT

Originally, the Charleston, Morehouse, and Advance lowlands had one feature in common—each was a swamp. Conditions were different in each area, however. The waters of the Charleston Lowland (Tywappity Bottoms) came from local rainfall and from overflows of the Mississippi and Ohio rivers. The land was flat, heavily forested except for some prairies, and there were no channels for runoff waters. Use of the 400,000 acres (162,000 ha) of land depended on construction of canals to carry off rainwater.

The Morehouse Lowland, known locally as the Little River Basin, begins at the Ozark Escarpment and extends south between Sikeston Ridge and Crowley's Ridge. The total area is 550,000 acres (222,750 ha). Castor River, Whitewater River (which becomes Little River in its lower reaches), Crooked Creek, Hubble Creek, and other streams drain waters from the Ozarks into the northern end of this lowland. Reclamation required the diversion of the Ozark streams out along the Advance Lowland to the Mississippi River about 5 miles (8.04 km) south of Cape Girardeau. The Little River Project, as it was known at its beginning in 1905, was the greatest reclamation area in the world. The lowlands were flooded repeatedly each year by the waters of the St. Francis, Black, and Whitewater rivers until ditches and levees were built.

For a century after the first settlements in the southeast Missouri lowlands, practically no progress was made in drainage, except on a very limited scale. Because timber was the chief resource, settlement was very sparse. About 1900 the dragline dredge was developed. This machine could move about 2,000 cu yd (1,530 m³) of earth a day and made possible both the building of adequate levees to contain the rivers and the cutting of ditches to drain the swamps.

The plans for drainage were similar for each lowland. North-south ditches, which followed the general slope, were cut about 1 mile (1.6 km) apart. These converged in main collector ditches that drained southwest toward the St. Francis River. In the Morehouse Lowland alone there are more than 1,200 miles (1,931 km) of ditches, and in the whole area the total exceeds 2,000 miles (3,218 km).

The enormous costs of rights-of-way, engineering, and construction were met by the issuance of bonds to be retired by drainage tax on the land benefited. Although drainage in the area is ever being extended and improved, most of the land became usable by the 1930s. Mosquito control was also made possible by drainage. Consequently, the "Swampeast," Missouri's last settlement frontier, became one of the most productive agricultural districts in the world. Land is used for cash crops: cotton, corn, soybeans, and wheat. In dry years the lowlands flourish, in wet years the sandy ridges do well, and in normal years the production is truly phenomenal. Many cases are on record in which the crops of two or three years are sufficient to pay the total cost of the land, at several hundred dollars an acre. Land values in the late 1970s ranged from about $1,250 for poorly drained land to $2,500 an acre (.405 ha) or more for well-drained "cotton land."

NOTES

1. Henry Rowe Schoolcraft, *A View of the Lead Mines of Missouri* (New York: John Wiley and Co., 1819), p. 15.

2. Ibid., pp. 65–67.

3. Henry Rowe Schoolcraft, *Journal of a Tour into the Interior of Missouri . . . Performed in the Years 1818 and 1819* (London: Phillips and Co., 1821), p. 15.

SELECTED REFERENCES

Campbell, Robert A. *Campbell's Gazetter of Missouri*. St. Louis: R. A. Campbell, 1875.

Gerlach, Russel. *Immigrants in the Ozarks: A Study in Ethnic Geography*. Columbia: University of Missouri Press, 1976.

————. "Population Origins in Rural Missouri." *Missouri Historical Review*, vol. 71, pp. 1–21. October 1976.

Fuller, Myron L. *The New Madrid Earthquake*. Reprint. Cape Girardeau, Mo.: Ramfre Press, 1966.

Haswell, A. W., ed. *The Ozark Region, Its History and Its People*. Vol. 1, Springfield, Mo.: Interstate Historical Society, 1917.

Hewes, Leslie. "The Oklahoma Ozarks as the Land of the Cherokees." *Geographical Review*, vol. 32, pp. 269–281. 1942.

Houck, Louis. *A History of Missouri*. Vols. 1–3. Chicago: R. R. Donnelley and Sons, 1908.

Paullin, Charles O. *Atlas of the Historical Geography of the United States*. Washington, D.C.: Carnegie Institute of Washington, 1932.

Rafferty, Milton D. *Historical Atlas of Missouri*. Norman: University of Oklahoma Press, 1982.

————. *The Ozarks: Land and Life*. Norman: University of Oklahoma Press, 1980.

Sauer, Carl O. *The Geography of the Ozark Highland of Missouri*. Geographical Society of Chicago, bulletin no. 7. Chicago: University of Chicago Press, 1920.

Schoolcraft, Henry Rowe. *Schoolcraft in the Ozarks*. Edited by High Parks. Van Buren, Ark.: Press-Argus, 1955.

Schroeder, Walter. "Spread of Settlement in Howard County." *Missouri Historical Review*, vol. 63, pp. 1–37. October 1968.

Shoemaker, Floyd C. *Missouri Day by Day*. Vols. 1–2. Columbia: State Historical Society of Missouri, 1942.

Shortridge, James R. "The Expansion of the Settlement Frontier in Missouri." *Missouri Historical Review*, vol. 75, pp. 64–90. October 1980.

Williams, Walter. *The State of Missouri*. Columbia, Mo.: E. W. Stephens Press, 1904.

CHAPTER 5

POPULATION: CHARACTER AND DISTRIBUTION

The earliest settlements in Missouri were along the two major navigable rivers—the Mississippi and Missouri—and until the latter half of the nineteenth century these rivers and their tributaries were the main avenues for immigration. Except for foreign immigrants, the population was largely from the states of the upper South and lower Middle West until about 1870. By 1860, 99,814 immigrants had arrived in Missouri from Kentucky, 73,954 from Tennessee, 53,957 from Virginia, 35,389 from Ohio, 30,463 from Indiana, and 30,138 from Illinois. Southern planters who owned slaves and could afford the higher-priced lands settled near the Mississippi and Missouri. Mountain people from middle and east Tennessee were especially attracted to the Ozarks, where land was cheaper. Manuscript census records show that settlers in Shannon, Dent, and Carter counties between 1820 and 1860 originated in Tennessee (284), Illinois (171), Kentucky (63), Arkansas (54), Indiana (48), Alabama (38), Virginia (11), and North Carolina (4).

Most of the American immigrants in the pioneer phase were of Scotch-Irish stock. They were experienced frontier settlers, accustomed to the hardships of arduous travel, to starvation, and to the dangers of Indian raids. Strong, independent, resourceful, they possessed an amazing knowledge of how to wrest a living from the forest. The Scotch-Irish were known as Ulstermen, Presbyterian Irish, or simply as the Irish. After large numbers of Irish Catholics began to arrive in 1812, it was necessary to distinguish between the two groups, so the immigrants from northern Ireland became known as the Scotch-Irish.

The yeoman farmers who settled in the Ozarks and the hilly districts in northern Missouri, notably the Lincoln and the Chariton River hills, possessed only a few tools and livestock. Data from the manuscript census of 1870 for Richwoods Township in Miller County provide an overview of the population at the end of the primary phase of settlement. Demographically the frontier had many similarities with today's Third World countries. There were 1,361 people in the township, most of them under forty years of age.

In fact, only one person in eight (12.5 percent) was over the age of forty, and 63 percent of the population was twenty years old or younger. Three-fourths of the population was literate; but among the people over thirty years of age, the illiteracy rate increased to more than 30 percent. The average household had 5.3 persons, but the households ranged in size from one to thirteen. There were only two octogenarians in the entire township. Three-fourths of the residents had immigrated from Tennessee and Kentucky, or from other parts of Missouri. There were only five foreign immigrants. The occupation breakdown yields 199 farmers, 17 farm laborers, 15 domestic servants, 12 widow ladies, 11 housekeepers, 6 teachers, 3 blacksmiths, 3 physicians, 2 dry-goods merchants, 2 store workers, 2 sawers, one each of the following: shoemaker, harnessmaker, retired farmer, miller, and minister of the Gospel. There was little wealth aside from the land; more than 30 percent of the population listed between six hundred and one thousand dollars as the value of their real estate, and only seven residents had landholdings assessed at more than two thousand dollars. As for personal property, the largest number of people had between three and four hundred dollars worth, so that the average settler was worth perhaps one thousand dollars to fifteen hundred dollars in terms of real and personal property.[1]

Many of the planters who settled the better-drained Missouri and Mississippi river bottomlands possessed slaves, usually less than ten, but sometimes more. They raised hemp, tobacco, wheat, and corn, which could be readily shipped to market on flatboats and later on steamboats. Their cattle, hogs, horses, and mules could be shipped by boat or driven to market in St. Louis or Kansas City. The belt of counties that stretched across Missouri, including the Missouri valley and a tier of counties north of it, became known as Little Dixie. Apparently the term was first used shortly after the Civil War to denote the Missouri midsection where southern sympathies, slavery, and Democratic politics were prevalent. The name has been popularized through politics.

Once peaceful conditions resumed following the Civil War, a period of railroad construction began stimulating immigration. The railroads greatly improved connections with the remainder of the Middle West. By 1890 the lower Middle West had replaced the upper South as the leading source of immigrants to Missouri. Illinois (with 135,585 immigrants) was the leading state followed by Kentucky (99,985), Ohio (84,907), Indiana (70,563), and Tennessee (67,591).

Blacks comprised only a small part of the immigration. Slave labor was not well adapted to the Ozark agricultural systems; nor was it used in mining activities to any great extent. In 1860 most of the black population of the Ozarks was on the eastern and northern borders. Slaves accounted for as much as 10 percent of the total population in only four Ozark counties: Washington, St. Francois, Cole, and Greene. Greater numbers were found on larger farms along the Mississippi and Missouri rivers.

FOREIGN-BORN SETTLERS

Germans comprised the largest immigrant non-English-speaking people in Missouri (Figure 5.1). The Polish and Bohemian settlers in Franklin and Gasconade counties, the Italians at Rosati, and the French at St. Louis and other river towns were nearly negligible by comparison. Most of the German farmers located in the Missouri and Mississippi border regions in compact settlements. Large numbers of Germans settled in St. Louis. By 1900, south St. Louis had become widely known as a German community. Even now the city is known for its fine German restaurants, traditional music, and customs that have to some degree been preserved. The 1980 St. Louis telephone directory lists thirty-three pages of names beginning with *Sch.*

The earliest German settlers were the so-called Whitewater Dutch who settled in Bollinger County just prior to the end of the eighteenth century. These colonists did not immigrate directly from Germany; and because they had no contact with other German groups, they gradually dropped the use of the German language.

Many German settlers were attracted to

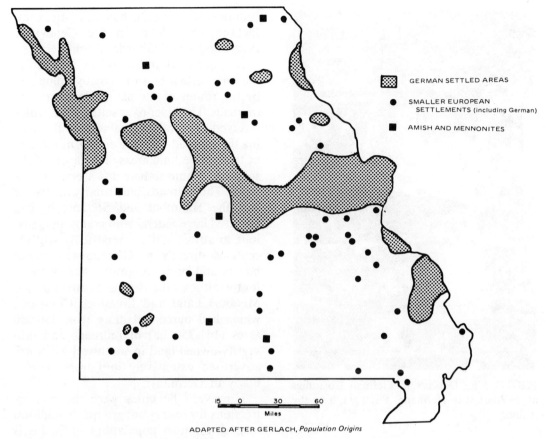

GERMAN SETTLED AREAS

SMALLER EUROPEAN
SETTLEMENTS (including German)

AMISH AND MENNONITES

15   0   30   60
Miles

ADAPTED AFTER GERLACH, *Population Origins*

FIGURE 5.1. Rural Population Origins.

Missouri by a book written by Gottfried Duden, *Riese nach den Westlichen Staaten* ("A journey to the western states"). Duden had lived for a time near Dutzow in what was later Warren County and described the land and living conditions in glowing terms. Between 1830 and 1850 large numbers of Germans immigrated to the Missouri and Mississippi valleys and bordering uplands. They were primarily of four types: (1) educated men and women of the Jungdeutschland movement who had been suppressed by a reactionary government; (2) romanticists who wished to escape a convention-ridden society; (3) religious separatists, who sought to escape the repression of an established church; and (4) the common people who sought to improve their economic situation. Immigration societies were active in settling Germans from their homeland and from crowded slums in cities in the East.

The Germans who settled prior to the Civil War were a mixed lot. Catholics settled at Westphalia in Osage County; at Taos, Richfountain, Loose Creek, Lustown, and Frankenstein in Cole County; at New Offenburg and Zell in Ste. Genevieve County; and in several localities in western Perry County. Protestant separatists settled at Wittenburg, Altenburg, and Frohna in Perry County. This latter group nurtured the Missouri Synod Lutheran Church.

Germans were attracted to Missouri by the low cost of land, the accessibility by navigable rivers, and the favorable reports about the soil and climate. Usually they settled on the cheaper land on the bluffs bordering the Missouri and Mississippi rivers. From this base they gradually expanded

PHOTO 5.1. Dancers in German Costumes at the Maifest in Hermann. Photograph by the Author.

from poorer to better land, accumulating wealth with which they bought out their American neighbors. As communities became more German in character, many Americans reportedly sold out because they did not want to live among the Germans.

According to the census of 1860, Jefferson City was half German and Boonville one-fourth; Hermann and Washington were predominantly German towns. German was taught in the public schools in the larger towns, and in the classrooms of some rural schools German was used more than English. By 1870 people of German birth or parentage composed more than 20 percent of Osage, Franklin, Warren, St. Charles, and St. Louis counties. These counties, along with the city of St. Louis, made up the core of the so-called Missouri Rhineland. German-born settlers made up a substantial portion of the population of other Missouri and Mississippi river border counties including Buchanan, Platte, Clay, Jackson, Cole, Jefferson, Ste. Genevieve, Perry, and Cape Girardeau counties.

As Figure 5.1 indicates, the location of the early settlements was greatly influenced by the routes of the navigable rivers and railroads. The older river settlements, which received a second wave of immigrants during the railroad-building era, form the core of the rural ethnic areas. The larger of the scattered ethnic settlements are along railroads. The railroads, particularly the Pacific and the Hannibal and St. Joseph, had acquired large federal land grants and, anxious to attract settlers, reportedly sent executives directly to Germany to recruit buyers and promote growth and business for their lines. Likewise, the Scottish-owned Missouri Land and Livestock Company, which had purchased more than 350,000 acres (141,750 ha) of railroad- and university-owned land in southwest Missouri, advertised extensively in Europe, particularly in Germany.

However, the cities were the real attractions for immigrant groups. In addition to large German populations in St. Louis and Kansas City, Irish, Italian, and Jewish neighborhoods formed. By 1980 the Jewish Employment and Vocational Service in St. Louis had become a big employer, providing jobs for 1,000 workers. "The Hill" in St. Louis is a well-known Italian settlement near the old Manchester Manufacturing District where Italian customs have recently revived. Over the past fifty years, Spanish-Americans from Mexico have moved to Missouri's two largest metropolitan areas where Spanish-speaking neighborhoods have been established. In the last twenty-five years, refugees from South Korea and Southeast Asia have added to the ethnic diversity of Missouri's large cities.

BLACK POPULATION

The migration of thousands of Blacks away from the rural South into the urban North has been one of the major shifts in the national population since World War II. Missouri has been very much a part of this shift.

In 1980, the nonwhite population of Missouri comprised 514,274 Blacks, 23,108 Asians, 12,319 American Indians, and 21,476 people of other races, including refugees from Korea, Southeast Asia, and Latin America—especially Mexico. According to the census, there are 51,667 persons of Spanish origin who may be of any race.

Missouri's urban areas, like most large urban areas, have experienced an increase in Black population. Between 1940 and 1980, the white population increased only 27 percent, whereas the nonwhite population increased 128 percent. Although nonwhite is a broader category than Black, 90 percent of Missouri's nonwhite population is Black. The increase in nonwhite population has been mostly in the cities. In 1980 only 8 percent of nonwhites residing in Missouri were in rural areas compared to 22 percent in 1940.

In the two largest cities, the proportion of the population that is nonwhite has significantly increased. In St. Louis, nonwhites constituted 47.6 percent of the population in 1980 as compared to 13.4 percent in 1940. In Kansas City nonwhites constituted 33.4 percent of the population in 1980 compared to 10.5 percent in 1940. In each case nonwhites are concentrated mainly in segregated neighborhoods in the inner cities.

Outside of the major urban centers Blacks in Missouri are found in significant numbers in two widely separated parts of the state (Figure 5.2). One concentration is in counties of central Missouri near the Missouri River. Southern planters settled this region, known as Little Dixie, prior to the Civil War and established a plantation economy based on slavery. Most of the slaves in Missouri resided there.

The other concentration of Blacks in Missouri is in the delta region of southeast Missouri. The movement of Blacks into this region is largely a twentieth-century occurrence. In fact, the progress of settlement of southeastern Missouri is unlike that of any other section of the state. Because of the difficulty of converting the vast swamps into productive farmland, the region remained sparsely settled until the 1920s. When the fertile bottomland soils were provided with artificial drainage, southern cotton planters moved into this region bringing with them large numbers of Blacks. However, the delta region has experienced a significant emigration of Blacks since about 1950.

The Missouri portion of the Corn Belt and that of the Ozarks are conspicuous by their absence of Blacks. In both cases, settlement was primarily by whites not involved in the slave economy of the South. The Corn Belt was populated by immigrants from the northeast. The Ozarks were settled largely by yeomen farmers from the hill country of Appalachia, few of whom owned slaves.

POPULATION TRENDS

Missouri has experienced a long period of population growth. From 1810, when the population was 19,873, until 1890, when the population was 2,679,185, the percentage increment averaged 94.5 for each decade. In the period 1890 to 1980, when the population reached 4,916,686, the percentage of growth averaged 9.5 for each decade (Figure 5.3). This steady increment of population is striking, especially since Missouri is a population-exporting state; that is, there are more people emigrating then immigrating.

There have been four significant geographical growth patterns in Missouri since 1890. The northern and western plains regions have the topography, soil, climate, and other conditions conducive to the profitable mechanization of farms. In these sections of Missouri the classic push-pull theory of population movement has been clearly exhibited. The surplus agricultural labor coupled with the growing economic opportunities in cities have brought sig-

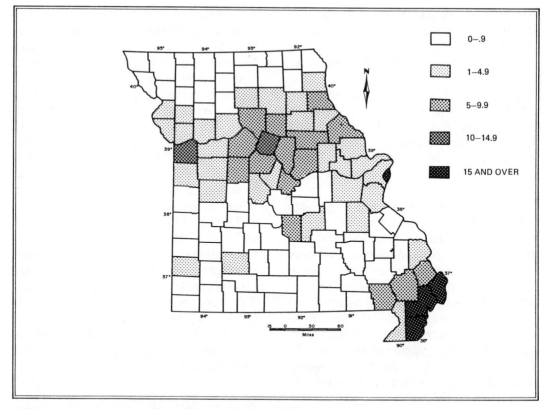

FIGURE 5.2.   Percentage Nonwhite Population, 1980.

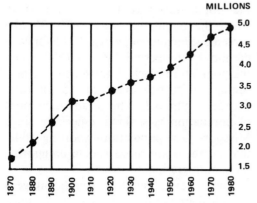

FIGURE 5.3.   Missouri Population, 1870–1980.

nificant decreases in population. Many counties in northern Missouri have lost population each decade since 1900 (Figure 5.4). This decline contrasts with the growth of population during the eighty-year period preceding 1900, when new farms and towns were laid out.

The Ozark Region stands in stark contrast to northern and western Missouri. The region has many small farms on steep slopes so that as a whole the agriculture of the Ozarks has not been mechanized to the degree of other areas. The population of most Ozark counties has been stable or has grown slightly. In the 1960s and 1970s some of the counties that have attracted second-home, retirement, and recreation development have experienced remarkably rapid population growth. Likewise, the counties near the region's major growth center, Springfield, have grown rapidly.

In the Southeast Lowlands, a high percentage of cultivated land is in cash crops, particularly cotton, soybeans, and corn. Until about thirty years ago the farms remained rather small, mainly because cotton harvesting and tillage had not been mechanized. Since 1950, farm mechanization (particularly the development of a

71

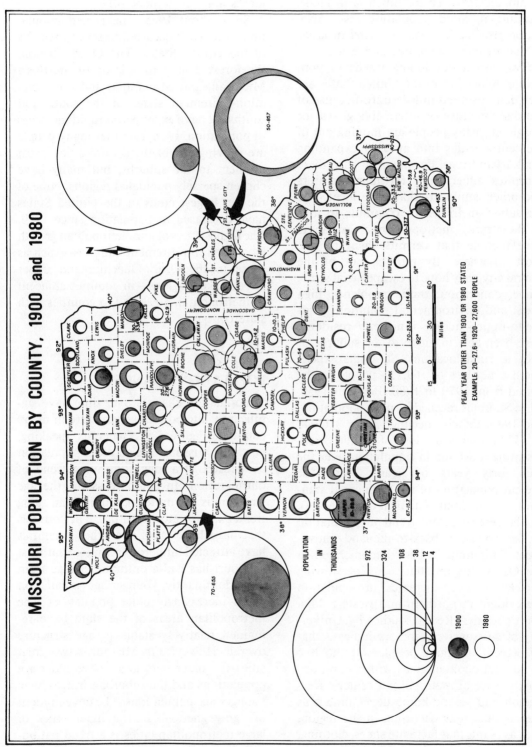

FIGURE 5.4. Missouri Population by County, 1900 and 1980.

successful mechanical cotton picker) has eliminated the need for much farm labor, resulting in rapid population loss. Also, cotton growing has been reduced in favor of that of corn, soybeans, and wheat.

Two recent developing trends in population relocation in the United States are well demonstrated in Missouri. Because of the diseconomies of urban living, real or imagined, many people are moving out of the central cities into an ever expanding rural-urban fringe. For the most part, these urbanites either work for manufacturers and other employers that have located in the suburban fringes or commute to jobs in the nearby metropolitan areas. Some have income that permits them to live most anywhere. By moving out of the central city, they hope to escape racial strife, crime, congestion, traffic problems, high taxes, and environmental pollution. Middle-to-upper-income inner-city residents have been able to move to the suburbs or even to rural locations. St. Louis experienced a net loss of 169,151 people in the period from 1970 to 1980. Between 1950, when St. Louis reached its peak population, and 1980, the city declined from 816,048 to 453,085 for a net loss of 362,963, representing a decline in population over the past forty years of nearly twice the present population of the Springfield standard metropolitan statistical area (SMSA).

The second recent trend in population is the so-called back-to-the-land movement. This trend is best demonstrated in the Ozark Region, but signs of slowing decrease, or even increases, in population are evident in northern and western Missouri counties. Recent studies by University of Missouri researchers indicate that 85 percent of young people want to live in nonmetropolitan areas within commuting distance of metropolitan centers. Recreation and second-home development as well as light manufacturing in the region, such as plants that fabricate shoes, clothing, plastics, and household electrical appliances, have created jobs for long-time residents and newcomers alike.

Since about 1965, unexpected population shifts have occurred in several regions of the United States. The Ozark Region; the forested land in Wisconsin, northern Michigan, and Minnesota; and the recreation-retirement states of the south and southwest have experienced rapid increases in population. It appears that many people are moving out of the central cities, most of them to the suburbs, but many have chosen sparsely populated regions. Nine of the ten largest cities in the United States have decreased in population since 1970. The highest rates of nonmetropolitan growth have been in retirement counties—such as those in the Ozark-Ouachita and upper Great Lakes regions—in counties adjacent to metropolitan areas and in counties with state colleges.

EFFECTS OF POPULATION CHANGE

Population changes over time have significantly altered the age structure in many counties (Figure 5.5). Generally speaking, northern Missouri has an older population as a result of a long continuing trend of outmigration. In south Missouri the age structure is not uniform, although an aging trend exists in most counties. The counties that have large lakes and other amenities have attracted numerous retirees. Southeast Missouri has had a dramatic change from a predominantly younger-age population to an increasingly older population. The metropolitan areas of the state have remained relatively stable in age structure overall. However, in Missouri's two great cities the older core areas have older-age populations and the suburban fringes have younger-age populations. The development of "gray ghettos" in the inner cities of large metropolitan cities is a trend nationwide.

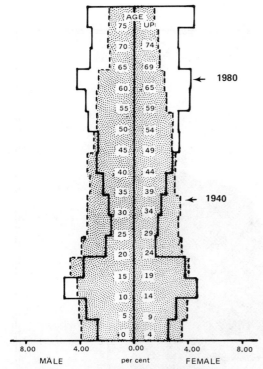

FIGURE 5.5. Population Pyramids, Mercer County, 1940 and 1980.

CURRENT POPULATION CHARACTERISTICS

The final population count for 1980 indicates that Missouri's population is now 4,906,480, which represents an increase of 5 percent over 1970. Missouri ranks thirteenth among the fifty states in both area and population and twenty-seventh in population density.

Missouri has never experienced a net decline in population from one census period to the next; however, the state has never during this century experienced as rapid a rate of population growth as has the United States.

During the decade from 1970 to 1980, ninety-four counties experienced growth while twenty counties plus the city of St. Louis showed a decline in population (Figure 5.6). These figures contrast with data for the 1960–1970 decade that indicate only

fifty-one counties showing growth. In the decade of the 1950s only thirty counties experienced growth. All of the Ozark counties, with the exception of Pulaski County, grew in population during the 1970s. The decline in population in Pulaski County can be attributed largely to cutbacks in military and civilian personnel at Fort Leonard Wood. Census reports also indicate that Missouri now has fifty-one communities with a population of 10,000 or more as compared with only thirty-seven communities in 1960.

Since the 1970 census, Missouri added another standard metropolitan statistical area. An SMSA, defined by the Bureau of the Census, is a city with at least 50,000 inhabitants or two contiguous cities that constitute, for general economic and social purposes, a single community of at least 50,000, the smaller of which must have a population of at least 15,000. Figure 5.7 indicates the six SMSA areas of Missouri. Joplin is the newest addition to the SMSA classification.

Missouri's population, according to the Bureau of the Census, is now 68 percent urban, compared to 70 percent in 1970. The two major metropolitan areas—Kansas City and St. Louis—account for more than 55 percent of the state's population. When combined with the other four SMSAs, the metropolitan areas account for more than 65 percent of the total.

The population center of the United States continues to move westward and is currently approximately 30 miles (48 km) south of St. Louis. The 1980 census indicated that the population center had for the first time moved west of the Mississippi River.

NOTES

1. Milton D. Rafferty, *The Ozarks: Land and Life* (Norman: University of Oklahoma Press, 1980), pp. 60–61.

74

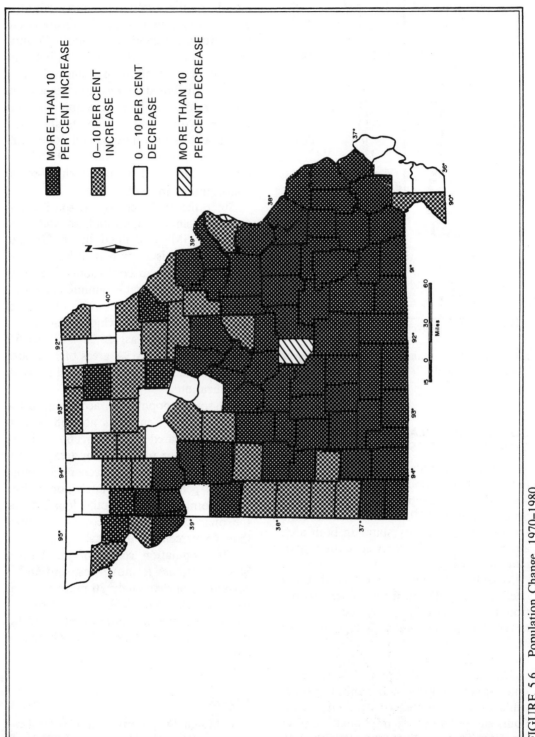

FIGURE 5.6. Population Change, 1970–1980.

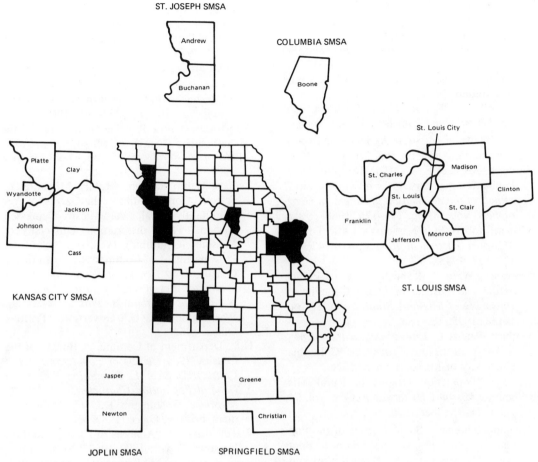

FIGURE 5.7.   Standard Metropolitan Statistical Areas.

SELECTED REFERENCES

Ashley, John W. "Profile of Poverty in Missouri." *Missouri Economic Study,* no. 7. School of Business and Public Administration, Research Center, University of Missouri (Columbia), 1965.

Augustin, Byron, and Kenneth E. Reger. "Rural Villages in Decline: Nodaway County, Missouri." *Transactions.* Missouri Academy of Sciences, vol. 6, pp. 11–18. 1972.

Baker, Thomas E., and Rex R. Campbell. *Race and Residence in Missouri Cities.* Jefferson City, Mo.: Missouri Commission on Human Rights, 1971.

Braschler, Curtis. *Regional Growth in Missouri.* University of Missouri Agricultural Experiment Station, bulletin SR 153. Columbia, 1973.

Bratton, Samuel T. *The Geography of the St. Francis Basin.* University of Missouri Studies, vol. 1. Columbia, Mo., July 1926.

Burt, Henry J. *The Population of Missouri. A General Survey of Its Sources, Changes, and Present Composition.* University of Missouri Agricultural Experiment Station, bulletin 188. Columbia, 1933.

Campbell, Rex R. "Conditions of Population Change in Missouri." *Business and Government Review,* vol. 4, pp. 14–21. Business and Public Administration Research Center, University of Missouri (Columbia), 1963.

_____. *Negroes in Missouri: A Compilation of Statistical Data from the 1960 United States Census.* Jefferson City, Mo.: Missouri Commission on Human Rights, 1967.

_____. *Negroes in Missouri—1970: An Analysis of the Racial Characteristics of the Missouri*

Population Using the 1970 Census of Population. Jefferson City, Mo.: Missouri Commission on Human Rights, 1972.

———. *Population Pyramids for Missouri Counties.* Miscellaneous Publication 317. Extension Division, University of Missouri (Columbia), 1973.

Campbell, Rex R., and John J. Hartman. *Missouri Population Characteristics and Changes.* University of Missouri Agricultural Experiment Station, bulletin 765. Columbia, 1964.

Coulson, Michael R. C. "The Distribution of Population Age Structures in Kansas City." *Annals of the Association of American Geographers,* vol. 58, pp. 155–176. 1968.

Crisler, Robert M. "Missouri's Little Dixie." *Missouri Historical Review,* vol. 42, pp. 130–139. 1948.

Dorrance, Ward A. "The Survival of French in the Old District of Sainte Genevieve." *University of Missouri Studies,* vol. 10, pp. 1–133. 1935.

Gerlach, Russel L. *Immigrants in the Ozarks: A Study in Ethnic Geography.* Columbia: University of Missouri Press, 1976.

———. "Population Origins in Rural Missouri." *Missouri Historical Review,* vol. 71, pp. 1–21. October 1976.

Glennon, Thomas. "Some Aspects of the Population Geography of the Missouri Bootheel." Master's thesis, Southern Illinois University, 1962.

Rafferty, Milton D. "Population and Settlement Changes in Two Ozark Localities." *Rural Sociology,* vol. 38, pp. 46–56. 1973.

———. *The Ozarks: Land and Life.* Norman: University of Oklahoma Press, 1980.

Rafferty, Milton D., and Dennis J. Hrebec. "Logan Creek: A Missouri Ozark Valley Revisited." *Journal of Geography,* vol. 72, pp. 7–17. 1973.

Sauer, Carl O. "Status and Change in the Rural Midwest—A Retrospect." *Mitteilungen der Oesterreichischen Geographischen Gesellschaft,* vol. 105, pp. 357–365. 1963.

Shortridge, James R. "The Expansion of the Settlement Frontier in Missouri." *Missouri Historical Review,* vol. 75, pp. 64–90. October 1980.

Tadcos, Helmi Ragheb. "Return Migration to Selected Communities in the Ozarks: A Predominantly Rural, Economically Depressed Region." Ph.D. dissertation. University of Missouri (Columbia), 1968.

U.S., Department of Commerce, Bureau of the Census. *1980 Census of Population. Vol. 1 Characteristics of the Population, Chapter A Number of Inhabitants. Part 27 Missouri.* Washington, D.C.: U.S. Government Printing Office, 1982.

U.S., Department of Commerce, Bureau of the Census. *1980 Census of Population. Vol. I Characteristics of the Population, Chapter B General Population Characteristics, Part 27 Missouri.* Washington D.C.: U.S. Government Printing Office, 1982.

Walker, Marcial. "Analysis of Changes in Two Missouri Towns, 1890–1960." Master's thesis, University of Missouri (Columbia), 1964.

West, James. *Plainville, U.S.A.* New York: Columbia University Press, 1945.

Zoubek, Linda, comp. *Missouri County Data Book.* Jefferson City, Mo.: Missouri Division of Commerce and Industrial Development, 1972.

CHAPTER 6

MINERALS AND MINING

The discovery of mineral deposits in Missouri began almost as soon as the white settlers entered the area. As early as 1673, the French explorers Père Marquette and Louis Joliet reportedly saw iron ore deposits along the Mississippi River near Apple Creek. By 1723, de LaMotte Cadillac, a French mineral expert, and Philip Renault had located and begun to work the famous Mine La Motte lead deposits in Madison County.

Iron smelting was begun near Arcadia on Stout's Creek in Iron County in 1815, and copper deposits were exploited in 1837 in Shannon County. The zinc deposits of southwest Missouri, discovered around 1851, were of such importance that by 1875 the area was starting to win wide renown as a great zinc-producing region.

Coal mining was under way in Missouri by 1840, and the first "wildcat" oil well was drilled in Jackson County in the late 1860s. Limestone, clay, barite, and other stone materials were mined before 1870, and the Portland cement industry developed in the state soon after.

COAL MINING

Since World War II, oil and gas have continued to grow in the U.S. energy market until in 1976 they represented 79 percent of the total energy consumed in the country. Coal and lignite accounted for 15.5 percent, water power 3 percent, and nuclear power 2 percent. An important factor favoring coal in long-range competition with the other fossil fuels for the energy market is the vast reserve tonnage available. It has been estimated that coal makes up approximately 90 percent of the world's total reserves of potential fossil fuel energy.

About four-fifths of Missouri's electrical power is produced by coal, and the demand for this energy source is expected to double by 1990. In 1981 the Missouri Department of Natural Resources estimated the state's coal production at 5,340,944 tn (4,855,403 t) worth $133,523,600. However, this figure amounted to only about 40 percent of the coal consumed in Missouri. The remaining 8 million tn (7.2 t) were imported. Illinois supplied about 90 percent of the imported coal and most of the remainder came from Oklahoma and Kansas. Illinois coal commands a large market in Missouri for two reasons. First, the Illinois coalfields lie at the very edge of Missouri's principal coal-consuming region, the St. Louis area, whereas the active coalfields of Missouri are located some distance to the west and northwest (Figure 6.1). Second, Illinois has a larger reserve of coal than Missouri and the coal beds are generally thicker, two

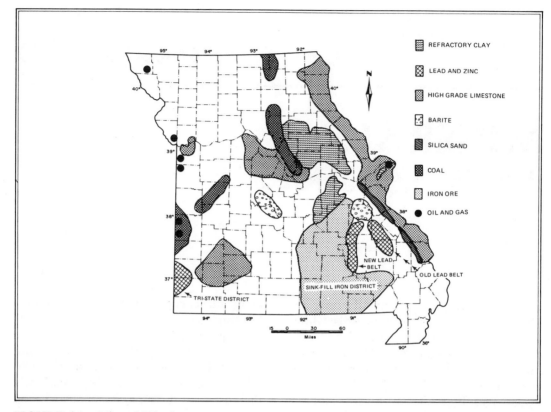

FIGURE 6.1.   Mineral Districts.

conditions that facilitate mining on a large scale.

The growing population centers of western Missouri, however, lie within the Missouri coal-producing area and will in the future draw upon this supply for their energy needs. Presently Missouri coal faces strong competition from the Kansas and Oklahoma fields. Peabody Coal Company in Oklahoma supplies the Sibley, Missouri, generating station in Jackson County with coal that has a higher Btu rating per pound than Missouri coal. City Utilities of Springfield purchases coal from mines in Oklahoma and Kansas for the same reason. Nevertheless, the future coal needs of western Missouri must be supplied in large part by Missouri coal.

Shaft mines, some of the first mines in Missouri, were opened in Ray and Lafayette counties in the early 1840s to recover easy-access coal. As a result of these op-

erations, Missouri led all other states west of the Mississippi River in total production until 1874. The majority of Missouri coal has been mined from five different coalfields: the Southwest Field, the Tebo Field, the Lexington Field, the Bevier Field, and the Mendota-Novinger Field.

The Southwest Field is located in western and southern Bates County and in Vernon and Barton counties. Bates County was once the leading coal-producing county in Missouri, but now its shallow coal seams have been exhausted. In 1891 over thirty mines were in operation in Bates County. Mining was by drift, shaft, and stripping operations. The Tebo Field, located in Henry, southwest Johnson, and northwest St. Clair counties, was a major producer of coal in 1891. Production today, as throughout the state, is from stripping away of overburden to expose the Tebo coal seam and other lower seams of coal.

PHOTO 6.1. "Brutus," an Electric Shovel Operating in the Pittsburg-Midway Coal Mine near Liberal, Barton County. Photograph by the Author.

Shaft and tunnel mines, where vertical shafts are sunk and tunnels dug along the seams of coal, were operated by Stealy and Fowler Company in the Lafayette Field near Higginsville as early as 1847. Getting into the mines, hauling up the coal, and transporting it to market were all tasks accomplished with teams of horses. Such subsurface mines in all of Missouri's coalfields were later modernized with steam and then with electric-powered equipment; but because of hazards, and the greater expense in recovering coal by these methods, underground mining is no longer done.

OIL AND GAS

Oil and gas have been produced in Missouri since the earliest drilling in the Kansas City area shortly after the Civil War. Some of the early wells were drilled to supply individual homes and communities with natural gas. Several of the fields in western Missouri (Figure 6.1), opened in the late 1800s and early 1900s, are now depleted. Among the more recent strikes in the state are the Tarkio Pool (1942) in Atchison County, the Florissant Pool (1953) in St. Louis County, and the Turney Gas

Pool (1952) in Clinton County. Missouri's oil production in 1979 amounted to 226,206 bbl and $7,221,000 (Table 6.1). No gas has been produced commercially since 1976.

Missouri's oil and gas are produced from strata mainly of the Pennsylvanian period. The Florissant Pool produces from the Ordovician period Kimmswick formation. Most of the oil and gas production in Missouri is associated with small domal or anticlinal structures. The shallow wells in western Missouri are classed as "stripper" wells and have averaged less than 10 bbl (2 kl [kiloliter]) per day. These wells produce by means of secondary recovery techniques: water or gas pumped into the rock layers forces the oil out.

Very-low-gravity, high-viscosity oil has been known in western Missouri for at least a hundred years. It has been described as tar springs, pitch, asphalt, or simply as heavy oil. This material ranges from true oil at shallow depths—less than 300 ft (91.44 m)—to a bituminous or asphaltlike residue developed where the oil-bearing rocks occur near the surface. Due to the rising energy costs of the 1970s and 1980s, this very heavy oil and the tar sands in the southwest part of the state are being studied intensively.

FIRECLAY

Clays include a wide variety of materials that are best described as hydrous aluminum silicate compounds of extremely small particle size. Fireclay is nearly all clay that fuses at temperatures above 2,770°F (1,521°C), and its most abundant mineral is kaolinite. The uses of clays for different products depend upon individual physical and chemical properties. The principal products manufactured from clay and shale in Missouri are refractory brick, common brick and tile, pottery, absorbent clays, and fillers. Clay is also one raw material used in the manufacture of cement. In 1979, Missouri's production of clay and shale amounted to 2,351,000 tn (2,137,272 t) valued at $20,522,000.

TABLE 6.1

Mineral Production in Missouri, 1979

Mineral	Quantity		Value
Barite	89,000tn	(80,900t)	$ 3,679,000
Cement	4,512,000tn	(4,101,818t)	198,444,000
Clays	2,351,000tn	(2,137,272t)	20,522,000
Coal (1981 est.)	5,340,444tn	(4,855,403t)	33,523,000
Copper	14,323tn	(13,021t)	26,705,000
Crude oil (1981 est.)	226,206bbl	(47,126kl)	7,221,000
Lead	519,259tn	(472,054t)	547,824,000
Lime	1,790,000tn	(1,627,272t)	70,187,000
Sand and gravel	12,558,000tn	(11,416,363t)	31,310,000
Stone	56,380,000tn	(51,254,000t)	140,029,000
Zinc	67,850tn	(61,682t)	50,723,000

Source: Missouri Department of Natural Resources, Division of Geology and Land Survey (1981 estimates). Mineral Yearbook. Washington, D.C.: Department of Commerce, Bureau of Mines, 1981.

The first clay to be mined and fashioned into pottery in Missouri was that Indians mined long before the arrival of the first Europeans. The manufacture of common brick for chimneys and buildings began with the settlement of the first French communities along the Mississippi River.

The first firebrick plant in Missouri was built in 1845. The industry continued to expand steadily until the Depression of the 1930s. Today the refractories business is well established with seven companies and ten plants operating in the state. The A. P. Green Refractories Company plant at Mexico in Audrain County is one of the largest facilities of this type in the United States. Refractory plants are also located in Calloway, Montgomery, and St. Louis counties.

Deposits of clays occur in three areas: the Northern Fire Clay District in Audrain, Boone, Monroe, Calloway, and Montgomery counties; the St. Louis District, and the Southern Fire Clay District made up of part of Gasconade, Franklin, and Crawford counties. Bentonite and other non-refractory clays are mined in the Bootheel area.

LEAD AND ZINC MINING

Lead and zinc ores are usually found in close association. Historically there have been three main lead-zinc belts in Missouri: the Old Lead Belt in St. Francois and Washington counties; the Tri-State District of southwest Missouri and adjacent parts of Kansas and Oklahoma; and the Central Mineral District, which consisted of smaller and more scattered mines in Camden and Maries counties. Smaller deposits of lead and zinc have been mined at various times and various locations in southwest Missouri. The most important of these mines were located along Pearson Creek southeast of Springfield and at Aurora. In the 1960s the mines in the New Lead Belt in Iron and Reynolds counties were opened, enabling Missouri to regain first rank among the states as a lead producer. In 1979, Missouri produced 519,259,400 tn (472,054,000 t) of lead valued at $547,824,000 and 67,850 tn (61,682 t) of zinc concentrates worth $50,723,000.

The Old Lead Belt

For more than a century following the discoveries of the Renault party, the mines

PHOTO 6.2.   A. P. Green Refractories Company, Mexico. Courtesy A. P. Green Refractories Company.

of St. Francois and Washington counties were worked in a rather casual manner. Smelting was improved when Moses Austin introduced the reverberatory furnaces at Potosi, which in turn led to an increased demand for lead ores, increased prospecting, and new discoveries. The introduction of the diamond drill, which permitted exploratory core drillings in the bedrock, was a major event in the history of lead mining. After 1869, large deposits of rich ores were discovered at greater depths. Because of the increased costs of underground mining, the holdings were consolidated and outside capital attracted. Company towns were built near the mines, the tunnels were extended, and hundreds of miles of undergound rail lines were laid. In St. Francois County

numerous closely spaced towns were founded from north to south: Bonne Terre, Flat River, Elvins, Desloge, Leadington, and Farmington. Fredericktown, in Madison County, was near the southern limit of the district.

For more than fifty years the Old Lead Belt was the leading lead-producing district in the United States. By 1950, most of the lead and zinc ores were mined by only a few very large corporations. The St. Joseph Lead Company, organized in 1869 to mine in the vicinity of Bonne Terre, had grown to be the largest producer; while a subsidiary company, the Mine La Motte Corporation, ranked second. Most of the lead concentrates were smelted at Herculaneum. Production reached a peak during World

War II; but gradually thereafter the larger, richer, and most accessible deposits were worked out, resulting in increasing costs, declining production, and the closing of mines. The last mine in the Old Lead Belt was closed in 1973.

The Tri-State Zinc-Lead District

The development and decline of the Tri-State District occupied much less time than did the mining cycle of the Old Lead Belt. Lead in the western Ozarks was first recorded by H. R. Schoolcraft in December 1818, when he visited the Indian "diggings" on Pearson Creek near the present site of Springfield.[1] Small mines were worked in Greene and Webster counties in the early forties, and near Joplin in 1848. The initial discovery at Granby in Newton County was made in 1849, and the large deposits in that field were discovered in 1854. By 1857 hundreds of cabins had been built and scores of shafts sunk. Prior to the Civil War the Granby lead was hauled by wagon to Boonville on the Missouri River, to Linn Creek on the Osage River, and to Fort Smith on the Arkansas River for shipment to outside markets.

The arrival of the Atlantic and Pacific Railroad in Joplin in 1870 coincided with the discovery of the superb mineral deposits in that district. In 1870 there was not a house in Joplin, but by 1874 Joplin was a city of 3,000 people, with 1,000 miners and thirteen furnaces. Rich deposits of lead caused the settlements of Oronogo, Webb City, and Carterville to spring up in quick succession. By 1872 a process for the treatment of zinc blend was discovered and in a matter of ten years zinc production became more important than lead. Zinc and lead were discovered in 1886 at Aurora and on Pearson Creek at Springfield.

Peak production for the Missouri districts came prior to World War I. As new deposits were discovered in Kansas and Oklahoma, the old mines in Missouri were shut down. Some mines were kept open long after their peak, but by 1960 the last

PHOTO 6.3.   Chat Piles and Mine Dumps near Carterville in the Tri-State District. Photograph by the Author.

mines in Missouri were closed. In 1968 the final chapter of the Tri-State District was written when the last producing mine at Miami, Oklahoma, closed.

The Central Mineral District, which includes Morgan and Camden counties and much of the Osage-Gasconade Hills, was never as important as the other two lead-mining districts. The mines, being small and scattered, were not consolidated and mechanized. Nevertheless, they influenced the geography of settlement, determining the location of towns in the Osage River basin. By 1910 the district was essentially defunct although some mining continued as late as World War II, when lead and zinc prices were high.

The New Lead Belt

The New Lead Belt in western Iron County and northern Reynolds County (see Figure 6.1) was explored in the 1950s and developed in the 1960s and 1970s. Ore bodies as much as 140 ft (42.6 m) thick and 3,000 ft (914 m) wide lie in flat beds approximately 900 (274 m) to 1,000 ft (304.6 m) beneath the surface. The ores, primarily lead with some zinc, copper, and silver, are deposited in a buried offshore reef, which lies embedded in the Cambrian-period Bonne Terre formation.

The mines, which were opened in the

PHOTO 6.4.   St. Joe Minerals Corporation Brushy Creek Mine in Reynolds County. Courtesy St. Joe Minerals Corporation.

1960s, employ the most modern machinery and technology. Room-and-pillar mining provides space for diesel-powered rubber-tired trucks to haul the ores to underground crushers. Repair and maintenance shops are located beneath the surface. At the surface, ores are pulverized and the lead and zinc concentrates are separated from the powdered ore by "flotation," a process in which the ore is treated with chemicals and the lead and zinc, in sequence, are floated from the rock waste. The lead concentrates are smelted near the mines at Bunker and Buick and at Herculaneum on the Mississippi River. The zinc concentrates go to East St. Louis or to Europe to be smelted.

The economic benefits of mining in the New Lead Belt are substantial. Except for management and technical personnel, the mines employ local people from surrounding towns and farms. The population of Reynolds County decreased from 8,923 in 1930 to 5,161 in 1960; but after mining was developed in the 1960s, the population had increased to 7,231 in 1980. Lead valued at more than $470 million recovered from mines provides large tax incomes for Iron and Reynolds counties.

IRON MINING

The first iron furnace to operate in Missouri was built in 1815 or 1816 at the Stout's Creek Shut-in by Corbin Ashebran. In 1823 Springfield Furnace, on Furnace

PHOTO 6.5.   Wheel Loader in the St. Joe Minerals Corporation Viburnum No. 28 Mine. Courtesy St. Joe Minerals Corporation.

Creek, about 6 miles (9.7 km) south of Potosi, was founded, and in 1846 the first furnace was built at Iron Mountain. Iron ore for these furnaces was hematites mined from the igneous rocks of the St. Francois Mountains. Waterwheels powered the blowers, hammers, and other machinery. These first iron plantations were nearly self-sufficient communities.

The frontier iron foundries operated with a profit because of the high value of their product. Missouri iron was shipped not only to St. Louis and other Missouri cities, but as far east as Cincinnati and Pittsburgh. In the 1840s there was wild speculation in the Iron Mountain District, as the area came to be known. Elaborate plans were drawn for "Missouri City," a utopian community to be located at the base of Iron

Mountain. The mines and smelters were expected to pay for schools, colleges, hospitals, large public parks and yield an annual profit for investors of $108 for every $100 invested.

Although the ore bodies proved to be less rich than the first wild reports claimed, several furnaces were built and the two mining towns of Iron Mountain and Pilot Knob grew and flourished. After the Civil War several new furnaces were built at the mines and at Carondolet near St. Louis. By 1870 the Iron Mountain District had produced more than 90 percent of the state's output. By 1875 the shortage of timber for fuel at the mines necessitated the establishment of additional furnaces in St. Louis, which could be easily supplied with Illinois coal. Eventually, when the

PHOTO 6.6.   Herculaneum Smelter, St. Joe Minerals Corporation. Courtesy St. Joe Minerals Corporation.

furnaces at Carondolet became obsolete, large modern furnaces were built at Granite City, Illinois.

The sink-fill hematite ores in Phelps, Crawford, and Dent counties supplied more than a dozen frontier iron furnaces that were built in the remote Courtois Hills (see Figure 6.1). Apparently the first furnace was founded around 1819–1820 on Thickety Creek in Crawford County and operated until about 1830. Thomas James and Samuel Massey of Ohio established the Maramec Iron Works, or Massey's, at Meramec Spring about 6 miles (9.7 km) southeast of St. James in 1827. The site provided a large hematite ore body, water power from Meramec Spring, limestone for flux, and a large supply of hardwood timber for charcoal.

The Maramec Iron Works, organized as an iron plantation, had many characteristics of a feudal manor. All lands, buildings, and equipment belonged to the partners, and the 100 or so workers and their families lived on the hill west of the furnace. Charcoal was made by piling oak and hickory cordwood on a level piece of ground and allowing it to char in a low-oxygen environment. Hematite was dug from a large sinkhole, shoveled into wagons, and hauled to the furnace. The company operated retail stores in St. Louis, Hermann, Jefferson City, Boonville, Brunswick, Independence, Warsaw, Lebanon, and Springfield where kettles, ovens, stoves, and tools were sold. Cannonballs, railroad equipment, bars, blooms, and pigs were shipped to St. Louis by way of the Old

PHOTO 6.7.   Iron Furnace at Meramec Park near St. James. Courtesy Walker—Missouri Division of Tourism.

Iron Road to Hermann or via the Springfield Road to Paydown on the Gasconade River. The ironworks closed in 1876 because of financial problems.

Several other smelters in the sink-fill iron district gradually went out of business as ores and fuel were depleted and improved transportation brought competition with the large ironworks and steelworks. The Sligo Furnace in eastern Dent County was one of the largest, and because of low-cost fuel and labor, the furnace continued to produce iron bars for blacksmiths' forges until the 1920s. In addition to the two main iron-mining districts, the brown ores in the southern part of Missouri were mined until recent years.

During the 1960s and 1970s, Missouri again became a producer of iron ore. None

of this ore is smelted in the state. The Hanna Mining Company, which took over operations at Pilot Knob in the 1960s, opened up new hematite deposits nearly 900 ft (274 m) beneath the base of the mountain. The ores, previously mined by open pit on the top of the mountain and by a shaft sunk in the western slope, were now milled at the mine and shipped in pellet form. The Pilot Knob mine closed in 1981, however, when low prices and foreign competition in the steel industry reduced demand for iron ore. The Pea Ridge Mining Company discovered a second major ore deposit south of Sullivan with the use of magnetic measurements and core drilling. The company subsequently developed the mine in the sixties. Although the mine was located not far

PHOTO 6.8.   Mine Pits and Sediment Ponds in the Barite Mining District in Washington County. Photograph by the Author.

from the old Maramec Iron Works, no relationship between the ores that were mined for the Maramec furnace and the Pea Ridge ores existed. The new ores were magnetite embedded in igneous rocks approximately 900 ft (274 m) beneath the surface. Once hoisted to the surface, milled, and roasted into pellets, the ores were shipped out to various locations. In 1977, the Pea Ridge iron mine and pellet plant also closed because of competition from foreign steel, reduced domestic steel production, and the high costs of operation created by the large amount of water flowing into the mine. It was reorganized, however, as the Pea Ridge Iron Ore Company, Incorporated, and reopened in 1979.

OTHER MINERALS

Barite (tiff) is a relatively soft, heavy, white-to-gray mineral. About 90 percent is used in oil drilling operations to hold gas pressure; the remaining 10 percent is used as filler in paint, ink, paper, textiles, and asbestos products.

In early days, many farmers found it possible to supplement their income by small-scale barite mining. Many of the French who settled in the vicinity of Old Mines eked out a living digging tiff after the mines closed. The common method of

obtaining barite is first to dig the barite-bearing clay from surface excavations; the material is then placed in a device known as a log washer, which separates the clay and barite by knocking and rolling the material about. The barite freed from the clay is collected, and the clay is allowed to accumulate in a tailings pond. In recent years the independent operator has been forced out of the tiff diggings by a few larger and more efficient operators.

In Washington County thousands of acres have been mined over, giving the area a blasted appearance. The huge tailings impoundments undoubtedly contain large quantities of barite and will probably be "mined" as the better deposits of barite ore are depleted.

More barite is produced in Missouri than in any other state. The deposits are exploited in two areas: the Washington County District and the Central Mineral District in Cole, Miller, Moniteau, and Morgan counties. In 1979, barite production amounted to 89,000 tn (80,900 t) at a value of $3,679,000. The Washington County District is one of the leading barite districts in the United States. The deposits of the Central Mineral District are scattered and can support only small operations.

Tripoli, a porous, decomposed siliceous rock, is mined in Newton County, Missouri, near Seneca and Racine. It is used in the manufacture of filters, abrasives, and polish.

Silica sand, or glass sand, is mined in the eastern part of Missouri. This sand, or sandstone, has chemical and physical specifications that can be used for a number of industrial purposes, although the bulk of production is used to make glass. The prime requisite is that it is essentially pure. The largest production in Missouri comes from the St. Peter sandstone along the Mississippi River border in Jefferson and Ste. Genevieve counties. It was first mined in large quantities when the Pittsburgh Plate Glass Company was built at Crystal City in 1874. The sandstone is soft and easily quarried.

Granite is quarried at Graniteville in Iron County near the famous Elephant Rocks. The first quarries were opened in 1869. The stone, marketed under the trade name Missouri Red Granite, became a popular building and paving stone. It was used extensively for building in St. Louis, and the waterfront docks at St. Louis and at Cape Girardeau are paved with "Missouri Red." The famous Monadnock Building in Chicago, a nineteenth-century architectural masterpiece, was built of this excellent Missouri stone. One of the main quarrying companies was founded by B. Grats Brown, then governor of the state. Only one quarry is operating at present, producing stone primarily for monuments.

Limestone and dolomite are abundant in Missouri. Several of the limestones and dolomites are of excellent quality for chemical limestone. The Burlington limestone is particularly known as an excellent chemical stone, so much so that a shaft 900 ft (274 m) deep has been sunk in the Kansas City area to recover the stone. One of the first industries of the state was the manufacture of lime from stone quarried from a number of formations bordering the Mississippi and Missouri rivers and in southwest Missouri near Springfield. This lime was manufactured in the rudest manner. Log heaps were built and blocks of limestone were thrown on them and burned. Later the lime was burned in small kilns. A few of these structures still stand in various states of decay.

At present, limestones and dolomites are quarried near the major population centers, where they are used for building stone, lime, cement, and refractory purposes. They are mined primarily in a belt paralleling the Mississippi River, in counties bordering the Missouri River, and in a six-county area in southwest Missouri near Springfield. In 1979, Missouri's production of lime and cement amounted to 6,302,000 tn (5,729,090 t) valued at $264,631,000.

THE ECONOMIC AND ENVIRONMENTAL EFFECTS OF MINING

Probably the most important results of mining in Missouri have been the stimulation of the economy, the building of roads and railroads to serve the mines, and the attraction of immigrants. In the older mining districts where ore deposits have been depleted, the local economy has usually undergone a period of decline, accompanied by outmigration. If transportation linkages to the industrial centers are good, however, some districts, such as the Old Lead Belt and the Tri-State District, have recovered by attracting various types of manufacturing.

In the less-developed mining areas, surprisingly few traces of the mining era remain. Production from many of the mines was never large enough to play a dominant or even significant role in the local economy. Where the mines were important, certain economic adjustments have lessened the impact their decline might otherwise have had. (These adjustments include population decline, the decline in retail business, the shift to mainly service and farm retailing, and the growth of small-to medium-sized manufacturing plants to provide employment.) The overall economic health of Springfield was not appreciably disturbed by the closing of the Pearson Creek District, partly because the decline was gradual and partly because the mines never played a dominant role in the economy of the city. Aurora was hit hard by the closing of the mines; but now with economic adjustments, little in the present economic infrastructure can be traced to the mines. Undoubtedly, significant effects of the mining activity are the size and spacing of the towns in the mining districts. Had mining not stimulated an economic boom, attracting many people, the towns would probably not have grown as large so rapidly. In the Joplin area and the Old Lead Belt, they border one another, creating a nearly continuous urban area.

The most salient evidence of the mining

era in the defunct lead-zinc districts and in the Tiff Belt (Washington County District) is the blasted appearance of the landscape. In the oldest of the districts, the mines were small so that there was no great accumulation of chat, and the shafts in many cases have been clogged with debris. But in the Old Lead Belt and the Tri-State District, considerable visible evidence of the mining era remains, and the mined-over lands present a persistent problem of land and resource use.

The mined-over lands have been modified little since the mines were closed except by the forces of nature. In most areas, however, the very large chat piles, which accumulated adjacent to the ore concentrators, have been hauled away, primarily to be used as road macadam. Without these piles, which served as landmarks for the mining districts, the mined-over areas have a cratered and brush-covered landscape, forlorn and desolate. Unused, water-filled pits and gaunt, abandoned shafts are interspersed with low chat piles, which have been mantled with a cover of scrubby timber and a tangled growth of blackberry, gooseberry, and similar brushy vegetation. Much of the undergrowth is thorny and weedy, and the footing is rough and sometimes dangerous. The signs of decay are evident everywhere. Worn-out mining equipment is scattered among the monolithic foundations of stamp mills and the rotting timbers of crushers and loading docks.

Little use is made of these lands at present. In the Tri-State District, much of the land is in the hands of private individuals who have established low-cost residences on small acreages at the outskirts of the towns. For the most part, the land is unfenced, and where fencing exists, its condition is poor. Some cattle are run on the unreclaimed land, and in rare cases grass has been sown, which has converted to wild pasture, resulting in some improvement. Frequently the old mines are used as landfills or simply left to uncontrolled dumping of trash. Whole areas are strewn with litter, tin cans, rolls of wire fencing, discarded household appliances, and old automobile bodies. These mined areas are mazelike networks of tree-shaped automobile lanes, with nearly impassable chuckholes that fail to discourage young people from courting and a few fishers from frequenting some of the larger water-filled pits.

A small amount of the mined-over land has been reclaimed for agricultural purposes. Near Bonne Terre a high-rent residential development has been built on mined-over land, and the St. Joe Minerals Corporation has deeded a large tract to the state for a park. The cost of redeveloping the land nearly precludes extensive redevelopment for agricultural purposes.

The casual visitor to the New Lead Belt will find surprisingly little tangible evidence of mining industry. There are no large chat piles such as those that served as landmarks in the Old Lead Belt and in the Tri-State District. Lacking also is the cratered and brush-covered landscape. Such characteristics of the old Ozark mining districts are avoided because the tailings are normally deposited out of sight in a nearby valley. There is talk of using the mine tailings as backfill in the mines. As for the buildings, only the hoist houses, where the ore is brought to the surface, stand well above the greenery. The office buildings and buildings for processing ore are mainly concealed behind trees.

NOTES

1. Henry Rowe Schoolcraft, *Journal of a Tour into the Interior of Missouri*, in Hugh Park, ed., *Schoolcraft in the Ozarks* (Van Buren, Arkansas: Press-Argus Printers, 1955), p. 113.

SELECTED REFERENCES

Buckley, Ernest R. "Geology of the Disseminated Lead Deposits of Washington and St. Francois Counties." *Missouri Bureau of Geology and Mines.* 2d series, vol. 9. 1908.

Buckley, Ernest R. and H. A. Buehler. "The Geology of the Granby Area." *Missouri Bureau of Geology and Mines.* 2d series, vol. 4 1905.

Crane, G. W. "The Iron Ores of Missouri." *Missouri Bureau of Geology and Mines.* 2d series, vol. 10. 1912.

Cuff, David, and William J. Young. *The United States Energy Atlas.* New York: Free Press, 1980.

Daniels, Stephen E. "Coal Mining in Northeast Missouri, 1850–1920." Master's thesis, Northeast Missouri State College, 1968.

Gibson, Arrell M. *Wilderness Bonanza: The Tri-State District of Missouri, Kansas, and Oklahoma.* Norman: University of Oklahoma Press, 1972.

Gist, Noel P., ed. *Missouri: Its Resources, People, and Institutions.* Columbia: Curators of the University of Missouri, 1950.

"The History of St. Joe." *St. Joe Headframe.* Special edition. Bonne Terre, Mo.: St. Joe Minerals Corporation, 1970.

Houck, Louis. *A History of Missouri.* Vol. 1. Chicago: R. R. Donnelley and Son, 1908.

"Indian Creek—The Prototype Operation." *Engineering and Mining Journal,* vol. 165, p. 89. April 1964.

Johnson, Hugh Nelson. "Sequent Occupance of the St. Francois Mining Region." Ph.D. dissertation, Washington University (St. Louis), 1950.

Jones, J. Wyman. *A History of the St. Joseph Lead Company.* Published for private circulation. New York: St. Joseph Lead Company, 1892.

McMahon, David F. "Tradition and Change in an Ozark Mining Community." Master's thesis, St. Louis University, 1958.

Megee, Mary C. "The Geography of the Mining of Lead and Zinc in the Tri-State Mining District." Master's thesis, University of Arkansas, 1953.

"Meramec Iron Ore Project Starts Production at Pea Ridge." *Engineering and Mining Journal,* vol. 165, pp. 93–108. April 1964.

Missouri State Highway Commission and the Writers' Program of the Works Progress Administration. *Missouri: A Guide to the "Show Me" State.* American Guide Series. New York: Duell, Sloan, and Pearce, 1941.

Norris, James D. *Frontier Iron: The Story of the Maramec Iron Works, 1826–1876.* Madison: State Historical Society of Wisconsin, 1964.

Rafferty, Milton D. *Historical Atlas of Missouri.* Norman: University of Oklahoma Press, 1982.

———. *The Ozarks: Land and Life.* Norman: University of Oklahoma Press, 1980.

———. "Persistence Versus Change in Land Use and Landscape in the Springfield, Missouri, Vicinity of the Ozarks." Ph.D. dissertation, University of Nebraska, 1970.

Robertson, Charles E. *Mineable Coal Reserves of Missouri.* Missouri Geological Survey and Water Resources, report of investigations no. 54. Rolla, Mo., 1973.

Rogers, Nelson F. *Strip-mined Lands of the Western Interior Coal Province.* University of Missouri Agricultural Experiment Station, research bulletin 475. Columbia, 1951.

Roome, Charles C. "Selected Aspects of the Southeast Missouri Mining Region." Master's thesis, University of Missouri (Columbia), 1962.

Sauer, Carl O. *The Geography of the Ozark Highland of Missouri.* Geographic ociety of Chicago bulletin no. 7. Chicago: University of Chicago Press, 1920.

Schroeder, Walter A. *The Eastern Ozarks.* National Council for Geographic Education Special Publication no. 13. Normal: Illinois State University, 1967.

Thoman, Richard S. *The Changing Occupance Pattern of the Tri-State Area of Missouri, Kansas, and Oklahoma.* University of Chicago Department of Geography research paper no. 21. Chicago: University of Chicago Press, 1953.

Thompson, Henry C. *Our Lead Belt Heritage.* Flat River, Mo.: News-Sun, 1955.

Vickery, Margaret Ray. *Ozark Stories of the Upper Current River.* Salem, Mo.: Salem Publishing Company, no date.

Wharton, Hayward M., et al. *Missouri Minerals—Resources, Production, and Forecasts.* Missouri Geological Survey and Water Resources Special Publication no. 1. Rolla, Mo., 1969.

CHAPTER 7

AGRICULTURE: DEVELOPMENT AND GEOGRAPHY

For nearly a century and a half, agriculture was the chief business of Missouri, and it is the third-ranking economic activity today. In the years prior to the Civil War, the state was experiencing the first wave of settlement. During the decade of the 1850s, the industrial capital of the United States increased from a little over $500 million to over $1 billion. Most of this was in the northern states, including Missouri. The railroads were expanding and opening new lands for settlement.

AGRICULTURAL EXPANSION

The first settlers from east of the Mississippi engaged in pioneer subsistence farming, although some surpluses were shipped from the more accessible river settlements. In the forested areas the cultivation of crops was supplemented by hunting, fishing, and the gathering of honey, berries, nuts, fruits, and greens. An unlimited supply of game and fish was close at hand. Pigeon, wild turkey, and deer were plentiful. An abundance of mast and prairies of bluestem grass provided food for the cattle and hogs so that it was unnecessary to cultivate more than a few acres of basic crops.

Statistics for the very early years are unavailable. A farmer's own tally of livestock would have been an approximation anyhow, for practically all stock ran at large on the range. Hogs, in particular, were killed for meat according to the need with no account taken. Gradually, livestock came to be "marked," usually with a cut in the ear, to denote ownership.

Corn, a staple for man and beast, became the most important crop the first settlers cultivated. They also grew wheat for white bread and biscuits. Because of the isolated area and the primarily subsistence economy, nearly all the pioneer farms produced some tobaccco, flax, hemp, and cotton for domestic use. The women spun wool or cotton for clothing. As late as 1869, Lawrence County farmers grew sixty-six bales of cotton.

The farmers plowed their fields with a bull tongue, a single blade attachment preceded by a sharp steel prong or coulter, which either cut the roots or caused the plow to jump over them. It was well suited for use on rough land and for opening new fields. In the first years it was drawn by oxen, later by horses or mules. The farmers leveled the land by harrowing or by dragging heavy brush over it and after harrowing, laid the land out in squares with the bull tongue plow. Then they dropped corn in by hand at the intersections, covering the seed either by a hoe or by dragging a rock or log down the rows.

Farming practices during the first 100 years of Missouri agriculture were much different than those used today. They were labor intensive and cooperative labor was very common, particularly for major tasks. House building, barn raising, hog butchering, horseshoeing, soap making, candle making, pressing apples for cider, canning and drying vegetables and fruits, cutting, shocking, and threshing grain were often undertaken cooperatively by several families in a rural neighborhood.

Continuous improvements in farming machinery and methods encouraged agricultural expansion. The cast-iron plow replaced the old wooden plow with a steel point. The famous one-horse double-shovel plow, which required but one round to cultivate a row, was a major innovation. Homemade wooden peg harrows replaced the drag harrow made of brush. In the 1850s the reaping machines Cyrus McCormick, Obed Hussey, and others invented replaced the cradle and scythe for cutting grain and hay. In the same decade, threshing machines were introduced, replacing the flail and winnowing methods of separating the grain. The steam-powered dragline dredge was an important invention that made possible the drainage of the Southeast Lowlands.

Hybrid corn and grain sorghum were not developed until the twentieth century, but methods to improve crops and strengthen animals by selective breeding were understood and used prior to the Civil War. Several different varieties of corn had been developed by selective breeding, and good farmers were selecting what they considered the best ears for planting. In a similar way some farmers were working to develop better strains of wheat, oats, and rye.

Apparently little effort was made in Missouri in the early days to use regular cropping systems such as those adopted in Indiana, Ohio, and other eastern states where agriculture was older. In Missouri, where the soils were newer, the plan was still largely to cultivate corn three or four years; then oats, wheat, or grass; and then corn again. Only the more progressive farmers were including red clover as a regular crop.

The most important early breed of cattle was the shorthorn, a type of general-purpose dairy and beef breed. There were a good many shorthorn breeders of prominence, several of them near the center of the state in Boone and Cooper counties. From these sources, shorthorn cattle gradually spread over the state, where they maintained their status well into the present century. Good breeds of hogs were not introduced until the late 1800s. Poland China became the most popular in the state. Horses came in originally with the pioneers and some of really good quality were introduced before 1850. The opening of the Santa Fe Trail and subsequent growth of trade with the Spanish led to the development of a market for mules. Central Missouri earned a wide reputation for its excellent mules. Buyers from the cotton states attended the large mule auctions and droves of mules were herded each year from Missouri's Little Dixie area to plantations in the South.

Agricultural societies and fairs were organized to share and disseminate information on improved methods and advances in technology. In 1853 the Missouri State Agricultural Society formed and by 1860 there were thirty-five or forty county agricultural societies. A fair was held in St. Charles County in 1821. In 1853 a fair at Boonville was promoted as a state fair. Several major fairs in central Missouri, where agricultural displays were featured, competed as state fair until 1899, when the State Board of Agriculture held an official state fair at Sedalia.

As agriculture expanded in the years prior to the Civil War, slave holding declined in importance. The wealthier slave owners were farmers, particularly those on the larger farms or plantations along the Missouri and Mississippi rivers. To a considerable extent, however, slaveholding in Missouri had become more a mark of distinction among the large landowners than a source of farm labor. Many of the slaves were serving as house servants and coachmen. Of course, the landowners who established large hemp and tobacco farms in the river counties prior to the war used many slaves. Cotton growing in the Southeast Lowlands had developed to only a small extent at this time.

During the Civil War, Congress passed two acts favorable to agriculture. The first was the Homestead Act of 1862, which provided that any person twenty-one years of age and the head of a family could secure title to as much as 160 acres (64.8 ha) of government land by paying $10 down, living on it for five years, and paying the fees for its administration. Although little good land remained in Missouri, some settlers were attracted by this offer. More were attracted by the improved farmsteads many Missourians sold in order to take advantage of the free government land in Kansas and the other plains states.

The Morrill Act of 1862 was the second legislation passed beneficial to agriculture. This act granted an allotment of government land to each state, from the sale of which "colleges of agriculture and mechanical arts" were to be established. Unfortunately, in Missouri the allotted land was mainly in the rougher parts of the Ozarks where the value was low. As a result, it took seventy to eighty years to sell it. Over 260,000 acres (105,300 ha), however, were disposed of at an average price of $2.17 an acre (.405 ha). This amounted to over $560,000, the income of which has gone to the Colleges of Agriculture and Engineering, which were established as separate entities within the University of Missouri in February 1870. The work of the College of Agriculture has had profound influence on the state's agriculture during the years.

During the latter half of the nineteenth century, continuous advancements were made in agriculture. Horse-drawn tillage equipment was perfected; the portable steam engine, or traction engine, was developed and adopted for plowing, threshing, and hauling; stable cropping systems were introduced; the practice of selecting improved crop and livestock strains, known as breeding up, was expanded; more advanced cultivation techniques were developed; and a few commercial fertilizers were produced. Road improvements helped some farm areas, but on the whole agriculture suffered from poor roads.

During the twentieth century, agriculture in the United States has made greater progress than had been made since the first immigrants landed on the East Coast. Although the influx of people from other states and countries had, by 1900, greatly slowed and the percentage of people in rural areas—on farms and in small towns (2,500 and below)—steadily declined, advances in agricultural mechanization, technology, management, and marketing generated great change.

The crops grown during the early 1900s were not greatly different from those grown before that time. Corn, oats, wheat, and tame hay were the leading crops. The cotton acreage in the Southeast Lowlands increased as more swampland was rapidly cleared and drained. In livestock production, methods of dipping cattle for tick control were devised, serum for the control of hog cholera was discovered and produced, and improved breeds of cattle and hogs were developed. Hereford and Angus were the leading beef animals; Holstein, Jersey, and Guernsey were the leading dairy stocks; and Poland China, Berkshire, and Duroc Jersey became the most important breeds of hogs.

The scientific developments that followed World War I transformed agricultural technology and had a marked influence on Missouri farm people. The use of automobiles and trucks, refrigerators, telephones, and electrical appliances increased

PHOTO 7.1. (top left) Tractor and Field Disk, Wolf Island Farms, Mississippi County. Photograph by the Author. PHOTO 7.2. (top right) Harvesting Soybeans with a Combine. Courtesy Missouri Department of Agriculture. PHOTO 7.3. (below) Harvesting Corn with a Picker-Sheller Combine. Courtesy Missouri Department of Agriculture.

greatly during this period. Large federal and state expenditures on hard-surfaced roads served to put Missourians on rubber. Most farmers were no longer isolated, and the barriers between country and city people gradually began to break.

When the stock market collapsed in 1929, farm prices, along with the prices of all commodities, fell. With no adequate method of controlling the de-escalation, farmers simply continued to produce. Thus total farm production in the nation declined only 6 percent, while farm prices fell to heart-breaking levels. The total farm income dropped from $12,790 million in 1929 to a low of $5,560 million in 1932.

During World War II, 12 million men and women were in the armed forces. As young men enlisted, the shortage of labor on farms became severe. However, improved machinery, favorable weather conditions, and the labor of the whole farm family combined to increase agricultural production about one-third over the prewar output.

The most remarkable developments in farm mechanization have been during the past fifty years. The rapid progress of agricultural technology in this period has had a tremendous influence on the entire country, among country people and city people alike. The most far-reaching mechanical development has been the invention of the general-purpose farm tractor, which brought about a great change in Missouri agriculture—the decline in numbers of horses and mules. In 1900 the census reported their number at 1,150,995. By 1954 it was down to 125,495. Very few farms in Missouri today have a single draft animal on them. The decline in the numbers of these animals released close to 20 million acres (8,097,066 ha) of land, which formerly grew horse and mule feed, for food crop cultivation or for meat and dairy production.

A number of recent developments in mechanization stand out as labor savers. The most important of these are the combine, made in various modes for harvesting wheat, sorghum, soybeans, and corn; the forage harvester; the modern hay baler; large land-leveling equipment; modern milking equipment; chemical spraying equipment; terracing and earth-moving equipment; and the cotton picker. Also, the plans and actual construction of farm buildings have undergone numerous changes for greater efficiency. The Harvestor, a multipurpose grain and silage storage tank, is rapidly replacing the upright silo. Trench silos permit increased use of mechanical handling equipment, and improved milking parlors and stainless steel, refrigerated, bulk milk tanks have revolutionized dairy farming.

FARMING REGIONS

In 1979, cash receipts from farming in Missouri totaled $4.2 billion (Table 7.1). A wide range of crops is grown commercially in the state including such disparate commodities as small grains, corn, cotton, and tobacco. However, Missouri agriculture is definitely oriented toward livestock production. Approximately two-thirds of the state's total farm income is derived from the sale of livestock and livestock products.

The intensity of agricultural production varies significantly from region to region within the state (Figure 7.1). However, all of Missouri's 114 counties report over $440,000 in agricultural receipts annually. The areas of most intensive production are associated with the state's two great river systems: the highly productive loess areas of west-central and northwest Missouri along the Missouri River and the black, fertile alluvium of the Mississippi floodplain in the delta region of southeast Missouri. (Figure 7.2) Twelve of Missouri's top 13 agricultural counties lie in these two regions.

The west-central and northwest area specializes in livestock and livestock products. Cash grains, although well represented, are deemphasized in favor of animal feed crops such as corn. Northern Missouri falls within the famous Corn Belt, the nation's—if not

TABLE 7.1

Field Crops and Livestock Production and Value (State total, 1979)

	Acres	Hectares	Production (bu)	Value ($)
Wheat	1,780,000	720,900	70,400,000	267,520,000
Soybeans	6,000,000	2,430,000	186,795,000	1,139,450,000
Oats	90,000	36,450	2,025,000	3,038,000
Rice	35,000	14,175	1,333,000	14,663,000
Corn	2,220,000	899,100	228,660,000	537,351,000
Grain sorghum	720,000	291,600	59,040,000	128,707,000
Cotton lint	157,000	63,585	157,000(lbs)	46,497,000
Cattle and calves	5,550,000(head)			2,081,250,000
Milk cows	276,000(head)			160,660,000
Hogs and pigs	4,100,000			350,550,000
Sheep and lambs	126,000			6,363,000
Broilers	25,297,000			26,309,000
Turkeys	10,950,000			88,761,000

Source: Missouri Crop and Livestock Reporting Service. Missouri Farm Facts, 1980.
Missouri Department of Agriculture, Jefferson City, 1980.

the world's—largest, high-yield area for livestock feed and livestock production (Figure 7.3). When the Corn Belt is considered as a whole, 9 out of 10 bu (352 1) of corn cultivated are fed to livestock. The remainder is exported, consumed in foods, and used in the production of oils and alcohol.

A similar system of farming is practiced in the loess soils of the eastern and northern borders of the Ozark region, although the farms are somewhat-smaller. Many of the farmers are of German ancestry who practice a general farming system. The mark of successful parenthood among this ethnic group has been to raise young men and women who are equipped with the knowledge, skills, and mental attitude to be successful farmers. General farming, with its diversity of crops and livestock, has led to small farms that have some difficulty competing with large-scale farmers.

In contrast, the Southeast Lowlands produce primarily field crops for direct sale. The most important crop in this region has been cotton. However, the soybean is a strong competitor for first ranking, and corn and wheat are also widely grown (see Figures 7.4–7.6). In recent years rice growing has increased, probably because of the

proximity of the large rice region in the Grand Prairie of Arkansas.

Truck farming, or truck, is of some importance in the vicinity of Missouri's two major urban centers—St. Louis and Kansas City—and to a lesser extent around Springfield. The few remaining strawberry growers in the Springfield area are vestiges of a once important tomato- , strawberry- , and fruit-growing enterprise in southwestern Missouri and northwestern Arkansas. Cash-grain farming is also practiced in the counties under pressure from urbanization. Rising land values on the urban fringes discourage farmers from investing in expensive dairy or livestock-feeding equipment. Cash-grain farming is a suitable transitional system in areas where land is gradually being converted to urban uses.

Fifteen counties in southwest Missouri are the leaders in dairy farming (Figure 7.7). Commercial dairying began in the Springfield area shortly after 1900 and spread throughout southwest Missouri and into northwest Arkansas. The topography, water, grass, and forage crops are conducive to dairying, and reliable markets developed in Kansas City and St. Louis at an early date.

Dairy cattle numbers and production in Missouri reflect national trends. Missouri

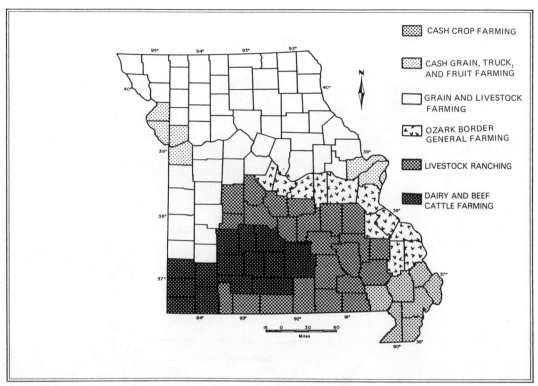

FIGURE 7.1. Agricultural Regions.

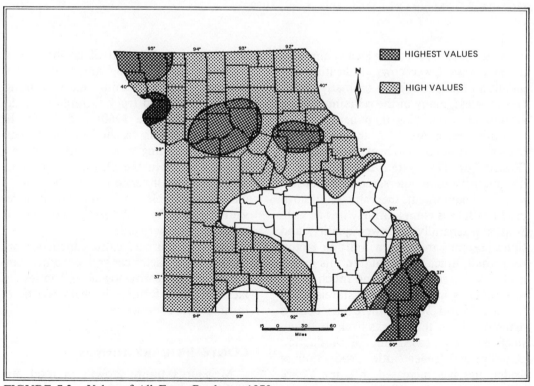

FIGURE 7.2. Value of All Farm Products, 1979.

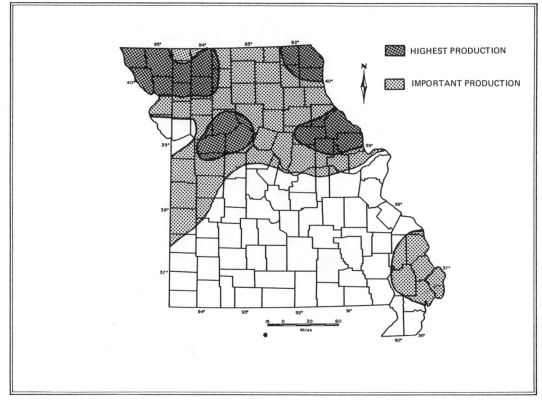

FIGURE 7.3.   Major Corn Production Areas, 1979.

dairy farmers are producing greater amounts of milk with fewer cows, indicating liquidation of that enterprise on many farms. Nevertheless, many of the remaining dairy farmers are expanding their herds.

Southwestern areas of the Ozarks in Missouri are devoted to beef cattle ranching (Figure 7.8). This system of agriculture is less intensive than others, requiring far less labor and equipment; the value of all farm products sold is comparatively less as well. Soils are generally of lower quality, and slope becomes more of a limiting factor. As a result, much of the land in this region is not used agriculturally, and much of the remainder is used only as pastureland.

Since World War II there has been a marked shift in the Ozarks back to a livestock economy based on the production of unfinished feeder cattle. Production of feeder pigs has increased in some Ozark areas, notably Howell County, but it is

small compared to that of northern Missouri (Figure 7.9). At the same time, general farming, poultry farming, dairy farming, fruit farming, and truck farming have declined. During the 1960s and 1970s the shift in emphasis reached major proportions, constituting a very important economic change in the Ozarks. High cattle prices made conversion of timberland to pasture profitable, and thousands of acres were cleared by bulldozing and aerially sprayed with herbicides.

Many of the beef cattle ranchers work part-time in factories and at other employment in nearby towns and cities. In fact, part-time farming is characteristic of most Ozark counties.

CONTEMPORARY TRENDS

Missouri's future growth in food and fiber production depends on many factors,

PHOTO 7.4. Mechanical Cotton Picker in Southeastern Missouri. Courtesy Walker—Missouri Division of Tourism.

of which two are major: (1) the comparative advantage Missouri has for producing a given commodity, and (2) how quickly Missouri farmers adopt new technological practices.

Soil, climate, and proximity to markets traditionally have strongly influenced what can be profitably grown in an area. These factors, along with the special skills and abilities of the individual farmer, have largely determined the comparative advantage and thus the commodity produced. As a result of technological advances, however, four additional factors have increasingly determined the comparative advantage of different areas: (1) increased specialization and dependence on other firms, (2) large-firm management of economies of scale, (3) the "footloose" nature of livestock and poultry production, and (4) improved transportation.

Specialization and dependence on other firms have greatly transformed agriculture since the days when farms produced a "near-final product." Dairy farmers in the early years, for example, utilized home-produced feeds, home-grown replacements, and family labor. As a result, they were basically self-sufficient. Today, with the use of mechanical milkers, concentrated feeds, specialized milking parlors, and bulk milk tanks, dairy farmers are dependent on their suppliers. In addition, the large investment such technology requires is justified only by bigger milking herds, which in turn lead to larger investments and greater specialization.

Even financing has become a specialized service. Broiler and turkey financing does not come from a general source of credit, but from large firms involved in the production and marketing process. Cattle feeding may now depend to a large extent on lenders who are specialists or big enough to employ specialists.

A rough measure of the interdependence of the production and marketing sectors of agriculture can be gained from an example. Farmers receive about thirty-seven cents of each dollar spent on food. But farmers pay out about 70 percent of this, or 26 cents, to buy production supplies. Thus only 11 cents of the consumer's dollar represents the value farmers add. The interdependence of farmers and farm-product marketing firms has been recognized by many attempts at coordination through contractual arrangements, what is loosely referred to as integration.

The continual substitution of larger and more automated machines for labor has brought large and indivisible inputs into each productive stage. A bulk milk tank or a cotton picker requires some minimal level of use for it to pay its way, thus encouraging large output. Bulk handling of feeds and fertilizers also raises the minimum operating scale while it reduces costs. In addition, larger operations that produce more can benefit from bulk discounts and cheaper transport for farm output.

Area specialization both supports and is supported by economies of scale. A

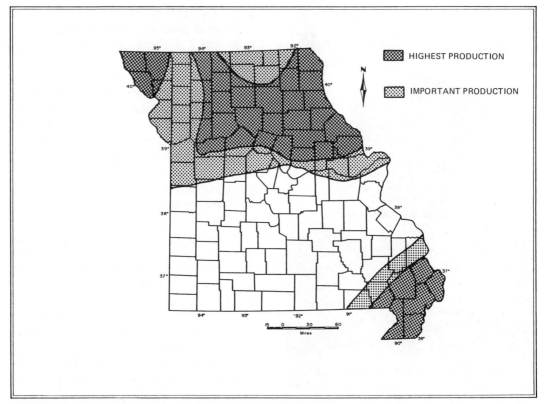

FIGURE 7.4. Major Soybean Production Areas, 1979.

veterinarian, for example, can specialize in treating diseases of one class of livestock. A lender can become especially competent in evaluating cattle-feeding operations if he has a large volume of such loans. All these economies of scale give producers in a specialized area many competitive advantages over producers in areas not so specialized.

Another factor that influences the comparative advantage of different areas is the gradual separation of livestock and poultry production from the land. Almost all concentrate-consuming livestock has become increasingly footloose, or independent of available land resources, especially broilers, layers, and turkeys. Even the large feedlots of the Great Plains, although located in surplus feed grain areas, often buy all or most of their feed. Economies of scale in livestock feeding have tended to offset the disadvantages that separation from the land

and reliance on purchased feed create. Thus, farmers can no longer depend only on the "natural advantages" their areas provide to assure them a share of livestock production, except of pasture-dependent beef cows and ewes.

Finally, many improvements in transportation have influenced locational advantages in producing agricultural products. Greatest cost reduction occurs with long-distance hauls of large quantities in bulk, such as milk that moves in bulk from Missouri assembly plants into Texas. Less progress has been made in reducing assembly costs, however, and they remain relatively high.

In summary, agriculture is changing rapidly and will continue to do so. To improve or even maintain Missouri's competitive position with other regions, not only producers but all sectors of the food and fiber industry must adopt new technology as fast

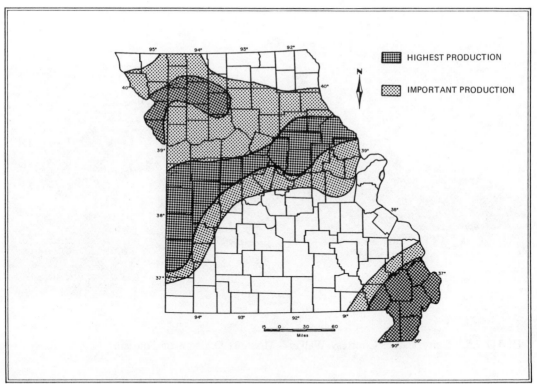

FIGURE 7.5. Major Grain Sorghum Production Areas, 1979.

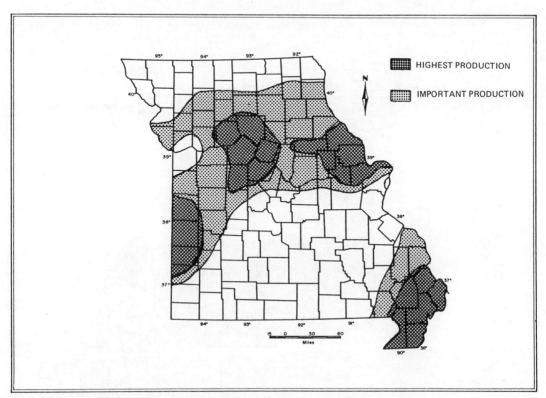

FIGURE 7.6. Major Wheat Production Areas, 1979.

102

PHOTO 7.5. Dairy Cattle. Courtesy Walker—Missouri Division of Tourism.

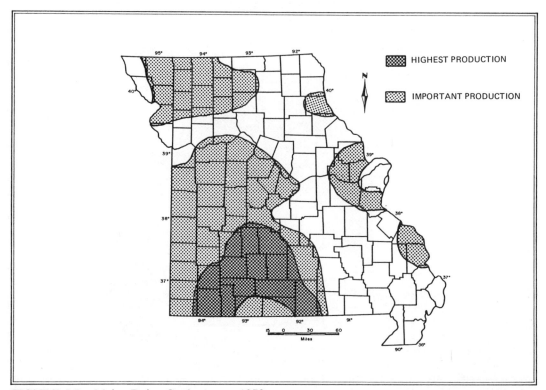

FIGURE 7.7. Major Dairy Cattle Areas, 1979.

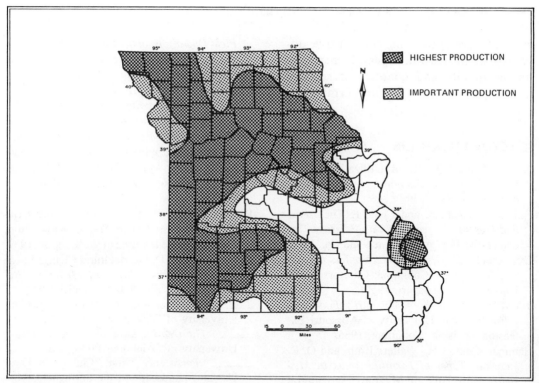

FIGURE 7.8. Major Cattle Production Areas, 1979.

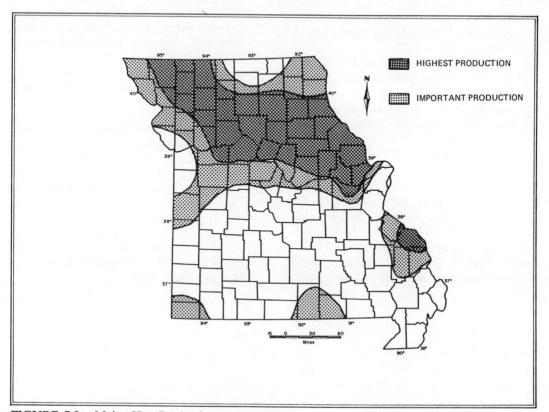

FIGURE 7.9. Major Hog Production Areas, 1979.

as it is developed. The competitive advantage of an area will depend increasingly on the quality and quantity of services from suppliers and marketing firms.

SELECTED REFERENCES

Bratton, Samuel T. "Land Utilization in the St. Francis Basin." *Economic Geography,* vol. 6, pp. 374–388. 1930.

Fairbanks, Jonathan, and Clyde E. Tuck. *Past and Present of Greene County, Missouri.* Indianapolis, Ind.: A. W. Bowen and Co., 1915.

Gist, Noel P., ed. *Missouri: Its Resources, People, and Institutions.* Columbia: Curators of the University of Missouri, 1950.

A Guide for Growth in Missouri's Food and Fiber Industry. University of Missouri Extension Division. Columbia, 1966.

Hammar, Conrad H., Walters Roth, and O. R. Johnson. *Types of Farming Areas in Missouri.* University of Missouri Agricultural Experiment Station, bulletin 284. Columbia, 1938.

Hewes, Leslie. "Cultural Fault Line in the Cherokee Country." *Economic Geography,* vol.19, pp. 136–142. April 1943.

_____. "Tontitown: Ozark Vineyard Center." *Economic Geography,* vol. 29, pp. 125–143. April 1953.

Kersten, Earl W., Jr. "Changing Economy and Landscape in a Missouri Ozarks Area." *Annals of the Association of American Geographers,* vol. 48, pp. 298–418. December 1958.

McFarlane, Larry A. "The Missouri Land and Livestock Company, Limited, of Scotland: Foreign Investment on the Missouri Farming Frontier, 1882–1908." Ph.D. dissertation, University of Missouri (Columbia), 1963.

Marbut, Curtis F. "Soil Reconnaissance of the Ozark Region of Missouri and Arkansas."

Field Operations of the Bureau of Soils, 1911. Washington, D.C.: Bureau of Soils, U.S. Department of Agriculture, 1914.

Meyer, Duane. *The Heritage of Missouri: A History.* St. Louis: State Publishing Co., 1963.

Miller, M. F. *A Century of Missouri Agriculture.* University of Missouri Agricultural Experiment Station, bulletin 701. Columbia, 1956.

"Missouri's War Against Texas Herds." *Springfield* (Mo.) *News and Leader,* January 30, 1977.

Paullin, Charles O. *Atlas of the Historical Geography of the United States.* Washington, D.C.: Carnegie Institute of Washington, 1932.

Rafferty, Milton D. "Agricultural Change in the Western Ozarks." *Missouri Historical Review,* vol. 69, pp. 299–322. April 1965.

_____. *Historical Atlas of Missouri.* Norman: University of Oklahoma Press, 1982.

_____. *The Ozarks: Land and Life.* Norman: University of Oklahoma Press, 1980.

_____. "Persistence Versus Change in Land Use and Landscape in the Springfield, Missouri, Vicinity of the Ozarks." Ph.D. dissertation, University of Nebraska, 1970.

Rafferty, Milton D., Russel L. Gerlach, and Dennis Hrebec. *Atlas of Missouri.* Springfield, Mo.: Aux Arc Research Associates, 1970.

Rafferty, Milton D., and Dennis Hrebec. "Logan Creek: A Missouri Ozark Valley Revisited." *Journal of Geography,* vol. 72, pp. 7–17. October 1973.

Riggs, Margaret. "Valley Contrasts in the Missouri Ozarks Region." *Journal of Geography,* vol. 35, pp. 351–359. December 1935.

Sauer, Carl O. *The Geography of the Ozark Highland of Missouri.* Geographic Society of Chicago, bulletin no. 7. Chicago: University of Chicago Press, 1920.

Steyermark, Julian A. *Vegetational History of the Ozark Forest.* University of Missouri Studies, vol. 31. Columbia: University of Missouri Press, 1959.

County pineries, the town of Chadwick became a sawmill boom town. The Hobart-Lee Tie and Timber Company operated shipping docks and company stores at Chadwick, Sparta, and a half dozen other locations in southwest Missouri.

Capitalists located their sawmills in Missouri because of the low cost of stumpage, or standing timber, in the area. White pine stumpage in Michigan and Wisconsin cost more than $3.00 per 1,000 bd ft (29.4m³) whereas the pine of Missouri averaged $1.22 for stumpage. The Missouri Land and Lumber Company purchased thousands of acres in Shannon, Ripley, and Carter Counties for prices ranging from $0.25 to $1.00 per acre (.405 ha). Some land that yielded about 4,000 bd ft (117.6m³) of shortleaf pine to the acre was purchased for as little as $0.125 per acre. The forests in the Southeast Lowlands sold for similar prices.

The impact of the large lumber companies on the economy, politics, and social life of the region was substantial. The Himmelberger-Harrison Lumber Company built large mills at Morehouse. The company owned timberland in various parts of the Southeast Lowlands and manufactured boards, posts, shingles, shooks, and staves. Log trains brought most of the saw timber to the mill at Morehouse from cuttings as far as 25 miles (40.22 km) away. The company had extensive lumber-producing machinery at Morehouse, as well as extensive drying yards. The quality of the timber available determined the products of the mill. From the larger trees high-grade timbers, boards, and shingles were produced; whereas the small, inferior trees were made into posts, less desirable lumber, and barrel staves and heads.

Some of the lumber the mill produced was sold locally. Products that were not marketed in the immediate vicinity were shipped by rail mainly to St. Louis, or to Memphis, and from these points distributed to consumer areas. Several of the large mill operations in the Ozarks, such as the Missouri Lumber and Mining Company, Cordz-Fisher Lumber Company, and Ozark Land and Lumber Company, marketed

PHOTO 8.2.   Oak-Hickory Forest and Bald Knobs in Taney County. Photograph by the Author.

CHAPTER 8

THE LUMBER INDUSTRY

Forests were both friend and foe to the early settlers in Missouri. There is ample evidence that the settlers used timber for buildings, fences, farm implements, and tools. At the same time, they struggled to clear forestland for the cultivation of corn, wheat, and other grains. When the Spanish commandant at New Madrid, Don Tomas Portell, was assigned the task of establishing farms and plantations to help support and feed the Louisiana government at New Orleans, he submitted a long list of tools considered necessary for such an undertaking. Axes, crosscut saws, adzes, and ripsaws indicate the abundance of the forests; and the cypress barracks, cypress clapboards, cypress flatboats, and cypress planking on wharves provide a fairly clear picture of the lowland timber species available.

Even though St. Louis and Hannibal were well-established lumber mill towns during the days of river transportation, the great lumber boom in Missouri actually occurred from the latter part of the 1800s to about 1920. As eastern settlers and European newcomers were attracted to the Midwest and Great Plains, the new settlements created a vast market for lumber for building houses, barns, and stores. At the same time, railroad construction, which required 3,000 crossties for each mile of track, proceeded at an unprecedented rate.

These factors, coupled with the general growth of the U.S. population and economy, created a strong demand for lumber and timber products, accounting for the exploitation of the vast hardwood forests of Missouri, as well as the less extensive Ozark pine forests.

The lumbermen who entered Missouri in the years following the Civil War were pioneers primarily looking for profits. In a capitalistic economy, they played the same role in the social and economic development of the frontier as cotton farmers, ranchers, and miners, who sought material gain by the exploitation of the natural wealth of the wilderness.

Large-scale lumbering was inaugurated when railroads were extended into the forests of the Ozarks and Southeast Lowlands, providing easy and low-cost transportation for bulky lumber products. By 1882 the Kansas City, Fort Scott, and Memphis Railroad had built a line from Springfield to Memphis, Tennessee, through the eastern Ozark pineries, and the St. Louis and Iron Mountain Railroad had laid tracks through the eastern pine timber to Poplar Bluff. In the delta Louis Houck was busy building a railroad empire to tap the giant oak and hickory timber in the swamps.

Missouri forests were an excellent source of lumber and railroad supplies for both the Great Plains and the eastern markets.

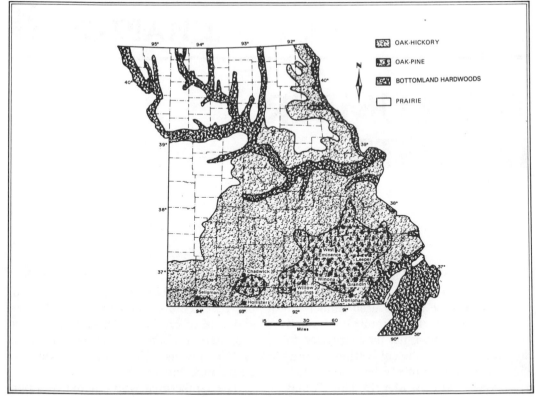

FIGURE 8.1.   Forest Types and Lumber Mill Towns.

Eastern investors purchased large acreages of shortleaf pine and oak timber. The cost of stumpage was low, from a few cents to a dollar per 1,000 bd ft (29.4m³), and the open winters permitted year-round logging.

Following practices established during the exploitation of the eastern and northern hardwood and pine forests, the lumber companies quickly built large sawmills, constructed logging railroads, and began cutting timber for manufacture into lumber. Shortleaf pine forests were exploited for lumber; oak timber was used for flooring, barrel staves, and railroad supplies; gum and other bottomland hardwoods were sawed for pallets, boxes, and crates. Large sawmills were built in New Madrid, Pemiscot, Dunklin, Stoddard, Ripley, Oregon, Reynolds, Carter, and Shannon counties. Large companies such as the Himmelberger-Harrison Lumber Company, Gideon-Anderson Lumber Company, Chicago Mill and Lumber Company, Missouri Lumber and Mining Company, Ozark Land and Lumber Company, the Cordz-Fisher Lumber Company, the Current River Land and Cattle Company, the Culbertson Stock and Lumber Company, the Clarkson Sawmill Company, and the Doniphan Lumber Company were founded to exploit southern Missouri's timberlands. Company towns such as Grandin and West Eminence were built by some of the companies, but many places—Doniphan, Leeper, Winona, Birch Tree, Sikeston, Bernie, Morehouse, and Kennett, to name a few—were known as sawmill towns. At the turn of the century, the lumber companies and such investors as Louis Houck owned as much as a third of the land in several southeastern Missouri counties. Lumbering operations were smaller in the western Ozarks, but when a branch line of the Frisco Railroad was built from Springfield to the Christian

PHOTO 8.1.   Virgin Pine on Highway 19 in Shannon County. Courtesy Mi
Tourism.

PHOTO 8.3. Whiskey-Barrel Manufacturing at the Independent Stave Company in Lebanon. Courtesy Independent Stave Company.

their products as a consortium in Kansas City.

In addition to the few large sawmills, there were many small ones called peckerwood mills. These small mills used the few large valuable trees and the poorer-quality trees the commercial companies left, together with the larger second-growth trees. Their products were mostly second-class boards, railroad ties, and poles. Some of the small mills were located along the railroads and thus had access to market. Others relied on wagon transportation to the towns or to railroad shipping points. In the swamps of southeastern Missouri the lumber wagons were constructed with solid, wooden, wide-tire wheels, made by boxing an ordinary spoked wheel. The wide tire cut less deeply than a narrow tire, and

the solid wheel prevented mud from accumulating between the spokes.

Logs a distance of a mile or more away were brought on wagons, or on carts. One end of the log was suspended from the axle of the cart and the other dragged on the ground. In the swamp country, logs were quite easily dragged in shallow mud runways. A team of mules, or a single mule, walked by the side of the mud slide. Some trained mules, knowing where to go and how to get there, could take a log along a slide without the direction of a driver.

Whenever a small peckerwood mill exhausted the local supply of timber, it moved to another site; or if no site was available, the mill went out of business. This process is still under way in the Ozarks. In more than a few places, abandoned mill sites are a common sight, with rotting piles of sawdust, strewn slabwood, a few pieces of abandoned machinery, and perhaps a dilapidated shed or two.

The lumber workers were a rough lot, many of whom apparently found the lumber camps a refuge from the law. Sheriffs from adjoining counties seldom sought out fugitives working in the camps. For the most part, the workers were poor people who came from hardscrabble hill country and were accustomed to the hard work their employers demanded. A few large landholders and sawmill operators in the Bootheel area brought in Blacks from the South to help in clearing the land, but this work was performed primarily by people from the hill country.

DISPOSAL OF CUTOVER LAND

Within a relatively short period, the entire landscape changed. Where once the sunlight had been unable to reach the forest floor, it now burned down on entire watersheds. The last of the lumber rafts floated down the Ozark streams and the southeastern swamps were drained to make the land suitable for agriculture. Timber companies sold their cutover land to development companies, ushering in an era of land speculation. An advertisement the Himmelberger-Harrison Land and Investment Company at Cape Girardeau circulated in the early 1920s illustrates the frantic dealing that occurred in cutover lands.[1]

Skillful manipulators offered for sale poor cutover Ozark land using half-truths and well-selected illustrations. They conjured up visions of comfortable country homes in the minds of city clerks and traders who had tired of the routine or instability of their occupations. The land was laid out in small tracts of 5 (2.02 ha) to 40 acres (16.2 ha) and sold for fruit orchards and chicken farms. Often it was so poor that trees could have been planted only by blasting holes or so remote and inaccessible

that products could be marketed only at great cost.

With the virgin forest removed, the sunlight shining on the denuded Ozark hills brought forth a profusion of oak sprouts. The brush soon choked out the annual grasses that had sprung up when the timber was first cleared. Soil erosion was accelerated and dirt washed down from the hillsides, filling the stream valleys. Ex-woods workers were by necessity now attempting to feed their families by farming those dry, gravelly bottoms and by grazing cattle on "company" hill lands. A sprouting axe became a tool that every child born on an Ozark hill farm learned to hate. Burning off the Ozarks became a custom. Initially a means to reduce hardwood competition with annuals, this practice eventually became a prescription for "greening up" each spring.

According to estimates, the annual burning off eventually blackened some 5 million acres (2,024,291 ha) of Ozark land each year. The destruction to the trees, watersheds, forest game habitat, and soil finally reached the point that even the most worthless annuals had difficulty pushing their heads through the rocks. Unfortunately, the damage to the land resulted in lowering the health, education, and general living standards of the people. Financially as poor as the hills they attempted to farm, the hill people became a symbol for pity and even comedy. The original 30 million acres (12,150,000 ha) of high-quality forests were reduced to some 15 million acres (6,075,000) ha of abused lands supporting very little that could be called a forest.

ERA OF FOREST MANAGEMENT

The era of forest management dates from the 1930s, when national forests were established and the Missouri Department of Conservation was created. Progress in management and improvement has since been continuous.

Beginning in 1933, the U.S. Forest Service purchased approximately 1.3 million

---

LAND VALUES MUST GO UP

We are offering the lands of the **Himmelberger-Harrison Lumber Company,** the finest body of cut-over land in Southeast Missouri in tracts of 20 acres and up, at reasonable prices, 10 percent cash, balance 10 years after date at 6 percent interest. **WITHOUT ANY INTEREST THE FIRST TWO YEARS,** if you improve the property.

We are also offering the lands of the **A. J. Mathews and Company, Inc.,** the finest body of improved lands in the state of Missouri, embracing many of the choicest farms in Cape Girardeau, Scott, Stoddard, and New Madrid Counties. Most of this land is on hard-surfaced roads, and nearly all of it is located adjacent to the thriving and prosperous towns of Oran, Randles, Perkins, Sikeston, Libourn, Malden, Parma, Gideon, and Risco, Missouri. We are subdividing this property and selling it in farms to suit the purchaser in tracts of 20 acres and up, at reasonable prices, 20 percent cash and the balance like rent.

Anyone who is a hustler and has a little to start with can make good on one of these tracts of land. Don't throw your hard-earned money away. Think of yours and your family's future. Buy you a home (it will do you more good than a flivver, Victrola, or piano), work hard and under present conditions you will soon pay for it. You will then be your own boss, independent and happy, with no one to take orders from except yourself.

Text of an early 1920s' flier distributed by the Himmelberger-Harrison Land and Investment Company.

acres (526,500 ha) and immediately started a basic forest improvement program. Mark Twain National Forest, which now includes the districts that formed the Clark National Forest, stretches across the Ozarks from McDonald County to St. Francois County. The national forest contains much private land, primarily the cleared valleys and the land along the well-traveled roads that follow the ridges. The U.S. Forest Service controls most of the upland area, especially away from the better roads.

During nearly fifty years of forest management under the multiple-use sustained-yield principle, much has been done to restore the forests to a condition similar to the original forest. Fire control, pruning, thinning, harvesting damaged and diseased trees, planting starts of pine and walnut, and controlled grazing have greatly improved the quality of the forest.

In 1936 a Missouri constitutional amendment provided for the creation of the Missouri Department of Conservation, with the Missouri Conservation Commission as its supervisory body. The commission is responsible for the fish, wildlife, and forest resources of the state and, through the Division of Forestry, provides technical assistance and administers joint federal and state conservation programs for the 13.7 million acres (5,548,500 ha) of Missouri's forestlands. Since 95 percent of this acreage is under private ownership, the commission programs are directed primarily toward privately owned lands.

Technical advice on timber management is provided through the Farm Forester Program. Missouri forestry laws provide incentive for long-range managment of farm woodlands. Woodland tracts that meet certain qualifications may be declared forest cropland and are thereafter subject to minimal property taxation until the timber is harvested. When the timber is harvested, a yield tax, based on the value of the stumpage, is applied. These acts grant the state additional powers to assist landowners in the enforcement of state laws on timber theft, a continuing problem on both public and private land.[2] Unfortunately, the average holding of privately owned forestland is too small for profitable long-term management practices.

Solutions to the problem of managing forest resources and of producing and using wood products lie with timber owners and the industries that harvest and process these products. Nonfarm ownership of forestland, usually in tracts of 40 acres (16 ha) or less, is steadily increasing. Unless changes in ownership result in the consolidation of some of these holdings, the management decisions owners of small tracts of timber make will largely determine the future of the forest resources of the state.

NOTES

1. Charles E. Hudson, "A Geographic Study Examining the Major Elements in the Rise of Cotton Production in Southeast Missouri, 1922–1925" (Master's thesis, University of Missouri [Columbia], 1967), p. 64.
2. Milton D. Rafferty, *The Ozarks: Land and Life* (Norman: University of Oklahoma Press, 1980), p. 189.

SELECTED REFERENCES

Baver, L. D. "Soil Erosion in Missouri." University of Missouri Agricultural Experiment Station Research, bulletin 349. Columbia, 1935.
Beilmann, August P., and Louis G. Brenner. "The Recent Intrusion of Forests in the Ozarks." *Annals of the Missouri Botanical Garden,* vol. 38, pp. 261–282. 1951.
Bratton, Samuel T. "The Geography of the St. Francis Basin." *University of Missouri Studies,* vol. 1, pp. 1–54. 1926.
Britton, Wiley. *Pioneer Life in Southwest Missouri.* Kansas City: Smith Grieves Co., 1959.
Christian County: Its First Hundred Years. Ozark, Mo.: Christian County Centennial, 1959.
Cole, Lela. "The Early Tie Industry Along the Niangua River." *Missouri Historical Review,* vol. 48, pp. 264–272. Fall, 1953.
Ferguson, Judy. *The Boom Town of West Eminence and Its Lumbering Days.* Rolla, Mo.: Rolla Printing Co., 1969.
Ganser, David A. *Timber Resources of the Missouri Prairie Region.* Bulletin B797. Columbia: University of Missouri, July 1963.
——. *Timber Resources of Missouri's Northwestern Ozarks.* Bulletin B847. Columbia: University of Missouri, 1966.
——. *Timber Resources of Missouri's River Border Region.* Bulletin B846. Columbia: University of Missouri, 1966.
——. *Timber Resources of Missouri's Southwestern Ozarks.* Bulletin B845. Columbia: University of Missouri, January 1966.
Garland, John H., ed. *The North American Midwest: A Regional Geography.* New York: John Wiley and Sons, 1955.
Hill, Leslie G. "History of the Missouri Lumber and Mining Company, 1880–1909." Ph.D. dissertation, University of Missouri (Columbia), 1949.
Hudson, Charles E. *A Geographic Study Examining the Major Elements in the Rise of Cotton Production in Southeast Missouri, 1922–1925.* Master's thesis, University of Missouri (Columbia), 1967.
Kucera, Clair L., and S. Clark Martin. "Vegetation and Soil Relationships in the Glade Region of the Southwestern Missouri Ozarks." *Ecology,* vol. 38, pp. 285–291. 1957.
Liming, F. G. "The Range and Distribution of Shortleaf Pine in Missouri." Central States Forest Experiment Station, U.S. Department of Agriculture, Columbus, Ohio, 1946.
Martin, James W. and Jerry J. Presley. "Ozark Land and Lumber Company: Organization and Operations." Unpublished manuscript, School of Forestry, University of Missouri (Columbia), January 31, 1958.
Myers, J. K., and R. C. Smith. "Wood Products and Missouri's Forests." Missouri economic

study no. 6. Columbia: University of Missouri School of Business and Public Administration Research Center, 1965.

Rafferty, Milton D. *Historical Atlas of Missouri.* Norman: University of Oklahoma Press, 1982.

———. *The Ozarks: Land and Life.* Norman: University of Oklahoma Press, 1980.

———. "Persistence Versus Change in Land Use and Landscape in the Springfield, Missouri, Vicinity of the Ozarks." Ph.D. dissertation, University of Nebraska, 1970.

Schoolcraft, Henry Rowe. *Journal of a Tour into the Interior of Missouri and Arkansas in 1818 and 1819.* 1821. Reprinted in *Schoolcraft in the Ozarks,* edited by Hugh Park. Van Buren, Ark.: Press-Argus, 1955.

CHAPTER 9

TRANSPORTATION

Prior to and for several years after the Civil War, rivers were the main arteries of commerce in Missouri. Missouri's two large cities, St. Louis and Kansas City, as well as Hannibal, St. Joseph, and Cape Girardeau, had their beginnings as river ports. Before 1820, the mackinaw, a flatboat 40 ft (12.19 m) to 50 ft (15.24 m) long designed for downstream traffic; the smaller bullboat, constructed from buffalo hides stretched over a pole frame; and the keelboat, the most efficient of non-steam-powered river craft, served Missouri's most basic transportation needs. The keelboat was effective for both down- and upstream travel. Using various power sources, including oars, poles, sails, and the cordelle, the keelboat could move 20 tn (18.14 t) upstream at a rate of 10 miles (16.09 km) to 15 miles (24 km) a day. Boats could pass downstream from St. Louis to New Orleans in two weeks under good navigation conditions; the return trip often took months.

WATER TRANSPORTATION

The first steamboat on the Mississippi River, the *Zebulon M. Pike,* traveled from Louisville, Kentucky, to St. Louis in 1817, pushing upstream at the impressive rate of 3 miles (4.82 km) per hour. Two years later a specially designed shallow-draft steamer, the *Independence,* moved up the Missouri River to Franklin. In June of 1819 a military expedition under Major

Stephen S. Long steamed out of St. Louis in four boats to explore parts of the trans-Mississippi west. Long's flagship, the *Western Engineer,* was fantastically constructed with a bow resembling a serpent's head and a smokestack so situated as to give the appearance of smoke pouring from the mouth of "Long's Dragon." It was designed to scare the Indians, which apparently it succeeded in doing. Very soon regular packet service was established at most of the Missouri and Mississippi river towns. The usual ports of call on the Missouri were St. Joseph, Kansas City, Lexington, Glasgow, Boonville, Jefferson City, Hermann, Washington, and St. Charles. On the Mississippi the main ports were Hannibal, Louisiana, St. Louis, Ste. Genevieve, Cape Girardeau, New Madrid, and Caruthersville.

In 1832 St. Louis docks received 532 steamboats; in 1845 the number reached more than 2,000 and soon thereafter jumped to more than 3,000 annually. The tonnage these steamboats carried reached approximately 1,500,000 tn (1,360,500 t) in the mid-1850s. Kansas City reported 759 steamboat arrivals in 1857, and in 1858 there were at least 60 regularly scheduled packets operating on the Missouri River.

The wood-burning steamers were highly susceptible to explosion, particularly when a head of steam was made to fight a strong current or to run upstream in chutes. In April 1852, one of the worst steamboat accidents in Missouri history occurred at

Lexington. The side-wheeler *Saluda,* carrying 250 Mormons en route to Salt Lake City, met heavy ice and a strong current on the north side of the river, forcing it to return to Lexington for the night. The next day the *Saluda* again tried to round the point and was forced back. The captain then ordered all steam possible and made a third attempt. When the boat, loaded with passengers, was about 30 ft (9.2 m) from shore, the boilers exploded. Passengers were blown to bits and scattered over the river and banks. Only 100 were ever accounted for. Three years earlier a fire broke out on a steamboat at the waterfront in St. Louis, spread to adjacent boats, and eventually leapt ashore where it burned several blocks of businesses. The total loss was in excess of $6 million.

In spite of the problems of navigation and the danger of explosion, steamboats were a great improvement over keelboats and flatboats. Steamboats were faster, larger, and could carry heavier and bulkier cargoes. They could provide passengers with room, board, fashionable furnishings, and entertainment.

None of the tributary streams that drained northern Missouri were large enough to be navigated except for short distances during high water. A few of the largest streams that drained from the interior of the Ozark Upland could be navigated. During the fall and spring months, shallow-draft steamboats landed at Warsaw regularly and could reach Osceola when conditions on the Osage River were especially favorable. Similar boats were used on the Current River to serve Doniphan during high water.

Samuel Massey and Thomas James, owners of the Maramec Iron Works, were persistent in their efforts to improve navigation on the Meramec and Gasconade rivers. Although they managed to use flatboats successfully to transport iron blooms from Paydown on the Gasconade River to the Missouri River port of Hermann, all attempts to navigate the Meramec were unsuccessful.

The White River was the only stream flowing from the interior Ozarks large enough to become an important artery of commerce for steamboats. Shallow-draft boats of 50 tn (45.4 t) to 75 tn (68.1 t) could run the rocky shoals and chutes loaded with 75 to 100 bales of cotton. In 1859 the steamboat *Ray* reached the mouth of the James River, the farthest point ever reached on the White River by steamboat. The usual port of call en route from Batesville, Arkansas, to Missouri was Forsyth.

Nearly every permanently flowing stream in the Ozarks was used at one time or another to float crossties to shipping points on the railroads. Normally the ties were cut in winter and stacked alongside a stream to await the spring rise. Then they were floated downstream, sometimes individually but usually in the form of rafts. Interestingly enough, the criteria for streams that are legally navigable for the popular sports of canoeing and float fishing were established during the logging era. In a landmark case in 1954, *Elder* v. *Delcour,* the Missouri Supreme Court declared that all Missouri streams are open to canoeing and fishing because they are navigable waters by warrant of their use to float crossties.

At present the Mississippi River and its connecting waterway systems comprise a 22,000-mile (35,354-kilometer) expanding navigable network. The river has an improved 9-foot (2.74-meter) channel throughout its course in Missouri, and below St. Louis there are no locks or dams. The portion from St. Louis to New Orleans is open to navigation twelve months of the year and the upper portion from early March to mid-December. Navigation to Chicago via the Illinois River is open year-round. The Missouri River has a 7.5-foot (2.3-meter) channel and is normally open to navigation from late March to the end of November.

About ten common carrier barge lines serve Missouri. St. Louis is the largest river port with two public docks and thirty-seven private docks, whereas Kansas City

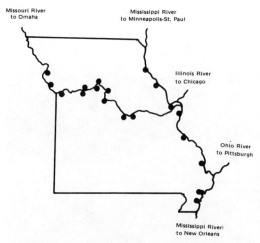

Missouri River
to Omaha

Mississippi River
to Minneapolis-St. Paul

Illinois River
to Chicago

Ohio River
to Pittsburgh

Mississippi River
to New Orleans

FIGURE 9.1.   Navigable Rivers and Docks.

has nineteen private docks (Figure 9.1). Other important river ports include Cape Girardeau with twelve docks; Caruthersville, eleven docks; New Madrid, five docks; and Hannibal, five docks. Towboats and barges are built at dry docks at St. Louis and Caruthersville.

Tows of eight to ten barges drawing 7 ft (2.1 m) of water can be taken from Kansas City to St. Louis in three days. The return trip requires about six days. Tows of forty or more barges, loaded to a draft of 8 ft (2.4 m) and powered by a large boat such as the Federal Barge Line's *United States,* can reach New Orleans in a week, stopping at various ports of call. The return trip requires about two weeks.

When speed in transportation is not essential, commodities and products can be moved inexpensively by water. The coal and steel industries particularly have profited from cheap water transportation. Petroleum products and agricultural chemicals move upstream whereas wheat, corn, and soybeans from the port hinterlands move downstream toward foreign markets.

ROADS

Land transportation developed slowly in Missouri. Road construction and maintenance were costly, and the few existing roads at the time of statehood were little more than poorly cleared trails. The first roads often followed the trails the Indians used in their hunting, warfare, and trading. In the early 1700s, roads were hacked through the country from Ste. Genevieve to the lead mines. Between 1776 and 1799, the Spanish laid out the King's Highway to link the Mississippi trading posts at New Madrid, Cape Girardeau, and Ste. Genevieve with St. Louis. The best-known route across the Ozarks was the Osage trail that led to St. Louis. This route, which followed the upland, was used by immigrants to the western Ozarks. It was known by various names: the Springfield Road, Ridge Road, and later, when a telegraph line was strung alongside it, Old Wire Road. Other early roads included the Boon's Lick Trail, which paralleled the Missouri River and connected a number of settlements established on the north bank of the river between Boon's Lick and St. Charles; the Old Iron Road, which linked the Maramec Iron Works with the Missouri River port at Hermann; and the Plank Road, over which iron was hauled from Pilot Knob to Ste. Genevieve.[1]

The 1st General Assembly of Missouri failed to provide state funds or to authorize any road taxes, but it did make all males from sixteen to forty-five years of age subject to road work and assessed fines upon those who failed to comply, with the payments on such fines going to the local road fund. Each male resident was obligated two days a year to assist a road supervisor in working the roads, or one day a year with a team of horses or mules. This system for the support of public roads was unpopular among farmers because the merchants, they believed, received the greatest benefit while they, the farmers, made the greatest contributions.

Many of Missouri's early roads were built as post roads to ensure the delivery of mail and to maintain communications with St. Louis, where a post office had been established in 1805. As early as 1810, several post roads had been laid to St.

PHOTO 9.1.   Towboat and Barges on the Mississippi River near Hannibal. Courtesy Walker—Missouri Division of Tourism.

Louis, and one connected Ste. Genevieve with Mine à Breton.

By 1819, Missouri could claim at least fifteen routes over which the mails were delivered once a week or once every two weeks. In 1857, after a long and bitter fight, the Butterfield Overland Mail Company headed by John Butterfield won the contract to establish mail delivery to California, backed by a $600,000 annual appropriation by Congress. Butterfield's line, with more than 100 Concord coaches, 1,000 horses, 500 mules, and 750 men, stretched from Memphis and St. Louis in the east to San Francisco in the west. Mail and passengers were transported from St. Louis to Tipton on the newly laid Pacific Railroad. There they transferred to stage coaches, which swung in a great arc through

Springfield to meet the Memphis stage at Little Rock and on through Preston, Texas, to San Francisco. Postage rate was $0.20 an ounce (28.3 g) for letters and passenger's fare was $100 in gold. On July 1, 1850, the first mail-carrying stagecoach between Independence and Sante Fe began its first trip to the far Southwest over the Sante Fe Trail, which Pedro Veal first marked in 1792–1793 and then William Becknell in 1821–1822. John Hockaday in 1858 joined the stagecoach entrepreneurs with a line from St. Joseph to the army posts in Utah. And in April 1860, the Pony Express kicked up its heels for a brief but colorful episode.

By mid-century, over 400 miles (644 km) of designated state routes had been laid, but the generally poor condition of

PHOTO 9.2.   Arrow Rock Tavern, Stagecoach Stop in Saline County. Courtesy Walker—Missouri Division of Tourism.

these roads made them difficult to use as arteries of commerce. Even in central Missouri, newspapers printed complaints that wagoners refused to haul goods over the roads. The need for more roads to open new areas was evident to most Missourians, especially short roads connecting the hinterland with the state's major waterways.

The economic recovery in the 1840s rejuvenated interest in internal improvements. Local government units remained responsible for roads, but some aid was obtained from revenues garnered from the sale of 500,000 acres (204,000 ha) of land the federal government granted the state in 1841.

Toll roads became something of a mania about mid-century and forty-nine companies were chartered in Missouri to construct plank roads. All but one were designed to connect some point in the state with the Missouri or Mississippi river.

Because of limited state and federal support for road construction, toll roads continued to be built linking large interior towns with the closest railroad towns. Some of the connecting toll roads remained in use until the 1930s.

Missourians built few bridges over major streams before 1850, relying primarily on ferries, which were usually operated as private business enterprises. County courts licensed the ferry operators and also set maximum-rate schedules for ferry trips. Gradually wooden bridges were built at key places to cross the larger streams. The smaller streams were generally not bridged before the automobile became common. As the wooden bridges washed out, high iron-trestle bridges replaced them.

Rural free delivery was inaugurated in Missouri on October 15, 1896, when three experimental routes were started at Cairo in Randolph County. By 1901 nearly

PHOTO 9.3. Pony Express Monument in Downtown St. Joseph. Courtesy Walker—Missouri Division of Tourism.

fifty communities, thirty-five north of the Missouri River, received this service. The Post Office Department requirement (1912) that new mail routes be established only on roads that were passable in all seasons of the year gave impetus to the movement for good roads.

The development of rural free delivery was coincident with the increased production and use of automobiles, which generated tremendous enthusiasm in Missouri. Some thirty automobiles were manufactured in St. Louis during this period. The names of the companies sound unfamiliar and exotic: Moon, Eureka, Clymer, Scott, St. Louis, American Morse, Darly, and Champion.

Automobile manufacturers and newspapers began to agitate for legislation to build and maintain roads. In 1907 the legislature created the Office of State Highway Engineer and set up a State Road

Fund using $500,000 from the federal government. In 1913 the 47th General Assembly created a State Highway Department with powers to designate selected inter-county roads as state roads. In 1916 Congress passed the Federal Highway Act, which provided for appropriations to the states based upon their size, population, and postal road mileage. By the Hawes Act of 1917, Missouri agreed to accept the federal funds and to provide matching funds for road projects. Road building was immediately accelerated; in 1917 alone, 122 projects were approved and, by the year's end, 11,400 miles (18,320 km) of inter-county-seat roads were dragged and improved. In 1921 the legislature passed the Centennial Road Act, which was designed to provide a network of roads connecting county seats. In 1927, Missouri voted to issue another $75 million in road bonds for construction of farm-to-market roads. These roads were

PHOTO 9.4. Covered Bridge at Paris, Monroe County. Courtesy Walker—Missouri Division of Tourism.

PHOTO 9.5. Riverdale Dam and Bridge on the Finley River, Christian County. Photograph by the Author.

mainly graveled, but well-engineered, highways through sections the primary roads did not reach.

The first bituminous-surfaced highways were constructed in the 1920s, and bituminous surfacing of county roads began shortly after World War II. In much of the Ozarks residual chert underlying the soil forms the surface of roads. After the overlying soil is bladed aside, the chert quickly becomes packed and hard, permitting all-weather travel. In northern Missouri the unsurfaced roads constructed on glacial till and loess are nearly "bottomless" after a heavy rain. Most of the farm-to-market roads are graveled or bituminous surfaced.

In the Ozarks, small streams are crossed most commonly by water gaps, or improved fords, where the gravel deposits in streambeds have been scooped out and replaced with concrete slabs. Unimproved gravel fords are still common in some of the poorer counties. The headwaters of the larger streams are crossed by concrete low-water bridges. Each year in the Ozarks several drownings occur when vehicles are swept from these picturesque crossings during times of high water.

Missouri's 32,000-mile (51,424-kilometer) state highway system is one of the nation's largest (Figure 9.2). Only six are larger—those of Pennsylvania, Texas, Virginia, West Virginia, North Carolina, and South Carolina. Missouri's system includes only about 27 percent of the approximately 117,000 miles (188,019 km) of roads, streets, and highways that cover the state. The county courts of Missouri's 114 counties have jurisdiction over more than twice as many miles of road as there are in the state system. In all, the county courts control more than 69,000 miles (110,883 km) of Missouri roads. They are the so-called CART miles, administered under the terms of the County Aid Road Trust Fund.

The interstate highways in Missouri maintain a pivotal position within the U.S. transportation system. Many of Missouri's interstate highways converge at St. Louis and Kansas City. The greatest volume of vehicular traffic is on Interstate 70, which connects these two cities. Interstate 29 links Kansas City with cities to the north in the Missouri valley, whereas Interstate 35 extends northeast to Des Moines and southwest to Kansas and Oklahoma cities. Interstate 55 connects St. Louis with Chicago and with Memphis and New Orleans. Interstate 44 links St. Louis with Springfield, Joplin, and the Will Rogers Turnpike in Oklahoma.

Probably the most important issue that has arisen over Missouri roads is that of adequate funding. In the 1970s rising petroleum prices reduced highway revenues in two ways: (1) gasoline consumption declined causing gasoline tax revenues to decrease; and (2) Missouri residents purchased smaller, lower-horsepower vehicles, thereby reducing automobile tag revenues. The decline in revenues has forced the Missouri Highway and Transportation Department to curtail highway maintenance and postpone construction of new highways.

While department revenues have been declining, the costs to operate the system have been rising. In 1979, the construction costs increased 42 percent. It cost $500,000 to construct 1 mile (1.6 km) of interstate highway in 1960, but $2,000,000 in 1979.

RAILROADS

When railroad construction began in Massachusetts, Pennsylvania, New York, Maryland, South Carolina, and other eastern states, Missouri had its advocates for the new means of reaching inland communities. The first railroad convention was held at St. Louis in 1836, and the general assembly showed enough interest to issue charters to a great variety of corporations, none of which was ready to build in the face of national depression.

A second railroad convention at St. Louis in 1849 explored the possibility of establishing a route from the eastern seaboard to the Pacific and quite naturally proposed

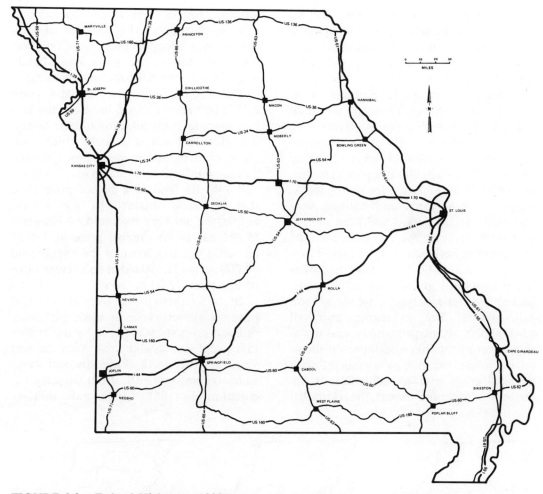

FIGURE 9.2. Federal Highways, 1980.

St. Louis as the most desirable point for a transcontinental line to cross the Mississippi. As it turned out, geography favored Chicago as the terminus of the line to the Pacific. Chicago was better located with regard to the industrial East and better aligned with the Platte River valley and the Wyoming basin, the best routes across the Great Plains and Rocky Moutains. Nevertheless, an enthusiastic legislature voted a grant of $1.5 million in bonds to the Hannibal and St. Joseph Railroad Company to construct its proposed line across the state between Hannibal and St. Joseph and a grant of $2 million to the Pacific Company to build from St. Louis to the western border of the state. By 1852 tracks

were laid and transportation began from St. Louis to Cheltenham, a distance of 5 miles (8.04 km).

In 1853, 32 miles (51 km) of track were added, and by 1856 the rails had been pushed westward to Jefferson City, a distance of 125 miles (201 km). On February 13, 1859, the Hannibal and St. Joseph Railroad was completed, the first across Missouri. The Pacific (now part of the Burlington Northern system) reached Kansas City in 1865. The southwest branch of this railroad in Missouri, running from the main line at Pacific, was extended to Rolla in 1861, and plans were made to extend it southwest by way of Springfield to the rich mineral resources of Jasper County, opening that area to settlement. The St. Louis and Iron Mountain Railroad, planned to connect St. Louis with southeast Missouri to serve the lead and iron industries of St. Francois, Iron, and Madison counties, was finished as far as Pilot Knob on April 2, 1858. From Mineral Point, on the main line, a spur was laid to Potosi (Figure 9.3).

Railroad building, however, required huge outlays of capital. Tracklaying alone cost $20,000 to $50,000 per mile (1.6 km), and millions were needed for rolling stock, shops, switching yards, and stations. Federal, state, and local aid had been offered generously for railroad construction. The U.S. government granted more than 3 million acres (1,215,000 ha) of land, and Missouri authorized an issue of state bonds, backed by first mortgages, to the several railroads at the aggregate sum of $24,000,000. Municipal, county, and township governments likewise indebted themselves. When the nation was beset with financial crises in 1861, all railroads operating in Missouri except the Hannibal

and St. Joseph were forced to suspend interest payments. The question of foreclosure was dropped until the Civil War was over, but in the years immediately after the war, the railroads went bankrupt.[2]

The Pacific Railroad obtained a grant of 125,000 acres (50,625 ha) from the federal government in addition to state bonds. The Hannibal and St. Joseph, which completed construction in four years, obtained a larger grant—611,323 acres (247,586 ha)— and sold its land at a higher price than that the Pacific obtained. In 1859, for example, the northern road sold 14,301 acres (5,792 ha) at an average price of $10.24 an acre (.405 ha), whereas the Pacific sold 78,000 acres (31,590 ha) at an average price of less than $2.00 an acre.

In the southern part of the state, railroad business slowed, and, in some instances, railroad property was seized by the armies that swept through the area. After the first year, railroads north of the Missouri River suffered relatively little from military occupation. In 1861, Confederate military

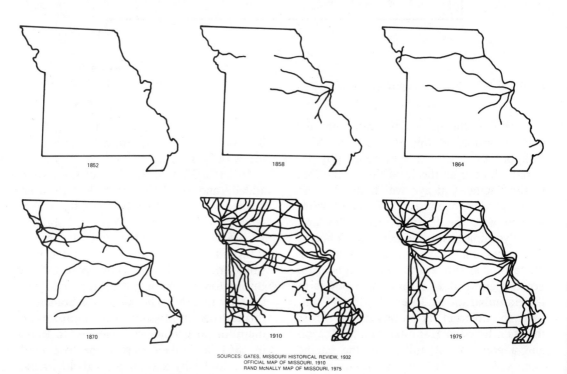

SOURCES: GATES, MISSOURI HISTORICAL REVIEW, 1932
OFFICIAL MAP OF MISSOURI, 1910
RAND McNALLY MAP OF MISSOURI, 1975

FIGURE 9.3.   Railroads, 1852-1975.

forces damaged or destroyed railroad bridges over the Gasconade, Osage, and Lamine rivers and the bridge over Gray Creek. During the same year Governor Clayborne Jackson ordered the destruction of the North Missouri Railroad, which resulted in property losses of $86,310. In 1864, General Sterling Price's raid brought further destruction of bridges and buildings on the Pacific, and damages of $100,000 to the North Missouri Railroad.

Ultimately, several factors caused the railroad companies to default: the lack of traffic, the steep, rocky land from the grants they received, the excessive cost of construction, and the loose management of finances. Actually, the looseness with which the companies' finances were conducted bordered on corrupt practices, and in some cases railroad financing was outright fraud. Several Missouri towns and counties raised funds, but never got a railroad. At one time, Dallas County, for example, owed bondholders more than the value of all property, real and personal, in the county. The Laclede and Fort Scott Railroad Company, which was to build a line from Lebanon through the county seat of Buffalo to Fort Scott, Kansas, received $235,000 from the sale of bonds; but the line was never completed.[3]

Though none of the Missouri railroads was to cross state border lines, it was expected that connecting lines would be built in the neighboring states, linking Missouri with the outside world. The first of these connections to be secured was with the East. By 1860 railroads had been built to St. Louis, which gave the city connections with Cleveland, Cincinnati, and Pittsburgh; and in 1863 a line from St. Louis to Chicago was completed, providing easier access to the Atlantic Coast. By 1870 rail lines were extended to New Orleans, Mobile, Nashville, Atlanta, Charleston, Des Moines, St. Paul, and Omaha.

Kansas City was by this time evolving into a railroad center. Many of the new rails in Kansas were laid to Kansas City, where connections were established with the newly built railroad to the Pacific coast. By means of the Missouri, Kansas, and Texas, and other railroads built through to Texas, a large trade hinterland was captured for Missouri's two major railroad cities.

The railroads proved to be an indispensable means of developing the resources of Missouri, and a network of them was built over the state, which in 1914 amounted to 8,208 miles (13,207 km). By 1918 every one of the 114 counties except Ozark, Dallas, and Douglas had at least one railroad passing through it.

Around the turn of the century, not all of the lines that had been built could be operated at a profit. The sheer complexity of management and transfer of goods worked toward the consolidation of numerous short lines and the abandonment of others (Figure 9.4). Since 1914 the railroad mileage in Missouri has declined by more than 1,500 miles (2,413 km) to approximately 6,700 miles (10,780 km). The abandoned lines can be categorized into three groups. The first consists of lines that ran parallel to other lines and competed for traffic—the Kansas City, Clinton, and Springfield for example. This line was abandoned after it was purchased by the Frisco system, which already had a line between Springfield and Kansas City. The second group consists of short spur lines that were designed to serve a major town, such as the Missouri Pacific branch line from Crane to Springfield; and the third includes short lines mining and lumbering companies built to exploit raw materials. Many abandoned lines in Missouri were laid to serve mines or to serve small sawmills. For example, several spur lines in Phelps, Crawford, and Dent counties were built to tap iron ore deposits and were abandoned when the ores were depleted or when the charcoal-fueled furnaces shut down. The Missouri Southern Railroad was an extensive logging railroad built between 1886 and 1910. By 1930 the timber was cut out, and ten years later the system was completely defunct. Several railroads that served the coal mines

126

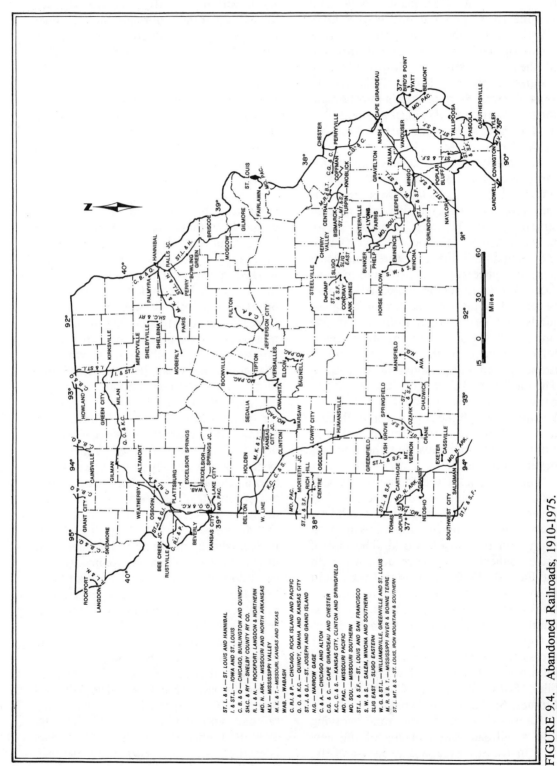

FIGURE 9.4. Abandoned Railroads, 1910-1975.
Source: Milton D. Rafferty, *Historical Atlas of Missouri* (Norman: University of Oklahoma Press, 1982). Reproduced courtesy of University of Oklahoma Press.

in northern and western Missouri were abandoned when the mines shut down. The Iowa and St. Louis Railroad was constructed from Sedan, Iowa, south through Worthington and Novinger to Elmer in Macon County. The coal mines along its route were the largest producers of revenue for the railroad for many years. In the 1930s, however, the mines started to close, and the railroad was abandoned section by section until the last tracks were removed in 1947. In a similar way many miles of track gradually fell into disuse over the years as mines closed in the Old Lead Belt and in the Tri-State Mining District.

Today, the number of passengers traveling by railroad is a small fraction of the traffic fifty years ago. Amtrak service from St. Louis and Kansas City provides connections to the East and West coasts. Most of the railroad revenues come from hauling freight. Food and farm products account for more than 35 percent of the total freight Missouri railroads haul. Other important rail cargoes originating in the state include stone and refractory products, metallic ores, nonmetallic minerals, chemical products, transportation equipment, and primary metal products. Nearly one-third of the rail shipments terminating in Missouri are of coal, mainly from Illinois and Kansas fields.

AIR TRANSPORTATION

Many pioneers in the development of aviation in the United States have been Missourians. Major Albert B. Lambert, a balloonist and enthusiastic supporter of air flight, helped found the St. Louis Aero Club, which did much to interest Missouri in the frontier of the skies. In 1910 the first international aviation meet was held at Kinlock Park between Ferguson and Florissant. When regular air mail service was instituted in the 1920s, among the first companies to provide it was the Robertson Aircraft Corporation of St. Louis, which in 1925 secured the franchise to carry mail between St. Louis and Chicago. Charles A. Lindbergh, a young first lieutenant in the

110th Observation Squadron of the Missouri National Guard, was one of the first pilots the company hired.

In 1939, James S. McDonnell, Jr., founded the McDonnell Aircraft Corporation, later known as the McDonnell-Douglas Aircraft Corporation, the largest aircraft industry in Missouri. The company started with two employees, received contracts to build airplanes during the war, and then obtained large contracts from the navy and air force in the postwar years. By 1962 the company had become the largest private employer in the state. During the sixties and seventies the company entered the competition for space hardware and built all of the Mercury and Gemini capsules that were flown.

As Missouri's location and physical attributes once encouraged early settlement in the late eighteenth century, its central location, temperate climate, and relatively hazard-free terrain have encouraged air travel to and within the state during the twentieth. Today twenty-three scheduled airline carriers serve the state. During 1975, nearly 6 million airline passengers enplaned in Missouri. St. Louis and Kansas City, centers for continental air traffic, accounted for 60 percent and 36 percent of the traffic respectively; Springfield for 2 percent; and all other cities another 2 percent. Lambert International Airport in St. Louis was the busiest airport and Trans World Airlines had the largest share of the passenger market—37 percent. The most active passenger route in Missouri, with forty-five direct flights daily, is between St. Louis and Kansas City. Direct flights from both cities are available to both coasts and to most major cities in the forty-eight contiguous states.

NOTES

1. Milton D. Rafferty, *The Ozarks: Land and Life* (Norman: University of Oklahoma Press, 1980), p. 105.
2. Ibid., p. 99.
3. Ibid.

PHOTO 9.6. Kansas City International Airport. Courtesy Convention and Visitors' Bureau of Kansas City.

SELECTED REFERENCES

Breuer, James Ira. *Crawford County and Cuba, Missouri.* Cape Girardeau, Mo.: Ramfre Press, 1972.

Buckley, Ernest R. *Public Roads, Their Improvement and Maintenance.* Missouri Bureau of Geology and Mines, 2d series, vol. 5. 1907.

Christian County: Its First Hundred Years. Ozark, Mo.: Christian County Centennial, 1959.

Cook, Delbert. "Abandoned Railroads in Missouri." Term paper, Department of Geography and Geology, Southwest Missouri State University, 1977.

Donnelly, Phil M. "Rural Free Delivery Service in Missouri." *Missouri Historical Review,* vol. 35, pp. 72–80. October 1940.

Fitzsimmons, Margaret Louise. "Missouri Railroads During the Civil War and Reconstruc-

tion." *Missouri Historical Review,* vol. 35, pp. 188–206. January 1941.

George, Floyd Watters. *History of Webster County.* Marshfield, Mo.: Historical Committee of the Webster County Centennial, 1955.

Gist, Noel P., ed. *Missouri: Its Resources, People, and Institutions.* Columbia: Curators of the University of Missouri, 1950.

Handley, Lawrence R. "A Geography of the Missouri and North Arkansas Railroad." Master's thesis, University of Arkansas (Fayetteville), 1973.

Ingenthron, Elmo. *The Land of Taney.* Point Lookout, Mo.: School of the Ozarks Press, 1974.

Meyer, Duane, *The Heritage of Missouri: A History.* St. Louis: State Publishing Company, 1963.

Miner, H. Craig. *The St. Louis–San Francisco*

Transcontinental Railroad. Lawrence: University Press of Kansas, 1972.

Missouri State Highway Commission and the Writers' Program of the Works Progress Administration. *Missouri: A Guide to the "Show Me" State.* American Guide Series. New York: Duell, Sloan, and Pearce, 1941.

Moser, David, ·et al. *Missouri's Transportation System: Condition, Capacity, and Impediments to Efficiency.* Jefferson City, Mo.: Office of Administration, Division of Budget and Planning, 1976.

Rafferty, Milton D. *Historical Atlas of Missouri.* Norman: University of Oklahoma Press, 1982.

_____ . *The Ozarks: Land and Life.* Norman: University of Oklahoma Press, 1980.

_____ . "Persistence Versus Change in Land Use and Landscape in the Springfield, Missouri, Vicinity of the Ozarks." Ph.D. dissertation, University of Nebraska, 1970.

_____ . "Trends in Ozark Roads and Bridges." *Ozark Mountaineer,* April 1974, pp. 21–27.

Sauer, Carl O. *The Geography of the Ozark Highland of Missouri.* Geographic Society of Chicago, bulletin no. 7. Chicago: University of Chicago Press, 1920.

U.S. Department of Commerce, *Interstate Commerce Commission Financial Dockets.* Nos. 14102, 20496, 12695, 10897, 12204, 12977, 12788, 19844. Washington, D.C.: Government Printing Office, 1936–1959.

Violette, Eugene Morrow. *A History of Missouri.* Cape Girardeau, Mo.: Ramfre Press, 1951.

Williamson, Hugh P. "Restrictions and Rights of the Missouri Sportsman." Missouri Department of Conservation, Jefferson City, Mo., no date.

Wright, Michael, ed. "Missouri Transportation Systems in Crisis." *Midwest Motorist,* vol. 52, pp. 2–3, 31. 1981.

CHAPTER **10**

AN ECONOMIC OVERVIEW

Since World War II, several of Missouri's economic sectors have experienced faster growth than the nation, namely farming, manufacturing, transportation, and communications and public utilities. Missouri's growth in manufacturing is easily the most important factor in the overall economic growth of the state. Although farm production in virtually all sectors has increased dramatically, the role of agriculture in Missouri's economy has decreased in significance as that of manufacturing and services has increased. The loss of over 124,000 farms from 1950 to 1978 and the accompanying outmigration has had an adverse effect on small-town retail trade, but has helped raise the overall per capita income. Growth in transportation, communications, and public utilities has been due to two factors: Missouri's strategic geographical location and rapid industrialization and urbanization.

Mining, contract construction, and finance in Missouri have kept pace with national expansion in these sectors. Following World War II, revenues from mining declined as the war-stimulated demand declined and as the better-grade ores were depleted. Over the past twenty years, large deposits of lead and zinc ores have generated a growth in revenues significantly faster than the growth rate of the nation. Wholesale trade has demonstrated some weakness as the states surrounding Missouri have matured economically. However, the Missouri Division of Tourism reported that the 1980 tourism and travel business reached $4.7 billion, placing it second to manufacturing in the state's economic hierarchy.

Six factors have greatly influenced Missouri's economy. The first of these factors is a peculiarity in the economic attitudes and expectations of the state populace. Whether through lack of information, isolation, or reticence, the modernization of agriculture in Missouri, especially in the southern half, lagged behind that of some adjacent states. Not until the later 1940s and early 1950s were horses traded for tractors and electricity introduced in the area south of the Missouri River.

A second factor, which has tended to lend stability to Missouri's agricultural income, is the specialization of Missouri farms in meat and milk production. A third factor, which has had a large impact of farming but also on manufacturing, is mechanization and automation. A fourth factor is the presence or absence of federal and state government employment. A fifth factor is the cost advantage or disadvantage of securing certain raw materials such as chemicals and leather. The sixth factor is geographical location with its associated market advantages and disadvantages.

MANUFACTURING

Probably the most important change occurring in the manufacturing sector of Missouri's economy since World War II has been the shift from the production of nondurables to durables. In 1939 the production of durable goods in Missouri was about 36 percent of total value added by manufacturing. By 1958 it was over 50 percent. The great increase in the manufacture of durables is the result of the production of transportation equipment, especially of military and civilian jet aircraft at the McDonnell-Douglas plant in St. Louis. Passenger automobile production, in which Missouri is one of the leading states, has been a stable sector until recent years; the rising prices for gasoline have brought increasing competition from foreign automobiles.

Passing agriculture as the state's major employer in the 1940s, manufacturing has become the dominant sector of the state's economy both in terms of employment and investment. In 1982 there were an estimated 425,000 persons employed in Missouri's diverse manufacturing activities, representing about 25 percent of the state's total work force. In terms of employment, the five leading manufactures are transportation equipment (57,500 employees); electrical equipment and supplies (53,100), food and kindred products (47,700); machinery, except electrical (36,600); and printing and publishing (34,200). During the past ten years expansions of existing manufacturers as well as new industries have added 13,918 new jobs each year. Approximately 55 percent of the new jobs were due to expansions and 45 percent were due to new industries.

Geographically, manufacturing employment in the state is concentrated in the metropolitan areas of St. Louis (48 percent), Kansas City (19 percent), Springfield (4 percent), St. Joseph (2 percent), and Columbia (1 percent) and in some nonmetropolitan areas (26 percent). The five manufactures that lead in value added by

manufacturing are transportation equipment, food and kindred products, chemicals and allied products, electrical equipment, and fabricated metal products (Table 10.1)

The decision a company makes to locate a plant or service facility in Missouri is usually based on a great number of factors. Some of the more important considerations are markets, a reliable energy supply, financing, natural resources, labor supply, transportation, and taxes.

Rural areas of Missouri are attracting mainly plants that employ a small number of workers, whereas the larger cities are getting the big plants. This is entirely as it should be. A large manufacturing plant can place undue strain on public utilities and the human resources of a small community. As for economic impact, a community of 1,000 that has obtained a manufacturer who will employ 20 people has improved its employment in the same proportion as a city the size of Springfield that has obtained a plant that will hire 2,000 employees.

Studies of manufacturing location in small Missouri towns indicate that most manufacturers do not have stringent requirements for raw material, market, or labor. Firms that locate in small towns expect to get along with fewer skills at the outset and are willing to train a large portion of their labor force. Generally they do not find it necessary to hire and keep top executives and professionals. Many are looking for one or more of the following benefits: lower local taxes, community support for plant construction, minimum land cost for expansion, relatively lower wage rates, and maximum labor stability.

Examination of geographical patterns over the past thirty years indicates conclusively that the food and kindred products, apparel and related products, lumber and wood products, and leather and leather products industries prefer (three to one or better) to locate in rural areas of Missouri. Other industries that appear willing to operate from rural areas are furniture and

TABLE 10.1

Manufacturing in Missouri, 1977

SIC Code	Industry Group	Value Added by Manufacture ($ million)	Value of Shipments ($ million)	Capital Expenditure ($ million)
20	Food and kindred products	1,529.2	5,905.5	99.6
22	Textile mill products	5.3	18.2	0.7
23	Apparel, other textile products	398.7	740.7	10.7
24	Lumber and wood products	161.4	357.1	11.8
25	Furniture and fixtures	152.7	295.8	8.6
26	Paper and allied products	348.1	837.3	31.7
27	Printing and publishing	733.0	1,280.8	35.3
28	Chemicals and allied products	1,277.0	2,523.7	130.2
29	Petroleum and coal products	161.3	684.1	13.1
30	Rubber and plastics products, NEC	D	D	D
31	Leather and leather products	308.2	575.0	4.5
32	Stone, clay, and glass products	434.3	827.4	33.8
33	Primary metal industries	629.1	1,468.0	112.7
34	Fabricated metal products	979.3	1,929.4	45.2
35	Machinery, except electrical	905.8	1,580.0	46.7
36	Electrical equipment and supplies	982.2	1,880.5	55.6
37	Transportation equipment	3,506.2	11,189.8	97.0
38	Instruments and related products	106.5	178.0	9.5
39	Misc. manufacturing industries	124.9	237.7	D

D = disclosure rule applies. (Data not revealed because too few units reported.)

Source: U.S. Department of Commerce, Bureau of the Census. Geographic Area Series, Missouri. Census of Manufactures, 1977. Vol. 3. Washington, D.C.: Government Printing Office, 1980.

fixtures, textile mill products, petroleum refining, and professional and scientific instruments.

The total effect a manufacturing plant has upon a community is much greater than just the creation of new jobs, investment, and facilities. The money a new or expanded industry introduces into an area causes a multiplier effect. According to a study the University of Missouri conducted, the multiplier value of each manufacturing dollar to a community varies from 1.1 to 3.2, depending upon the type of industry. Research data from the Missouri Division of Commerce and Industrial Development show the following increases would result from every 100 new jobs created: a population increase of 218; personal income increase of $618,200 per year; car registration increase of 113; bank deposit increase of $137,400; a retail sales increase of $519,600 per year; wholesale sales increase of $895,000 per year; and

service industry receipts increase of $81,600 per year.

ENERGY

On the whole Missouri manufacturers, business, and residential dwellers have access to reliable, competitively priced energy service. Missouri power plants generate ample electricity for virtually any size industrial customer. In 1975 Missouri utilities generated 9,446 megawatts (Mw) of electricity during peak demand periods. By 1983, Missouri power plants are projected to be able to produce 18,059 Mw.

The entrenched channels of the Ozark streams provide nearly ideal conditions for the development of dams and reservoirs for hydroelectric power. Large lakes can be created at relatively low cost and, because of forested slopes, the lakes are not subject to heavy siltation from eroded soils. The state's large reserves of coal combined with reliable water supplies, both in the

Ozarks and along the Mississippi and Missouri rivers, make development of thermal electric power less costly than in many other parts of the United States. Because Missouri power companies depend mainly upon coal for generation, the state has one of the most reliable electrical energy systems in the nation. In 1975 Missouri's two largest metropolitan areas, St. Louis and Kansas City, ranked second and fifth lowest in electric-utility costs among the twenty-three largest cities in the United States. The electric-power grid covers the entire state. Trunk lines supply the major urban centers, whereas smaller lines, many of them built by rural electric cooperatives under the Rural Electrification Administration (REA), serve small towns and farms.

Missouri is strategically located between the oil and natural gas fields of the southern Great Plains and the Gulf Coast. Trunk lines for oil and natural gas from the Great Plains fields to the industrial states to the northeast pass through central and northern Missouri. Feeder lines from these trunk lines branch out to serve towns and cities along the way. Similarly, the main natural gas and oil pipelines from the Gulf Coast oil fields pass up the Mississippi valley to the northeast, providing energy to southeast Missouri and St. Louis. The Ozark Region is conspicuous by the absence of natural gas pipelines. Only the eastern, western, and northern borders are served by natural gas. Many areas in northern Missouri are also without natural gas service.

The availability of natural gas service is extremely important for the development

PHOTO 10.1.   Power Plant Turbine at Stockton Lake. Courtesy U.S. Army Corps of Engineers, Kansas City.

of certain types of industries. Sources of reliable fuel supplies will undoubtedly continue to attract manufacturing; and, in all probability, the most reliable fuel supplies will be where large supply lines and storage facilities are in existence. Plans are under way to use salt dome structures in Texas and Louisiana as large-scale underground storage reservoirs for imported crude oil. Existing refineries and pipelines will refine and distribute the products.

Missouri has not been hit as hard as many states by the nationwide natural gas shortage. In nearly one-fourth of Missouri, new customers needing a moderate amount of natural gas are being accepted. Some sections of Missouri can offer large volumes of natural gas to new industrial customers. Gas is delivered to customers through 20,484 miles (32,958 km) of distribution mains and pipelines laced across the state. Latest reports show Missouri's natural gas consumption equals 366.2 trillion Btus annually, with 36 percent going to the industrial sector. In price, Missouri's natural gas ranks in the lowest half among the fifty states.

BUSINESS AND TRADE

Missouri is an excellent location for business and trade. Excellent facilities for highway, rail, water, and air transport, coupled with the state's central location, make Missouri one of the nation's most cost-efficient areas for sending and receiving goods. St. Louis and Kansas City are major convention centers, and Springfield, because of a favorable location in the scenic Ozarks, attracts considerable convention business. In 1981, travel and tourism generated an estimated $4.7 billion, edging ahead of agriculture to rank second to manufacturing as a revenue-producing industry.

The availability of financing can be tremendously important to today's businesses. Missouri offers a wide range of alternatives that helps companies meet their expansion capital requirements. Some of the financial alternatives are tax-free industrial development bonds; planned industrial development loans; and loans from local industrial development corporations, commercial banks, and insurance companies.

Companies locating in Missouri find a large, diverse labor supply. In 1982, approximately 2 million employees earned their living in Missouri. In the 1970–1980 decade, nonagricultural employment increased by more than 300,000 workers. Approximately 30,000 new high school graduates enter Missouri's labor force annually. The skills of the labor force are extremely diversified. No standard industrial classification has more than 15 percent of the state's employment.

Missouri's location in the middle of the nation, between the population center and the geographical center of the forty-eight contiguous states, provides advantages for marketing its own products. Almost half of the United States is only hours away by air, a day away by truck, or two days by rail. Consumer-oriented businesses find Missouri a prime location for reaching a vast concentration of U.S. consumers. The twenty states all or partly within 500 miles (806 km) of Missouri contain 95.8 million people, 91 of the nation's 200 largest cities, and $496 billion in annual personal income. The same twenty states annually account for 43 percent of U.S. food sales, 41 percent of U.S. general merchandise sales, 48 percent of U.S. automotive sales, 46 percent of U.S. building materials and hardware sales, and 42 percent of U.S. drug sales.

Beyond this rich regional area, national and international markets are within easy reach of Missouri. The state's transportation system allows companies to ship manufactured goods and raw materials throughout North America and the world. Air cargo service is available from all of Missouri's commercial airports, with convenient connections to most parts of the world.

Missouri's duty-free foreign-trade zones

in Kansas City, St. Louis, and Springfield offer special advantages to companies with worldwide markets and supplies. Chartered by the federal government, the zones enable international marketers to import goods for storage, processing, assembly, display, or combining with domestic components without payment of duty. Duties are not paid unless and until the goods enter the U.S. market. Those products reshipped abroad remain entirely free from import duties.

Many of the same factors that make Missouri an effective marketing and warehousing area also make it an excellent location for corporate headquarters. The state's centrality, complete transportation services, and outstanding quality-of-life features foster efficient office operations.

Missouri's major cities offer the full range of banking, legal, and consulting services vital to corporate management. The state's excellent higher education system assures a continuous source of professional personnel. Kansas City and St. Louis provide the sophisticated communication services needed for corporate headquarters. In these cities companies can utilize computer-age telecommunications and the latest in information management systems.

Missouri is home to the largest operating company of the AT&T conglomerate, the world's largest telephone-answering service operating toll-free twenty-four hours a day, and to two of the nation's largest centralized reservation centers (Sheraton and TWA). Twenty-five companies listed among the Fortune Double 500 are headquartered in Missouri (see Table 10.2). Numerous regional branch offices and association headquarters also are located in major Missouri cities.

Minimizing tax costs is an important consideration in new plant location. Missouri's tax structure for corporations is one of the most favorable in the nation. According to figures generated by the accounting firm Price, Waterhouse and Company, Missouri ranks second lowest in tax burden among twenty-three competing in-

dustrial states. Taxes considered were corporate income taxes, sales taxes, property taxes, unemployment insurance taxes, and franchise tax expenses.

In 1975 Missouri's average manufacturing wage ranked twenty-fourth among those of the fifty states. The average production worker in Missouri earned $4.75 an hour compared to the U.S. average of $4.81. However, most of Missouri's non-metropolitan counties have prevailing wage levels well below the state average; 71 percent recorded an average hourly wage lower than $3.50. In nonmanufacturing jobs, 71 percent of Missouri counties had average hourly earnings of less than $3.50 and nearly half were under $3.00.

Living costs remain reasonable in Missouri. In a 1975 study of 164 municipalities across the nation, Columbia and Springfield ranked seventh and eighth lowest, respectively, in cost of living. St. Joseph was among the lowest 12 percent. Costs are rising less rapidly as well. Even Missouri's two major cities, Kansas City and St. Louis, record a consumer price index below the U.S. average. Missouri's five SMSAs compare favorably with U.S. indexes in cost of living. Based on a value of 100 for the United States as a whole, the cost-of-living indexes for Missouri's SMSAs are Columbia—85.7; Springfield—86.9; St. Joseph—92; Kansas City—102.4; and St. Louis—102.4. Representative indexes for cities in adjacent states include Chicago—112; Des Moines—111; Little Rock—101.6; and Tulsa—98.6.

SELECTED REFERENCES

An Annotated Guide to Statewide Planning Documents and Research Materials. Jefferson City, Mo.: State of Missouri, Office of Administration, Division of Budget and Planning, 1977.

Gist, Noel P., ed., *Missouri: Its Resources, People, and Institutions.* Columbia: Curators of the University of Missouri, 1950.

Missouri Corporate Planner. Jefferson City, Mo.: Missouri Division of Commerce and Industrial Development, 1976.

TABLE 10.2

Fortune Double 500 Companies Headquartered in Missouri

Company	City
Monsanto Co.	St. Louis
McDonnell-Douglas Corporation	St. Louis
Ralston Purina Company	St. Louis
General Dynamics Corporation	St. Louis
Anheuser-Busch, Inc.	St. Louis
Farmland Industries, Inc.	Kansas City
Emerson Electric Company	St. Louis
Interco, Inc.	St. Louis
Pet, Inc.	St. Louis
Brown Group, Inc.	St. Louis
Interstate Brands Corporation	Kansas City
Kellwood Company	St. Louis
Butler Manufacturing Company	Kansas City
Laclede Steel Company	St. Louis
Mallinckrodt, Inc.	St. Louis
Seven-Up Company	St. Louis
Falstaff Brewing Corporation	St. Louis
Valley Industries	St. Louis
A. B. Chance Company	Centralia
Permaneer Corporation	Maryland Heights
Cook Paint & Varnish Company	N. Kansas City
Legett & Platt, Inc.	Carthage
Angelica Corporation	St. Louis
Petrolite Corporation	St. Louis
Rival Manufacturing Company	Kansas City

Source: Missouri Division of Commerce and Industrial Development. Missouri Corporate Planner. Jefferson City, 1975, p. 4 (Markets).

Missouri: Physical Characteristics and Constraints for Development. Part 2, Standards for Urban Development in Terms of Engineering and Environmental Considerations. Jefferson City, Mo.: Missouri Department of Community Affairs, Office of Planning, 1973.

1980 Missouri Directory, Manufacturing, Mining, Industrial Services, Industrial Supplies. St. Louis: Information Data Company, 1980.

Rafferty, Milton D. Historical Atlas of Missouri. Norman: University of Oklahoma Press, 1982.

White, Leonard A. and Richard E. O'Brien. An Income Study: The Growth of the Economy of Missouri Compared to National Growth, 1929–1960. Jefferson City, Mo.: Missouri Resources and Development Commission, 1961.

CHAPTER 11

POLITICAL AND SOCIAL GEOGRAPHY

The principle of local self-government is strongly entrenched in Missouri. This fact largely accounts for the number as well as the complexity of the state's local government units. There are 114 counties and 329 townships in Missouri. The township as a unit of local government is of minor importance. The most important units of local government in the state are the county and the city. Although the county is considered to be essentially a local government to serve rural areas, the activity of many of its officers affects urban as well as rural inhabitants. Incorporated municipalities such as cities and villages are subject to the government of the county within which they are located. St. Louis city, which was separated from St. Louis County in 1875, is an independent political unit with powers essentially equivalent to those of county governments.

Missouri's county seats are remarkably centrally located within the counties, due to the fact that they were established when travel by horse-drawn wagon was at a rate of 6 (9.6 km) or 7 miles (11.2 km) per hour. Only about 15 of the 114 county seats may be said to be asymmetrically located within the counties. Of these, 9 are towns founded on the Mississippi and Missouri rivers as ports and trading centers.

Missourians pledge considerable allegiance to home counties. Longtime residents of St. Louis, Kansas City, or of one of the large towns who once lived on a farm or in small towns often retain strong loyalties for their original home county. To stay conscious of place, to claim unofficial residency rights, is perhaps a way for those who live in large cities to maintain personal identity.

The voting districts for representative government are important elements in the political geography of Missouri. In addition to two U.S. senators, Missouri presently has nine representatives to Congress (Figure 11.1). Although Missouri's population increased about 5 percent during the 1970s, growth in the Sun Belt states was greater. As a result Missouri lost one seat in the U.S. House of Representatives when all of the data for the 1980 census had been tabulated.

Legislative power in Missouri is vested by the Constitution of 1945 in the General Assembly, more commonly known as the legislature, composed of the Senate and the House of Representatives. The Senate

FIGURE 11.1.   U.S. Congressional Districts, 1982.

consists of thirty-four members who are elected for four-year terms (Figure 11.2). The House of Representatives consists of 163 members elected for two-year terms (Figure 11.3). New senatorial and representative districts are established following each federal decennial census. The most recent redistricting was in 1981.

In 1969 twenty regional planning districts were delineated as quasi-political units made up of member counties. The functions of the various substate planning districts include comprehensive planning for such diverse things as public water systems, sanitary sewers, integrated transportation systems, orderly land-use arrangements, solid waste disposal, open space and rec-

reational areas, and the coordination of planning activities for all federal assistance. These planning districts, however, are much less important in the daily lives of people than are the counties.

POLITICAL CHARACTERISTICS

Missouri is nicknamed the Show-Me State, which suggests political skepticism regarding change, whether it be change in institutions or in accustomed patterns of action. Its government is more conservative than that of most other states, at least with respect to taxation, expenditures, and innovative programs. It is noted for its low tax effort and low expenditures, and

FIGURE 11.2.   State Senatorial Districts, 1982.

in 1976 ranked forty-fifth in state and local revenue effort (thirty-seventh in per capita expenditures for welfare, thirty-fourth in highways, forty-first in local schools, and forty-sixth in total education).

Missouri state administrations have been conservative, primarily because of the ability of outstate political forces to capture the gubernatorial office and the inability of the major metropolitan areas to settle on a gubernatorial candidate. Perhaps the competition between the state's two major metropolitan areas has been a factor in strengthening the hand of rural and small-city legislators and politicians in state matters. In any case, the majority of state administrators is usually recruited from outstate areas, especially from a relatively small radius around Jefferson City.

Outstate Missouri's traditionalistic politics are based on an elitist conception of the commonwealth community. Most of the state's voters are committed to preserving a privileged position for traditional elites or established old families. In this political system, hierarchy is accepted as the natural order and those at the top of the social structure are expected to play a dominant role in government. People are for the existing order and against change, and good government is government provided by the leadership of traditional elites.

Political parties are considered useful, but of secondary importance. Their func-

FIGURE 11.3.   State Representative Districts, 1982.

tion is to recruit candidates, but only those candidates considered acceptable by the leadership. The majority of Missouri's counties are essentially one-party systems—either Democratic or Republican. Party ties are highly personal and based upon family and social ties.

Missouri can be classified as a weak two-party state. Over the years one party—the Democratic party—has been dominant. The state has supported every Democratic presidential candidate since 1932 except Adlai Stevenson in 1952, Hubert Humphrey in 1968, George McGovern in 1972, and Jimmy Carter in 1980. The support for Richard Nixon and Ronald Reagan, however, is not surprising, given the prevailing conservatism in the state.

The Democratic domination has been even more noticeable in congressional elections. Approximately 80 percent or more of those elected since World War II have been Democrats. At the state and local levels, the Democratic dominance is most pronounced. Since 1900, Democrats have controlled the General Assembly, particularly the senate where they have been in the majority for seventy-two out of eighty years.

VOTING PATTERNS

The origins of regional voting patterns in Missouri can be traced back to the time of the Civil War, perhaps earlier. In general, Southern stock has meant Democratic allegiance; northern, Republican (Figure 11.4). The early settlement of Missouri focused on its two great rivers: the Mississippi and, particularly, the Missouri. A tongue of settlement extended across the state on both sides of this river even before the eastern border was completely occupied. The Missouri valley was inhabited primarily by pioneers of southern stock and was so southern in character that it was given the name Little Dixie. To this day, it remains the stronghold of Missouri Democrats. Because slaveholders were among the first settlers, this part of Missouri still contains a comparatively high percentage of rural Blacks. After 1830, large numbers of German immigrants entered Missouri and moved up the river from St. Louis, largely displacing the original settlers. The lower Missouri River counties, because of their German stock, are today among the strongest Republican districts of the state.

In northwest Missouri the old southern influence that settlers brought in by the Missouri River mingles with the old northern influence of immigrants from across the Iowa and Illinois prairies. The northern group was dominant in north-central Missouri in the counties that today form a part of the U.S. Corn Belt. This area constitutes by far the largest section of good farming land in the state and is heavily agricultural in its interests. The largely Republican character of this part of the state is analogous to the Republican character of the rural Corn Belt as a whole.

The Mississippi River Border of the Ozarks is of mixed political character and its inhabitants of mixed origin. A half century ago the area was largely Republican, reflecting the German migration to this region during the nineteenth century. At that time only Ste. Genevieve County with its large French Catholic and German Catholic populations could be counted as solidly Democratic. Since that time a new

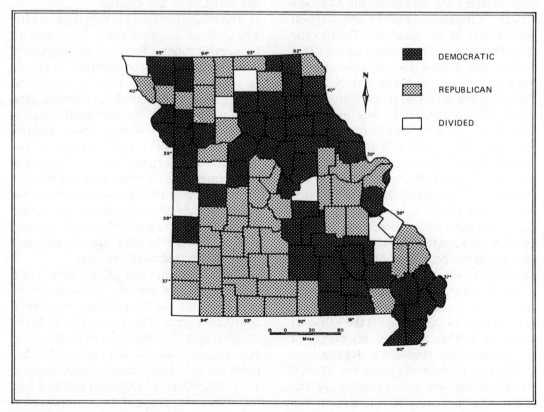

FIGURE 11.4. Voting Patterns.

infiltration of people with Democratic or Independent voting tendencies, resulting from increased manufacturing and service employment, has gradually diluted German Protestant strength in the area. Today only Perry and Cape Girardeau counties retain their Republican allegiance; the remainder of the counties in this area lean rather persistently toward the Democratic party.

The Republican character of the western half of the Ozarks is analogous to the Republican character of the hill districts of Kentucky and Tennessee, and the settlers of this region were in large part of the same ethnic stock, reinforced later by small farmers from northern states. Nearly all of these settlers were yeoman farmers and nonslaveholders, therefore, not tied to the Southern cause in the Civil War. Actually, these settlers migrated into the hill regions of Kentucky and Tennessee, prior to their movement into Missouri, largely from the North rather than the South.

A political fault line runs north and south through the middle of the Missouri Ozarks. In the eastern Ozarks, the roughest hill districts of the state, the Democratic party dominates. The amount of land that can be farmed there is small, consisting of limestone basins and alluvial bottoms. These limited tracts near the Mississippi were taken up at an early date by settlers of southern origin moving in from western Tennessee. The western half of the area consists largely of a strong Republican element from eastern Tennessee. Because relatively few new people have immigrated until recent times, the political loyalties are well established. There is a distinct division between the two areas, formed by the eastern boundaries of Miller, Camden, Laclede, Wright, and Howell counties.

The Democratic character of the counties south of Kansas City results from their settlement at an early date via the Missouri valley as well as a return movement of southerners from abolitionist Kansas.

The southeastern lowlands are alluvial accumulations, on a huge scale, of the Mississippi River and its tributaries. The land is superbly fertile, but most of it, in order to be farmed, has required artificial drainage. The crops cultivated on the drained land have been cotton and corn, typical of areas farther south. The agricultural population for this region was originally drawn primarily from areas farther south also, including a rather substantial Black population, who performed the heavy labor of growing cotton. The Democratic character of this region is unmistakable, reflecting the origin of its population.

The present-day distribution of political allegiancies in Missouri is a result of the history of settlement, which in turn, was affected by geographic conditions. The earliest immigrants were southern Democrats, and having the pick of the area, established themselves in the most accessible and most desirable locations. The later immigrants were largely Republican, including prosperous farmers from the prairie states who came into north-central and northwestern Missouri and to lesser extent into the border districts of the Ozarks.

The map of political preferences in Missouri, which is based upon votes cast in primary elections, shows that although there is a Democratic preponderance statewide in primary voting, as there is in general voting, approximately 40 percent of Missouri counties vote predominantly Republican (Figure 11.4). Most of these counties are in the southwestern Ozark area of the state and in northern Missouri. There has been remarkable consistency in county voting in the 1908–1972 period. Counties that voted heavily Republican in the earlier years are still doing so today, and the same is true for the heavily Democratic and more evenly balanced counties.

Only 3 counties out of 115 have had a clear-cut shift in primary voting behavior over the years: the three densely populated, contiguous areas of St. Louis city, St. Louis County, and St. Charles County. St. Louis city, once marginally Republican, has become strongly Democratic, especially since the 1950s, whereas St. Charles and St. Louis counties have changed from overwhelmingly Republican to marginally Democratic in primary voting. The dramatic changes in these counties are probably due to major changes in the composition of the population and the effect of the New Deal on the voting of such minority groups as Blacks, Jews, Catholics, and labor union members.

The gross data for the 1908–1972 period indicate that the Republican primary vote has increasingly become more of an outstate vote; that is, a vote from outside the St. Louis and Kansas City metropolitan areas. The Democratic vote, however, has changed from one that was primarily outstate to one that is concentrated in the urban-suburban Kansas City and St. Louis areas. This is not to say that outstate areas no longer vote heavily Democratic. The eastern Ozarks and Little Dixie, for example, still do. Rather, these outstate areas have declined in population over the years and are less important in statewide elections. Thus, the Democratic vote has, in a sense, followed the movement of population in the state, since the great bulk of growth in Missouri during the twentieth century has been in the half-dozen counties encompassing the two big metropolitan areas.

SOCIAL GEOGRAPHY

With the exception of the five or six largest cities, Missouri can be considered a rural, agricultural state. Nearly half of the 114 counties do not have towns with populations as large as 2,500, and only 18 counties have towns larger than 10,000 people. In the face of these statistics it is surprising that 7 out of every 10 Missourians live in areas of 2,500 population or more and are therefore considered urban dwellers.

Rural and *urban* are meaningful terms, but they are not discrete or truly accurate when applied statistically. The city of St. Louis is the epitome of urbanity in Missouri just as a farm in Davies County is unquestionably rural. But what about the subdivision of fifty homes that lies outside the boundaries of a small city? What of the farms in a township that has incorporated itself as a municipality to avoid annexation by a neighboring city? Are these areas and the residents of them urban or rural? There are no easy answers to such questions. People today live in a variety of situations that grade subtly from rural to urban.

Evidence drawn from the federal census and university research indicates that the quantity and quality of education, training, health, and housing fall short for rural Missourians when compared with the state as a whole. Rural people receive the benefits of a natural environment, but they have less access to cultural advantages—including libraries, live music and theatre, and local communications media. There are special problems of supplying each of these services and amenities in rural areas, and the problems are particularly serious for education despite some progress in school consolidation.

The characteristic differences between rural and urban people are disappearing in those areas of Missouri within 50 miles (80 km) of St. Louis, Kansas City, Springfield, St. Joseph, Columbia, Jefferson City, Joplin, and Cape Girardeau. Due to purchases, sales, and off-farm work, the economic ties farm families form are increasingly oriented to local towns or cities. Farm people, especially those whose incomes permit, build homes and buy furniture, appliances, food, and other items like those of city dwellers. Through relatives and local organizations, they have strong social ties with nearby cities.

At the same time, the automobile is making it possible for those whose livelihood is in town to reap the benefits of living in the open country. People who formerly would have had to live in town for work reasons are choosing to commute, living beyond the built-up areas and becoming increasingly interspersed with the farm population.

There are sections of Missouri, such as the interior Ozarks, the Bootheel region, and parts of northern Missouri, where the population is so sparse that some people live outside the easy commuting range of any large town or city. For people in these areas, special solutions are needed, possibly including mobile health and related services and special teachers who serve more than one school.

It is evident that the great physical and cultural diversity within rural areas of the state marks an outstanding characteristic of Missouri. Nevertheless, broad areas can be differentiated on the basis of physical, biological, social, and cultural homogeneity. Four broad social regions, corresponding in a general way to the major physiographic regions, can be recognized: the northern and western plains, the Missouri-Mississippi border, the Ozarks, and the Southeast Lowlands. The large metropolitan areas of Missouri form separate social regions (see Chapter 12).

The northern and western plains social area includes most of the counties north of the Missouri River and extends south along the western border to Jasper County. This area was settled fairly early on a permanent agricultural basis. The first immigrants came mostly from the southern states of Kentucky, Tennessee, and Virginia, followed later by substantial numbers from Illinois, Indiana, and Ohio. No large foreign groups settled in this section of the state with the exception of some German immigrants along the Missouri River. The rural population reached its peak from about 1890 to 1900 and has generally declined since that time

By all measures, the northern and western plains region has the highest level of economic and social well-being in the state. The standard of living of the farm population is higher than that of the other sections of the state. Some important indicators are the high availability and use of electricity, superior road conditions, low proportion of persons receiving public welfare funds, a highly productive mechanized system of agriculture, high land values and assessed value of property, a high regard

for education and achievement, and a tendency to maintain houses, buildings, machinery, and other property in a good state of repair. Social interaction seems centered on occupational and economic activities. The church, although an important institution, tends not to be the major focal point for social contacts, as in other areas of the state.

The Missouri-Mississippi border area begins with Cole County near the center of the state and extends along the Missouri and Mississippi rivers to Cape Girardeau County. The St. Louis metropolitan area falls geographically within this designation.

The first settlers of the region were the French, succeeded by the Germans. The Germans became the dominant group, and their cultural background is reflected in the present social structure of the area. The persistence of a high rural farm-population density is at least partially due to their strong belief in the value of farming as a way of life. Young men and women are raised to be progressive and productive farmers and, as a result, a large number of young people tend to take up farming on relatively small farms, although they find it increasingly difficult to compete in the agricultural marketplace.

In spite of the small farms, the living standards of the farm population are generally above the state average, but lower than those found in the northern part of the state. By producing food for home consumption, the thrifty German farmers manage to raise these standards somewhat. Canning vegetables and butchering hogs and cattle for meat are skills that many young people learn. Burning wood from the farm woodlots or timber tracts also increases the self-sufficiency of these people.

Although traditional elements of the old German culture are gradually being abandoned, many still persist. For example, the people have retained strong familial ties. Care for the aged is the responsibility of kin as well as that of public welfare agencies. The people also maintain strong affiliations with ethnic churches—the Roman Catholic, the Evangelical and Reformed, and the Lutheran—which have in turn been instrumental in preserving many ethnic cultural values.

The third social region consists of the Ozarks. The western Ozarks, much the better farming country, are more like northern Missouri than the interior areas. The Ozarks' heritage stems from the upper-south hill country. The first immigrants, mainly from Tennessee, Kentucky, and nearby parts of the southern Appalachians, were descended from hardy Scotch-Irish stock. Because for many years only a few outsiders entered the area, the values, beliefs, technology, and general life-style came to be patterned after those of the first immigrants. Even today most of the Ozark counties are more than 98 percent white, native born. Most inhabitants are Protestants who have clung to the traditional ways of their forebears. The Ozark social region has been, until recently, something of a backwater area, with a distinctive and unchanging cultural landscape.

When compared to the fluidity of social relations in other areas of the United States, the Ozark social system is stable. Kinship relations are strong and extend back generations. Social activities focus on churches and schools, which are dependable and predictable institutions. Among youth and adults alike, there seem to be few problems of identity or questions about belonging.

To gain an understanding of the society, it is important to recognize the extreme isolation that existed until the last fifty years or so. Generally, the rough topography and paucity of resources limited railroad building. Short branches were used to haul lumber and mineral ores from the area, but these were abandoned when the timber was cut and the mines worked out. Prior to the construction of highways and the use of automobiles and buses, there was little transportation in or out of the area, and thus little chance for social and technological innovations to reach the people. More recently the widespread use of automobiles—together with the telephone, radio, and television—has eliminated many of the barriers that once separated the people of this area from the greater society. In the vicinity of the large lakes, where second-home and retirement villages have been developed, the recent immigration of new people has altered the traditional social and political order. Despite these changes, the area remains relatively isolated.

The Southeast Lowlands comprise the fourth social area of Missouri. The level terrain and fertile soils make agricultural production and farm values as high as any place in the state. Until about thirty years ago the farms were relatively small, a reflection of the high amount of hand labor required for cultivating and harvesting cotton. During the first half of the twentieth century, large numbers of Blacks immigrated to the area from the cotton states in response to this need.

An important aspect of the area's social structure is the sharp differentiation in social class. In keeping with tradition, clear distinctions are drawn between white and Black as well as between wealthy, propertied whites and whites who are poor. Aquisition of property by the unpropertied is complicated by the high cost of land resources, including high taxes for the construction and maintenance of drainage ditches throughout the area. As a result, an upper and two lower classes have formed with relatively few people in the middle.

People of both the upper and lower classes are in general political conservatives and religious fundamentalists. Religion plays an important role in their lives. For the most part, they adhere to sects or to highly independent congregations of the Baptist and Methodist churches, preferring two Sunday services (one in the morning and one in the evening) and a mid-week church service (usually on Wednesday). They object to social dancing, drinking, and smoking. Much of the day-to-day social organization is built around the church and the school, two traditional groups that provide a wide variety of social needs.

SELECTED REFERENCES

Britton, Wiley. *Pioneer Life in Southwest Missouri.* Kansas City: Smith-Grieves Co., 1929.

Brunk, Ralph A. "The Gerrymander in Missouri." Master's thesis, University of Missouri (Columbia), 1930.

Cralle, Waldo O. "Social Change and Isolation in the Ozark Mountain Region of Missouri." Ph.D. dissertation, University of Minnesota, 1934.

Crisler, Robert M. "Republican Areas in Missouri." *Missouri Historical Review,* vol. 42, pp. 299–309. 1948.

Dohm, Richard R. *Political Culture of Missouri.* Extension Division, publication MP 228. University of Missouri (Columbia), 1978.

The Economic and Social Condition of Rural America in the 1970's. Economic Development Division, Economic Research Service, U.S. Department of Agriculture, Washington, D.C., 1971.

Friedman, Gordon D. "Voting Trends in Missouri Primary Elections, 1908–1972." Paper presented at the annual meeting of the Missouri Political Science Association, November 16, 1973, at Lodge of the Four Seasons, Lake of the Ozarks.

Gallaher, Art. *Plainville Fifteen Years Later.* New York: Columbia University Press, 1961.

Gerlach, Russel L. "Geography and Politics in Missouri: A Study of Electoral Patterns." *Missouri Geographer.* Fall 1971, pp. 27–36.

Gilmore, Robert K. "Theatrical Elements in Folk Entertainment in the Missouri Ozarks, 1886–1910." Ph.D. dissertation, University of Minnesota, 1961.

Gregory, Cecil L. *Rural Social Areas in Missouri.* College of Agriculture, research bulletin 665. College of Agriculture, University of Missouri (Columbia), 1958.

Harris, Morran D. "Political Trends in Missouri, 1900–1954; A Study of Local, Regional, and Statewide Political Trends Since 1900." Master's thesis, University of Missouri (Columbia), 1956.

Herlinger, Elizabeth. "Historical, Cultural, and Organizational Analysis of Ozark Ethnic Identity." Ph.D. dissertation, University of Chicago, 1972.

Kostbade, J. Trenton. "Geography and Politics in Missouri." Ph.D. dissertation, University of Michigan, 1957.

Meyer, Duane. *The Heritage of Missouri; A History.* St. Louis: State Publishing Co., 1973.

Parrish, William E., Charles T. Jones, Jr., and Lawrence O. Christensen. *Missouri: The Heart of the Nation.* St. Louis: Forum Press, 1980.

Rafferty, Milton D. *Historical Atlas of Missouri.* Norman: University of Oklahoma Press, 1982.

_____. *The Ozarks: Land and Life.* Norman: University of Oklahoma Press, 1980.

Rafferty, Milton D., Russel L. Gerlach, and Dennis Hrebec. *Atlas of Missouri.* Aux-Arc Research Associates, Springfield, Missouri, 1970.

Rural People in the American Economy. Agricultural Economic Report no. 101. Economic Research Service, U.S. Department of Agriculture, Washington, D.C., 1966.

Rural Poverty in Three Southern Regions: Mississippi Delta, Ozarks, Southeast Coastal Plain. Agricultural Economic Report no. 176. U.S. Department of Agriculture, Washington, D.C., 1970.

CHAPTER 12

METROPOLITAN CENTERS

Missouri has four large cities that have always been the state's leading centers of culture and industry. All are standard metropolitan statistical areas. St. Louis, the largest by far, and Kansas City are major metropolises that rank among the great cities of the United States. Springfield and St. Joseph are cities of regional importance, significantly larger than the remaining cities in the state.

ST. LOUIS

The largest city in Missouri lies along a crescent-shaped bend of the Mississippi River about 10 miles (16.1 km) downstream from the convergence of the Mississippi and Missouri. Seven bridges, including two carrying interstate highways, span the Mississippi, connecting the city with the industrial suburbs that face it across the river. The St. Louis SMSA encompasses the city of St. Louis and eight counties on both sides of the Mississippi River: St. Louis, St. Charles, Franklin, and Jefferson counties in Missouri and Clinton, St. Clair, Madison, and Monroe counties in Illinois. In 1970, the population of metropolitan St. Louis stood at about 2.4 million, but after 1970, St. Louis's population, like that in twenty-one other formerly growing SMSAs, began to decline, falling to 2,356,460 by 1980.

St. Louis was selected as the site of a trading post of the French trading firm of Maxent, Laclede, and Company in 1763. A year earlier, a few months previous to the Paris treaty, France had ceded to Spain the whole of its vast territory west of the Mississippi. By the 1763 Paris treaty, England acquired title to Canada and the territory east of the Mississippi River. Pierre Laclede Liquest selected the site for a trading post; and the beauty, as well as the commercial advantages of the country—bordered on the north by the Missouri, on the south by the Meramec, and on the east by the Mississippi—seems to have attracted the attention of the earliest voyagers. (In 1699, a Jesuit missionary station was established in the Mississippi valley, near the mouth of the River des Peres.) The location was strategic for command of the trade of the upper Mississippi, the Illinois, and the Missouri rivers.

For five to ten years, St. Louis was merely a trading post. Its first building was located on the block of ground now bounded by First, Second, Walnut, and Market Streets. Some of the settlers established themselves along the river above and below this area. The settlement was nicknamed Pain Court ("short of bread"), a name that apparently stems from the lack of agricultural land rather than from poverty. A narrow belt of timber extended along the river, as far back as what is now Fifth Street or Broadway. Westward and beyond lay an open prairie, long known as La Grande Prairie. Various parts of this prairie were given different names: St. Louis Prairie was near the town, Prairie des Noyers was to the southwest, and the space between was called Cul de Sac; to the south was Little Prairie and to the north was White Ox Prairie. The creek running through Cul de Sac, bordered by wooded and grassy banks, was known as La Petite Riviere. In order to secure water power for a mill, this creek, later known as Mill Creek, was dammed, and the pond that formed was called Chouteau's Mill Pond. The main St. Louis railroad yards, located south of the central business district, now mark this vicinity. Because of the large number of Indian ceremonial mounds built on the site of St. Louis, the city is sometimes referred to as the Mound City. As St. Louis expanded into the prairie, the mounds were destroyed despite attempts to preserve some of them.

The founding of St. Louis represented a further exploitation of the natural resources of the wilderness as well as an impulse toward home making and state building. In the forty years before the Louisiana Purchase, it became the center of exchange for the goods of hunters and trappers. It also developed important commercial relations with the Spanish Southwest over the Santa Fe Trail. It was the entrepôt for white settlement of the Mississippi valley region and the lands drained by the western tributaries. When Louisiana was purchased in 1803, French and Spanish—both recent arrivals from Europe and from the new world colonies—Blacks from Guinea or the Congo, Indians from nine to ten tribes, French couriers and voyageurs, Saxon hunters from the Appalachians, American flatboat men, Puritans, soldiers, politicians, and immigrants from England and Ireland all walked the streets of St. Louis. This polyglot society seeking the riches of trade was already under pressure, however, from a society of farmer–home builders. Although the Indian trade remained strong for many years afterward, the arrival of the steamboat *Zebulon M. Pike* in 1817 marked the beginning of a flood of new permanent settlers.

The close of the Indian wars in 1815 started a tide of emigration from Virginia, Kentucky, Tennessee, and from the north side of the Ohio River. Up to that time St. Louis was a French town with simple wood houses and a few large, plastered and whitewashed stone houses and forts, extending along the river in several long and narrow streets.

As new immigrants arrived, St. Louis began to lose its distinctive French character, though the impress left by its early settlers was such that it could never be entirely effaced. At the time of the U.S. occupancy of the territory in 1804, St. Louis probably contained fewer than 1,000 inhabitants. In 1808 St. Louis extended its boundaries west to Seventh Street and was incorporated as a village with 1,400 inhabitants. In the same year, Joseph Charless founded the first newspaper, the *Missouri Gazette*. In 1821, when Missouri became a state, the population was about 5,000. The population in 1833, according to the census, was 6,297; and in 1835, 8,316. By 1840, the population had reached 16,394. Caravans of settlers, sometimes thirty to fifty wagons a day, crossed the Mississippi at St. Louis on their way west. The flatboats of Missouri farmers, loaded with locally produced pork, hemp, grain, apples, and flour, passed through toward New Orleans in increasing numbers.

In the latter part of 1847, St. Louis was connected with the East by telegraph lines. Two years later, on October 15, 1849, a national railroad convention was held in St. Louis, at which plans were made for a network of railroads, including a transcontinental line, converging at St. Louis.

In 1849, fire and pestilence visited the city. On May 19 of that year, fire broke out in the steamboat the *White Cloud* at the levee, and some twenty steamers were consumed. The fire spread to the shore and swept through fifteen blocks of buildings. The loss was estimated at $3 million. A virulent cholera epidemic in the city that year claimed 4,557 lives. Nevertheless the city's population jumped to 75,000 by 1850, 160,000 by 1860, and 350,000 by 1880.

Craftsmen, their journeymen, and apprentices engaged in the first manufacturing in St. Louis. In small shops, they made tinware, shoes, furniture, pottery, bricks, and other necessities. Tobacco factories, manufacturers of lead pigments, tanneries, and other small plants were established by 1820. By 1850, St. Louis was well established as an industrial center. Nineteen flour mills were exporting 0.5 million barrels of flour annually.

About 1820, James Russell discovered coal in some gullies on his estate near what is now Tholozan Avenue just east of Morganford Road. Russell opened the first coal mine in the Old Gravois Digging, and until 1887 coal from the Russell mines supplied the city of St. Louis. Fireclay mining on the property began in the 1860s when the Oak Hill Fire-Brick and Tile Works was established. Several types of fireclay were discovered in the area now included in St. Louis and St. Louis County. The Cheltenham District was one of the largest fireclay mining areas. In addition to ordinary firebrick, the refractories produced tile; brick for rolling mills, blast furnaces, gas works, zinc furnaces, coke ovens; and ordinary building brick.

During the latter half of the nineteenth century, most of the older downtown buildings were razed and replaced by brick structures. As construction spread away from the riverfront to the north, west, and south, St. Louis became a city of red brick.

An unusual view of the landscape of St. Louis was recorded by Camille N. Dry in his perspective drawings of 1875. The long waterfront was lined with side-wheel and stern-wheel steamers with black smoke belching from tall twin stacks. Workers were loading barges of every description with lumber, casks of sugar, molasses, cotton bales, and barrels of flour and apples. From north to south, along the entire length of the broad waterfront, stood piles of wood products: poles, beams, dimension lumber, and railroad ties. At a half-dozen locations, there were large sawmills, where huge rafts of timber from the upper Mississippi country were tied up, waiting to be broken up and sawed into lumber products. There were shipyards and dry docks, hundreds of teams of horses pulling wagons loaded with goods, droves of cattle being herded down ramps to barges, and high-stepping pacers pulling the fragile carriages of waterfront entrepreneurs.

Parallel to the waterfront were the railroads—the Iron Mountain Railroad, the Chicago and Alton Railroad, and the St. Louis, Kansas City, and Northern Railway Company—with their switching yards, depots, and repair shops. Crowded close against the railroad tracks in a solid wall of brick three-to-five-story buildings was the manufacturing and business core of the city. There were cotton compresses, several dozen sawmills and lumberyards, wagon factories, plow manufacturers, iron and machine works, stove works, grain and hay warehouses, tobacco factories, chemical works, meat-packing houses, tool manufacturers, and dozens of processors of agricultural food products. Located behind the manufacturing plants in the downtown area were livery stables, hotels, wholesale houses, banks, retail stores, and office buildings. The newly constructed steel-span St. Louis (Eads) Bridge was jammed with traffic–trains loaded with coal from the Illinois mines on the lower level and drays, lumber wagons, a horse-drawn trolley, and dozens of carriages on the upper level.

The freight yards and depots of the Atlantic and Pacific, the Missouri Pacific and the Missouri, Kansas, and Texas (Katy) railroads were located just south of the central business district (CBD) in Mill Creek valley, bounded by Spruce Street on the north and Chouteau Street on the south. On either side and mixed in among the switching yards were warehouses, grain elevators, metal fabrication plants, sugar refineries, breweries, lumberyards, textile mills, shoe factories, distilleries, and food processors.

The city's neighborhoods were already differentiated into ethnic clusters, which generally revolved around a particular church. The south side was recognized as a German stronghold, where the newly formed Republican party had gained seats in the state legislature. There were Irish and Czechoslovakian areas as well as a Black ghetto near the waterfront industries. Large tracts of land at the edge of the city were scarred with shallow pits from which fireclays had been dug. The vicinity of the intersection of Arsenal and Iowa streets was a cratered landscape in the process of being converted to a residential neighborhood. A similar landscape had developed around the Cheltenham Fire Brick Works along Manchester Road.

The neighborhood around Lafayette Park was widely known for its marble-fronted mansions with private streets and carriage houses. Large estates were situated at the periphery of the city, with large houses set back from the thoroughfares on tree-lined lanes and surrounded by fruit orchards and meadows.

Although St. Louis lost its position as the "Midwest Metropolis" to Chicago—in part because of its tardiness in bridging the Mississippi River and in providing low-cost transshipment of rail cargoes to the eastern rail network—it became and still is a major manufacturing center. Coalfields close by in Illinois meet iron ore from the Ozarks in St. Louis. Its excellent transportation connections make the city a good location for major plants of manufacturers that distribute nationally. After Philadelphia, St. Louis is the second most diversified manufacturing city in the United States.

The plan of the city has undergone important modifications in the past several years. Along the Mississippi a granite-paved, almost deserted wharf stretches for 1.5 miles (2.41 km). Until fairly recent times, a closely packed belt of empty warehouses, commercial buildings, and factories, dating from the period following the great fire of 1849, bordered the wharf. Once the commercial core of the city, this section was virtually abandoned when St. Louis turned its back on the river. The heart of the present central business district lies several blocks to the west, and for many years the dead belt along the river was a problem. A solution has been found in the Jefferson Memorial Plaza. Buildings of historical significance, such as the Old Catholic Cathedral and the St. Louis County Court House, where the Dred Scott case was tried, have been preserved. At the same time, the Gateway Arch, Stauffer's Riverfront Inn, and high-rent apartments have been constructed. Close by is Busch Stadium where the St. Louis baseball and football Cardinals play their games.

The chief business district of St. Louis extends roughly from Fourth Street almost to Grand Boulevard and from Chouteau to Franklin avenues. The leading retail houses are in the downtown shopping district between Sixth and Eleventh, and Olive and Washington. West from Grand Boulevard in the center of the city are rows of substantial brick and mortar houses, many of them now boardinghouses, small display rooms, funeral parlors, or antique shops. Close to King's Highway these structures give way to large and fashionable apartment houses and hotels. In this section, centering on Euclid and Maryland avenues, is an exclusive shopping district where imported delicacies, rare silver, and exclusive clothing are sold. A little to the south is a large number of hospitals, clinics, and nursing homes.

West of King's Highway lies the broad expanse of Forest Park, bordered by fine older residential areas, especially in the north, where the well-to-do are guarded against the traffic by ornamental gates and insured against neighborhood changes by rigid building codes.

PHOTO 12.1.   St. Louis Waterfront and Skyline. Courtesy Walker—Missouri Division of Tourism.

Enclosing the CBD are the north and south sides, which have much in common. Each was once joined to the city along the business district by a slum area and a Black district, and each was settled in the main by lower-middle class and working families, predominantly German. The German element is particularly strong on the south side. Much of the poorer tenement housing has been cleared for urban renewal and for the new interstate and boulevard systems that converge on the downtown area.

Adjoining the south-side German community are Czechoslovakian neighborhoods. A fairly large Italian settlement is situated mainly between King's Highway and Sulphur Avenue, and Manchester Road and Arsenal. Originally many Italians worked in the nearby clay-products plants.

Clayton: A Developing Metropolitan Focus

The relative decline of the core city and of its downtown central business district has been a phenomenon common to almost every major metropolitan area in the United States since 1945. The CBDs of most of these large cities have experienced declines in total retail sales relative to total retail volumes in the metropolitan areas, and thus are no longer as strongly dominant as retailing centers.

Over the past twenty-five years, the city of Clayton has been transformed from a residential suburb of St. Louis into a retailing center and, in more recent years, into an office center. Its once small and limited business district now rivals downtown St. Louis. Major retailing growth began in the Clayton business district in 1946 and has continued steadily, making Clayton the retailing center of St. Louis County. Office-building construction began in 1948; and by the beginning of 1966 Clayton had fifty buildings with a total floor space of more than 2 million sq ft (186,000 m²). The coming of Famous-Barr Company to Clayton in 1949 gave to the development of retailing a strong impetus. The company selected Clayton because the city was considered the best location within a very good marketing area (west St. Louis and adjacent St. Louis County).

The pioneer office development occurred in 1948, when a group of doctors built the Clayton Medical Building on North Central Avenue, a block north of the courthouse. In 1951 the movement of the Brown Shoe Company to Clayton apparently had a strong psychological impact on the local business world, revealing that a suburban location might be acceptable to large St. Louis companies. Office-building construction advanced rapidly in the next few years. Between 1953 and 1964, forty-six structures were erected in Clayton according to city records, whereas only three new office buildings were built in downtown St. Louis between 1931 and 1961.

By 1982 approximately 3.5 million sq ft (325,278 m²) of office space had been built in Clayton, including offices housing the national headquarters of the Brown Shoe Company and the Seven-Up Company. Clayton continues to be the chief metropolitan subcapital, but the Westport area and the vicinity of Lambert International Airport have become important St. Louis County office clusters. Also, over the past twenty years, some fifty buildings and 7 million sq ft (650,557 m²) of office space have been built in the St. Louis central business district.

Although none of the other incorporated cities surrounding St. Louis can claim an office cluster similar to that of Clayton, several of them have very large shopping malls. In fact, as the metropolitan area has grown, fourteen major retail centers have been built (Figure 12.1).

Manufacturing in St. Louis

The key to the commercial and manufacturing continuity of downtown St. Louis is its position at the river on a long, narrow, upland spur—the Downtown Upland. Laclede selected the Downtown Upland for the site of a trading post in 1763 because it was the first flood-free land below the mouth of the Missouri River. The undercut ledge of St. Louis limestone made a natural landing place at which Laclede tied his boats.

Fur, hides, skins, and wool were traded at St. Louis on a large scale. Of the seventy firms dealing in these products, listed in a business directory in 1927, fifty-six were located in the wholesale district within a few blocks of the Mississippi River. This pronounced concentration was an inheritance of the fur-trading days, when fur-laden boats unloaded at the levee.

St. Louis became the terminus of several railroads traversing the wheat belt in Missouri, Oklahoma, Kansas, and Nebraska. Many of these railroads entered the St. Louis waterfront by way of the Mill Creek valley. In 1927, Lewis Thomas mapped thirteen grain elevators in the Mill Creek valley, eight on the riverfront on North Broadway, three on South Broadway, and eleven on the east shore.

By the 1920s the livestock industry had located chiefly in the National Stock Yards in National City and East St. Louis, Illinois, and handled 6.5 million head of livestock annually. There was one meat-packing plant in each of the west side districts: North Broadway, South Broadway, and Mill Creek. Lumberyards were concentrated in the North Broadway District, where rafts of logs were floated in earlier years. Six lumberyards had been established in the Northwest Industrial District along the belt railroad (Terminal Railroad Association) by 1927.

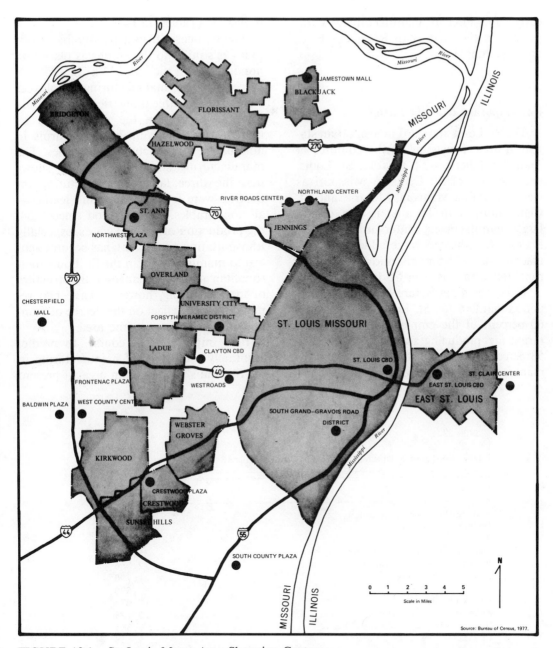

FIGURE 12.1.   St. Louis Metro Area Shopping Centers.

Heavy industry had its start with the iron furnaces at Carondolet in 1846, a location to which iron ore and pig iron could be shipped from the Iron Mountain District by rail and coal by way of the Mississippi River. The iron and steel business was gradually concentrated in East St.

Louis and Granite City to take advantage of the east side's assets for heavy manufacture. Coal costs were much higher on the west side due to the ferrying charges at the Mississippi River.

Chemical manufacturing was well established on both sides of the river at an early date. Fireclay manufacture was important in the vicinity of River des Peres and Cheltenham.

Contemporary Manufacturing

The St. Louis standard metropolitan statistical area, consisting of the counties of Franklin, Jefferson, St. Charles, St. Louis, and the city of St. Louis in Missouri as well as Clinton, Madison, Monroe, and St. Clair counties in Illinois, is one of the larger manufacturing centers in the United States. The adjusted value added by manufacture in 1972 for this midwestern metropolitan area was over $5 billion.

Today the manufacture of durable goods is dominant in the St. Louis SMSA. Over 60 percent of the employees in manufacturing are producing such goods, whereas 58 percent of the adjusted value added by manufacture is contributed by durable goods

industries (Tables 12.1–12.2).

The emphasis placed on durable goods today is similar to the emphasis placed on nondurables in the late 1930s. In 1939, 60 percent of the manufacturing employees were in nondurable industries. In this same year, 63 percent of the value added by manufacture was contributed by firms in nondurable manufacturing industries. The manufacturing structure for 1939 shows that the three largest manufacturing industries were food, apparel, and leather—all nondurables. In the period since 1954, the production of durable goods, especially transportation equipment, has become central to manufacturing in the St. Louis metropolitan area. The changes in the structure of manufacturing, however, have had remarkably little effect on the degree of manufacturing diversity in the area.

It is impossible, of course, to predict accurately the future of manufacturing in the St. Louis metropolitan area. If present

TABLE 12.1

Major Employers in the St. Louis Metropolitan Area

Company	Total Employees
McDonnell Douglas Company	107,503
Monsanto Company	64,604
Interco, Inc.	37,600
Emerson Electric Company	25,800
Ralston Purina Company	22,066
Brown Shoe Company, Inc.	21,700
Pet, Inc.	20,500
Kellwood Company	15,978
Anheuser-Busch, Inc.	10,723
Diversified Industries, Inc.	6,385
Granite City Steel Company	5,158
UMC Industries, Inc.	5,079
General Steel Industries, Inc.	3,700
Century Electric Company	3,535
Falstaff Brewing Company	3,239
Mallinckrodt Chemical Works	2,709
American Zinc Company	2,388
Laclede Steel Company	2,202
Huttly Sash and Door	1,000
Total	361,869

Source: 1980 Missouri Directory of Manufacturing, Mining, Industrial Services, Industrial Supplies (St. Louis: Informative Data Company, 1980), pp. 361-416.

TABLE 12.2

Industrial Growth in Metropolitan St. Louis: 1972-1977

SIC	Industry	Value Added by Manufacture ($ millions) 1972	Value Added by Manufacture ($ millions) 1977	Percent Change
20	Food and kindred products	570.7	680.0	+19.2
23	Apparel, other textiles	108.5	---	---
24	Lumber and wood products	32.1	35.9	+11.8
25	Furniture and fixtures	58.1	80.6	+38.7
26	Paper and allied products	111.9	159.8	+42.8
27	Printing and publishing	283.2	376.9	+33.1
28	Chemicals and allied products	489.2	931.7	+90.5
29	Petroleum and coal products	150.7	318.1	+111.1
30	Rubber, misc. plastic products	64.4	143.0	+122.0
31	Leather and leather products	47.4	58.8	+24.0
32	Stone, clay, glass products	161.1	223.0	+38.4
33	Primary metal industries	443.9	787.9	+77.5
34	Fabricated metal products	401.5	643.4	+60.1
35	Machinery, except electrical	359.6	576.9	+60.4
36	Electric, electronic equipment	247.1	379.8	+53.7
37	Transportation equipment	1,513.8	2,678.7	+76.9
38	Instruments, related products	52.7	71.6	+35.9
39	Miscellaneous manufactures	58.9	64.4	+9.3
	Total	5,154.8	7,530.5	

Source: U.S. Department of Commerce, Bureau of the Census. Geographic Area Statistics, Missouri, Part I. Census of Manufactures, 1977. (Vol. 3. Washington, D.C.: Government Printing Office, 1981), p. 26-21 to p. 26-24.

trends continue, however, it is highly probable that (1) durable goods will become of greater importance, (2) the significance of the transportation-equipment industry will increase, and (3) the industrial diversity of this metropolitan area will, as a result, decline.

Industrial Districts

Although manufacturing is distributed in many parts of metropolitan St. Louis, it is for the most part concentrated in clearly defined manufacturing districts. The location of these districts has been determined by geographical, historical, and economic factors: the access to water, rail, truck, and air transportation; the availability of level, well-drained land, of cheap and reliable sources of energy, and of an adequate supply of high-quality water; the proximity to raw materials such as fireclay and coal; and the existence of land-use controls such as zoning and building regulations.

The oldest and largest industrial area within the city of St. Louis is the *North Broadway District* (Figure 12.2). This district, which extends north from the central business district to beyond the city limits, is sandwiched between North Broadway Street and the Mississippi River. Sawmills and grain storage and milling began in this area at an early date. The district is now quite diversified with manufacturing plants producing food products, animal feeds, paper and plastics, light metal products, and chemicals. The southern part of the area is almost completely covered with four- to eight-story brick and mortar buildings and ancillary parking lots, loading docks, and railroad sidings. Although the district is extremely congested, several large truck terminals have been located in the North Broadway area to serve the large volume of business there. Although the

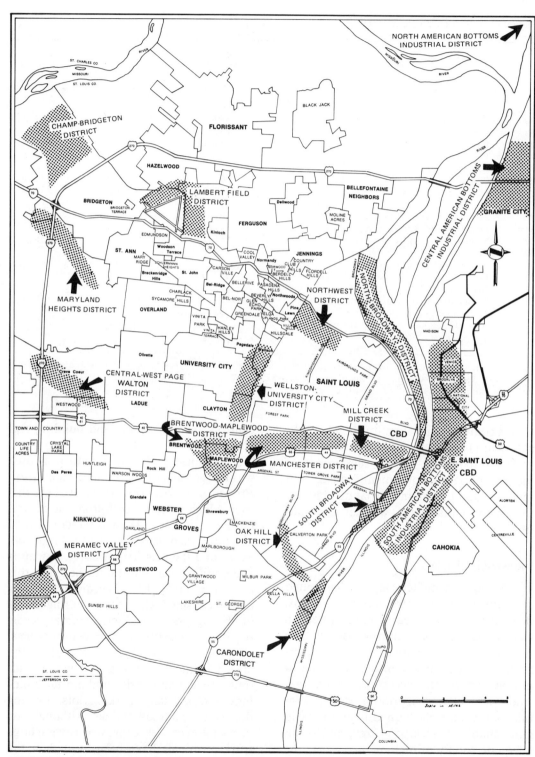

FIGURE 12.2. Industrial Districts in St. Louis.

area is already well developed in the southern section and under considerable construction in the central and northern sections, the district still contains some vacant land. This land, which was once subject to periodic flooding, is mostly north of East Grand Avenue.

The *South Broadway Industrial District* extends south from the central business district parallel to the waterfront to about Meramec Street. It is an old industrial area with a number of very large manufacturing firms. The most recent major expansion has been undertaken by Anheuser-Busch, Incorporated, by Monsanto Chemical Company, and by the Kosciusko redevelopment project.

At the southern limits of St. Louis, along the waterfront, is the *Carondolet District,* once the separate industrial city of Carondolet. Here the first coal-fired iron furnaces in Missouri were built in the 1870s and 1880s. Coal from Illinois and iron ore from the St. Francois Mountains made St. Louis

PHOTO 12.2. Monsanto Company's Queeny Plant in St. Louis. Founded in 1901, the Plant Produces Aspirin, Resins, and Food Ingredients. Courtesy Monsanto Company.

PHOTO 12.3.   Brewery Facilities of Anheuser-Busch, Incorporated, in St. Louis. Courtesy Anheuser-Busch, Inc.

the only nineteenth-century steel city west of the Mississippi River. The steel mills closed more than seventy-five years ago when new coke ovens and steel mills were built in the Illinois coal fields at Granite City. The area has long been stagnant as plants have been abandoned over the years without replacement.

The *Mill Creek District* is a light manufacturing and warehousing district built in the valley of Mill Creek just south of the central business district. The district developed lumber milling, grain milling, and light manufacturing even before the Civil War. Most of the area was built up as railroad switching yards; the main passenger depot was expanded in the latter half of the nineteenth century.

Another of St. Louis's major manufacturing areas, the *Northwest Industrial District,* follows the west belt connection of the Terminal Railroad Association and Interstate 70. The first development followed World War I. A second major expansion took place during World War II when the huge St. Louis Ordnance Plant was built on a 250-acre (101-hectare) tract. The largest employer at present is General Motors' Chevrolet plant.

The most spectacular industrial growth over the past forty years has occurred in the *Lambert Field Industrial District*. One of the largest industrial areas in St. Louis County in terms of acreage and by far the largest in terms of employees, the district is located in the northwestern part of St.

PHOTO 12.4.   McDonnell-Douglas Corporation Facilities Bordering Lambert International Airport in St. Louis. Courtesy McDonnell-Douglas Corporation.

Louis County, bounded by Interstate 270 on the north and west, Graham Road on the east, and the Lambert International Airport on the south. The development of the area parallels the growth of the McDonnell-Douglas Aircraft Corporation. Organized in 1939 by J. S. McDonnell with only two employees, the corporation has grown until it is now the largest private employer in Missouri. Among the better-known McDonnell aircraft have been the Phantom, the Demon, the Voodoo, the DC-9, and DC-10. In 1959, McDonnell began manufacturing spacecraft for the National Aeronautics and Space Agency. The sprawling McDonnell-Douglas Aircraft Corporation offices, manufacturing plants, and research facilities occupy about 50 percent of the manufacturing district. Also

located in the district is Ford Motor Company's assembly plant.

The remainder of St. Louis's manufacturing districts are small in comparison to these large districts, although collectively they produce more manufactured goods than any one of the four major districts. The *Manchester District* extends west from south King's Highway along the valley routes of the Missouri Pacific and the Burlington Northern railroads. It first developed as a clay mining and clay products area, the atmosphere of which it retains today. The *Oak Hill District* blossomed as a light manufacturing and warehousing area in south St. Louis after a branch line of the Missouri Pacific was put through the area in the late 1800s. Considerable new plant construction was added after World

PHOTO 12.5. Numerical Control Machine Tools, McDonnell Aircraft Company Division of McDonnell-Douglas Corporation in St. Louis. Courtesy McDonnell-Douglas Corporation.

War II. The *Brentwood-Maplewood District* and the *Wellston–University City District* were laid out along the Terminal Railroad Association belt line and the Norfolk and Western Railway right-of-way in eastern St. Louis County. Both areas are nearly fully occupied by light manufacturing and warehousing. Farther out in west-central St. Louis County, the *Central–West Page Walton District* and the *Maryland Heights District* were laid out beginning in the 1950s. The belt highways, U.S. 67 and Interstate 270 make these areas readily accessible by truck. Both districts contain within their boundaries a number of planned industrial parks. Many warehousing and light manufacturing companies from the inner city have relocated in these areas to take advantage of modern, one-story,

spacious buildings. In far northwestern St. Louis County, in the Missouri River bottoms, the *Champ-Bridgeton Industrial District* is being developed as a model industrial area along the lines of the Teterboro, New Jersey plan, but on a larger scale. The largest of the pioneer manufacturing plants in the district are Hussmann Refrigerator Company and the R. C. Can Company. In southwest St. Louis County, the *Meramec Valley Industrial District* is situated along Interstate 44 just west of the intersection with the belt freeway—Interstate 270. The first and largest industry in the district is Chrysler Corporation's St. Louis assembly plant, which was built in 1958.

Although East St. Louis, Alton, Granite City, and other industrial towns east of the Mississippi River are separated from

PHOTO 12.6.   The Emerson Electric Company Electronics and Space Division and World Headquarters in Jennings. Courtesy Emerson Electric Company.

St. Louis by a state boundary, they are economically interdependent with greater St. Louis. Many of the workers who fire the furnaces in Granite City's steel mills live in Missouri, and by the same token many of the workers in St. Louis's factories and office buildings commute from the Illinois suburbs. The Illinois industrial satellite cities are developed on the broad, level Mississippi alluvial plain, an area rich in groundwater and easily developed for industrial purposes. The area has been known as the American Bottoms since the days when St. Louis was Spanish territory. Three industrial districts are recognized in the American Bottoms.

The *North American Bottoms* lies east of the Mississippi River, including the industrial cities of Alton and Wood River.

Separated from the St. Louis urban area, this industrial district is dominated by large plants associated with old but successful businesses. Obsolescence is thus less a problem in this district than it is in the South American Bottoms. These large plants produce a variety of products—petroleum, ferrous metals, nonferrous metals, ordnance, paper, stone, clay, and glass.

The *Central American Bottoms* is a highly specialized industrial area, with metalworking the major occupation. It is also a growing area. A. O. Smith has built a plant in the area and the major employer, Granite City Steel, has invested large amounts of money in new equipment and new buildings.

The *South American Bottoms* includes East St. Louis and several nearby small incorporated towns. The heavy manufacturing in this district is due in large part to the advantages of the location, the existing transportation facilities, and the associated population clusters. Most of the large plants in this district had their origin before 1920. Today the area, with a number of closed plants, is a declining industrial district.

The growth of metropolitan St. Louis from 1940 to 1970 represents a draft upon the rural population hardly equaled anywhere in the United States during the same three decades. Half to two-thirds of Missouri's 114 counties experienced a net loss of population during this period and many of the emigrants settled in the St. Louis metropolitan area.

During the same period, the Black population in metropolitan St. Louis increased from 150,088 to 378,816, or 252 percent. The source of Black immigration, as of white, has been mainly rural. The new Blacks have come to St. Louis from the southern plantations, most from the southern Mississippi valley, and directly from rural environments. In the popular proverb, they are "from Mississippi," a state that has contributed substantially to their coming.

The metropolitanization of St. Louis has led to a serious and enduring political problem—the fragmentation of the area into a host of independent political units that rarely cooperate with each other. In 1876, St. Louis city separated from St. Louis County, thereby becoming one of the first cities in the United States to freeze its boundaries. St. Louis city includes an area of 61 sq miles (158.6 km²), less than one-fifth the area of Kansas City. The city gained a home-rule charter from which it was hoped more efficient government would emerge. The less progressive and poorer parts of St. Louis County would be excluded and thus no longer a tax burden for the city. Movements to consolidate the city and county have been brought to vote on several occasions, but tax-wealthy and high-assessed-valuation St. Louis County

residents have rejected the consolidation scheme, fearful that many of the expensive social programs in St. Louis city would raise taxes. Thus the situation has been reversed over a century of centrifugal movement of population, factories, businesses, and assessed valuation. In the past century of suburban growth, the territory around St. Louis has been balkanized into a shatter belt of small to medium-sized incorporated towns—first a belt of streetcar suburbs and then a layer or two of automobile commuter towns.

As early as the 1900 census of population, it was evident that parts of the city of St. Louis were losing population as residents moved to the western neighborhoods or to the suburbs. New, poor, industrial populations—mainly Blacks and southern and eastern European immigrants—had for some time begun to filter into habitations abandoned by their predecessors. They filled in the nooks and crannies among factories, railways, and wholesale houses. Many neighborhoods near the factory zones became blighted, and over the past fifty years there have been numerous attempts to rehabilitate such inner-city neighborhoods.

The most ambitious program was the building of the Pruitt and Igoe apartments just north of the central business district. The Pruitt apartments, completed in 1955 at a cost of $21,689,000, were a complex of twenty eleven-story high rises, originally intended for white tenants. The Igoe apartments, completed a year later for $14,438,000, were composed of thirteen eleven-story buildings for Black tenants. After the 1954 Supreme Court decision regarding nondiscrimination in housing, Pruitt-Igoe opened without racial quotas. In fact, almost all of the 11,500 residents of the thirty-three buildings were Black. Pruitt-Igoe, one of the largest and supposedly one of the best-designed public housing projects of the post–World War II era, quickly became a local and national scandal. By 1975, a contract had been let for its total demolition. Many problems

PHOTO 12.7. The Pruitt-Igoe Housing Development Shortly Before Demolition in the 1970s. Photograph by the author.

with the development had become apparent: there were no shopping facilities; no health services; inadequate transportation; a minimum of job opportunities; and almost nonexistent school, playground, and recreational facilities. Discontent, crime, vandalism, and low occupancy were correlated problems.

Blacks are most heavily concentrated in two areas in the St. Louis metropolitan area: in East St. Louis and in an east-west belt extending from the waterfront westward to beyond Forest Park. Historically, the movement in St. Louis has been westward, and the western frontier of mixed neighborhoods has spread as far as the city boundary and beyond to University City. Wellston, wedged between St. Louis and University City, is 87 percent Black.

Within the city there are many beautiful residential sections, which were laid out in the later part of the nineteenth century and in the first two decades of the twentieth century. The most fashionable districts were labeled places. Vandevanter Place, Westmoreland Place, and Portland Place seem to impress visitors the most.

The first place of any importance was Vandevanter, which Julius Pitzman designed and laid out in the 1870s. Pitzman's ideas were based on the successful example of Baron Haussman in Paris, where rigid

building restrictions were imposed on residential subdivisions. The concept became so popular that Pitzman was engaged to lay out other places throughout the city—Portland Place, Westmoreland Place, and Flora Boulevard. Eventually there were dozens of them in the city. They were carefully designed to take advantage of site characteristics, were built to take advantage of prevailing cooling winds, and were well planted with turf and trees.

During the later part of the 1800s a grand park was laid out in a direct line of the city's greatest growth. The park contained some 1,400 acres (567 ha) and included 1,100 acres (445 ha) of native forest for which it was named. Forest Park was established by a bill of the legislature in 1874 and in 1904 was the site of the world's fair—the Louisiana Purchase Exposition.

Satellites and Shatter Belt

Several industrial satellite cities grew up on the east side, the land on the Illinois side of the river. These water- and coal-rich river bottomlands were also known as the American Bottoms. East St. Louis, Madison, Granite City, National City, and Cahokia were not an overflow of St. Louis industry—only a few factories shifted their location from one side of the river to the other. Rather these cities exemplify a tendency for centrifugal growth, the use of cheaper, open land at the outskirts of cities for industrial growth. Cheap land and cheap coal were the greatest factors in attracting industries to the east side. In the removal of the St. Louis Stockyards to East St. Louis, for example, cheap land was of prime importance. In the heavy steel manufacturing, which played so important a part in the development of Granite City and other towns, cheap land in large tracts and a large supply of cheap coal were main considerations.

The industries of the east side required a large supply of unskilled labor. Very soon the east side cities attracted large Black and ethnic group populations. Granite City and Madison came to comprise one of the largest settlements of Bulgarians and Macedonians to be found in the United States. "Hungary Hollow" in Granite City gained a wide reputation as a blighted ethnic settlement. About 1910 more than 90 percent of the population of Hungary Hollow were men—some single, but others with families in the old country. In the fall of 1912, as many as 600 went back to fight in the Balkan War.

The political fragmentation of St. Louis County may be likened to the balkanization, or development of numerous political units, in eastern Europe. Kirkwood, founded in 1853 on the Pacific Railroad by St. Louis investors Hiram Leffingwell and Richard Elliot, was to be a suburb for families who desired pure air away from the contaminating influence of a large city. During the 1890s, mass transit facilities underwent the most spectacular growth in St. Louis history, as new trolley lines were laid into St. Louis County. Some of them real estate promoters built to increase the value and sales of new subdivisions. By 1902 St. Louis was connected with Jefferson Barracks, Webster Groves, Kirkwood, Meramec Highlands, Clayton, Overland, Creve Coeur Lake, St. Charles, and Florissant. Extensive interurban railroads also were constructed throughout the east side in Illinois. The St. Louis County units began to form as streetcar lines were extended out in a radial network. Some of the cities grew from the nucleus of a small hamlet or village—St. Ferdinand, Ferguson, Clayton, and Webster Groves, for example. Others grew as overflow residential suburbs in open country, such as University City, a municipality created through a series of real estate subdivisions beginning in 1904.

The growth of the industrial satellites and residential suburbs of St. Louis has contributed to the overall growth of the standard metropolitan statistical area. In 1970, the population of the St. Louis SMSA stood at about 2.4 million, increasing by 12 percent since 1960, a rate lower than the average national metropolitan increase of 17 percent. After 1970, population in metropolitan St. Louis, like that in twenty-one other formerly growing SMSAs, began to decline, falling to 2,356,460 by 1980.

St. Louis reached a peak population of 880,000 in the early 1950s. During the 1960s, St. Louis's population declined 17 percent while its suburban ring population increased 29 percent. The rush to the suburbs was most acute among whites. Between 1960 and 1970, a net 34 percent of the white city dwellers moved away. By 1980 St. Louis's population had declined to 453,085.

KANSAS CITY

Geographical Growth

Missouri's second largest city had its beginning as a shipping point on the Kaw Bend of the Missouri River, where the river turns sharply east on its way across the mid-section of Missouri. Although reports from a few explorers reported that the country around the big bend of the Missouri River offered great potential for agriculture, the image of the "Great American Desert" was difficult to shake off. The region known as Big Blue Country was occupied by the Kanza, or Kansas, Indians whose name supposedly means "people of the south wind." This peaceful group, which engaged in farming, fishing, and trapping, was quickly displaced when settlers moved into the area.

The first permanent settlers were French traders from St. Louis, led by Francois Chouteau, who settled in 1821 at a trading post at the mouth of the Kaw (Kansas) River. A lively "truck-and-dicker trade" soon developed with the neighboring Indians, the employees of the mountain traders and freighters, the Mackinaw boatmen, and others. The traders received ponies, pelts, furs, trinkets, and annuity monies in exchange for powder, lead, tobacco, sugar, coffee, candies, beads, and whiskey. The tribes trading at the bend of the Missouri River were the Delawares, Potawatomies, Peorias, and Weas.

FIGURE 12.3. Map of the Town of Kansas (Kansas City), 1846. Courtesy State Historical Society of Missouri.

Even before the first steamboat reached Kansas City in 1831, there was substantial commerce on the Missouri River. Because of the natural rock ledge, the site of Independence provided good wharfage, and, in 1827, the town was established to handle the increasing commerce of the region. A second town, Westport, grew up 4 miles (6.43 km) inland from the future waterfront site of Kansas City. Westport had been platted in 1835, 4 miles south of Chouteau's Landing to service the Santa Fe Trail, which in earlier years had been supplied by Independence, Fort Osage, and Franklin, Missouri. For a time Westport was the most important town near Kaw Bend, benefiting from commerce connected with the Mexican War of 1846 and the great gold rush to California in 1849 and 1850.

John C. McCoy—businessman, trader, real estate promoter, and founder of Westport—established a freight landing on the river where a flat rock slanted from the bank some 18 miles (28.96 km) above Independence and north of the present central business district. Westport Landing, as the settlement was known, was purchased in 1838 by the Kansas Town Company and by 1848 had grown to a population of 700. In 1850, it was recognized as the "Town of Kansas" by the Jackson County court (Figure 12.3). By that time the town's population had declined by about half because of a cholera epidemic. The Missouri General Assembly chartered the town in 1853 as the "City of Kansas," marking the beginning of a long period of prosperity and population growth.

At the time of its charter, the city comprised 0.98 sq miles (2.5 km²). In 1859, the city annexed land to the south extending its boundaries from Ninth Street to Twentieth Street, bringing the total area to 3.82 sq miles (9.8 km²). By 1860, Westport had declined to about 1,200 citizens, but Kansas City had grown to a population of 4,418. A bird's-eye map of Kansas City in January 1869 depicted seven steamboats on the waterfront.

The year 1869 was a benchmark in Kansas City's history. In July of that year, the Hannibal and St. Joseph Railroad bridge—the first built across the Missouri River anywhere—was completed, and by the end of the year there were seven railroads in Kansas City. In 1870, the stockyards were established in the Kaw Bottoms and the city's population reached 32,260. In 1881, there were fifteen railroads serving Kansas City. Millions of bushels of wheat and corn were marketed and milled in and shipped from the city. In 1873, in the middle of national financial panic, another 1.43 sq miles (3.7 km²) were annexed to the south and east, bringing the total area of the city to 5.25 sq miles (13.6 km²). In the face of a depressed national economy, the city continued to grow, reaching a population of 55,785 by 1880.

The U.S. decennial census of 1880 indicates that the residents of Kansas City were dominantly American stock, primarily from the upper South and lower Middle West. There were about thirty churches, more of which were Methodist and Presbyterian than of any other denomination. A sizable German population had settled along the Missouri River borderlands. Three German-language newspapers, including the *Herald des Westens* ("herald of the west") and *Westliche Volkszeitung* ("western folk newspaper"), were published in Kansas City for distribution in the city and surrounding area.

In 1885, the city annexed 7.72 sq miles (20 km²), more than doubling its size (12.72 total sq miles or 32.9 km²) and extended the boundaries south to Thirty-first Street and east to Cleveland (3800 east). During the 1880s, population growth was rapid. Many of the "movers and shakers" that would help shape the cultural landscape of the city arrived in this decade. Among them were William Rockhill Nelson and Samuel Morss, founders of the *Kansas City Star;* the architectural firms of Van Brunt and Howe from Boston, Burnham and Root from Chicago, McKim, Mead, and White from New York; and George Kessler, noted landscape engineer. The park board, a singularly progressive group, laid out elaborate plans and produced a map, "Showing the Proposed System of Boulevards and Park Reservations." In the 1880s, eight different companies—the Northeast Electric Railway, the Kansas City Belt Railway, the Interstate Elevated Railway, the Kansas City Cable Railway, the People Railway, the Grand Avenue Railway, and the Metropolitan Street Railway—expanded the street railway system. The lines were constructed to connect the residential areas, spreading mainly across the hills to the south, with the industrial river bottoms and the center of commerce near the present-day site of Interstate 70. The commercial and manufacturing businesses in the 1880s were mainly housed in two- to four-story red brick and wood-frame structures.

More land was annexed in 1897, four years after the national financial panic. By this time, real estate investment had regained strength, and several new subdivisions were added. The annexation of 1897 again doubled the size of the city, bringing the total area to 25.38 sq miles (65.7 km²), extending the boundary south to Forty-ninth Street and east to the Little Blue valley. By 1900 the population had reached 163,752. Kansas City had at this time assumed a central banking role. Local banks throughout the Southwest turned to Kansas City to finance the herds of the cattle kings. Kansas City was also the chief financier for the Midwest's grain elevators. Large mail-order houses had been established and Kansas City's wholesale houses dispatched salesmen into the Corn Belt, throughout the wooded Ozarks, and into the vast western plains.

At the turn of the century, Kansas City's trade market was equal to half the land mass of the United States. Some 50,000 miles (80,645 km) of railroad track radiated from the West Bottoms. According to a popular saying, if a grain car was set rolling on the Great Plains it would roll naturally to the terminals in Kansas City. The city was the largest lumber market west of St. Louis, and its stockyards and packing plants supported 50,000 people out of a total of 265,000. Manufacturing was becoming diversified as nationally known companies— Speas Vinegar, Loose-Wiles Biscuits, Dickey Clay Pipe, and Peet Brothers (later Colgate-Palmolive) soap—were established. Farm implements, awnings, brooms, boxes, bricks, beer, candy, carriages, copper items, clothing, furniture, flour, glue, harnesses, iron and steel, paint, shoes, and tinware were all manufactured in the city.

Residential growth paralleled the expanding manufacturing base and the multiplication of jobs. With a modest beginning—which proved to be a landmark event and harbinger of the expanding U.S. city— J. C. Nichols began his Country Club District—a planned shopping center with surrounding residential developments—with the purchase of 10 acres (4 ha) north and west of Fifty-first and Grand in 1905. At that time it was more than a mile past the end of the streetcar lines. The shopping center—Country Club Plaza, reportedly the first planned shopping center in the United States—included offstreet parking and management of pedestrian movement. The plaza, with its unusual Spanish motif, has held up remarkably well over the years and continues as a healthy commercial center.

By the time of his death in 1950, J. C. Nichols had built a company controlling about 5,000 acres (2,025 ha) and known throughout the country for its enlightened techniques for planning residential districts, with the appropriate shopping center, schools, churches, and country clubs. Nichols's ideas of planning had a great impact on the cultural landscape of south Kansas City and also spread far beyond the Kansas state line into northeast Johnson County. The Nichols company not only helped to shape the look of the land in Johnson County, but made it one of the most exclusive residential districts in greater Kansas City.

In 1909 an additional 34.26 sq miles (88.7 km²) were annexed to the city, again

PHOTO 12.8. The Country Club Plaza in Kansas City, First Suburban Shopping Center in the Nation. Courtesy Convention and Visitors' Bureau of Kansas City.

more than doubling the geographical area, bringing it to a total of 59.64 sq miles (154.5 km²). The annexation took more land to the north (between Cleveland and Booth avenues) and a great deal of land to the south and southeast. The south limit was extended to Seventy-ninth Street where it stayed nearly forty years, until 1947. By 1910, the city's population had reached 248,381.

The growth of Kansas City geographically has been strongly influenced by physical site and situation. Confined by the state boundary on the west and the Missouri River barrier on the north, the city spread for the first seventy-five years to the south and east. There was always a strong urge to break the Missouri River

barrier. The "Clay County Bottoms," in the shadow of downtown, were an attractive real estate plum to be picked by developers who could provide cheap, reliable transportation across the river. Old communities had existed north of the river for many years—an 1880 map shows fourteen square blocks platted in Harlem—but crossing the river meant taking the ferry boat until 1911, when the North Kansas City Wagon and Railway Bridge was completed. A consortium of Armour, Swift, and Burlington interests resulted in the construction of the "A-S-B Bridge" and the creation of North Kansas City in 1912 as a center of light industry, warehousing, and distribution. The first Missouri River bridge—"the Hannibal"—was replaced in

1917 by a new iron-trestle structure that many people still believe to be the 1869 structure. The 1887 Milwaukee Railroad bridge was converted into the Chouteau Bridge in 1953.

Over the past fifty years, several additional bridges have breached the river barrier. The Courtney Bridge (1929) linked Independence and Liberty, and the Fairfax Bridge (1935) connected the eastern edges of Wyandotte and Platte counties. A new bridge for the Milwaukee Railroad was built in 1945 and the Liberty Bend Bridge opened in 1949. The Paseo Bridge (1954), the Broadway Bridge (1956), the I-435 Bridge (1972) near Randolph, and the I-635 Bridge (1975) near Eighteenth Street in Kansas City, Kansas, are the most recent additions to the bridge system in greater Kansas City.

Several downtown skyscrapers were built between 1910 and 1930, along with the monumental Union Station and the Liberty Memorial. The population increased by 75,000 during the 1920s, but the factory closings and depressed economic conditions of the 1930s brought a small decline in population—the first in the city's history. Federally sponsored (Works Progress Administration and Public Works Administration, for example) construction projects during the "Boss" Pendergast political era of the 1930s changed the brick and mortar landscape of downtown Kansas City.

An annexation of 2.38 sq miles (6.7 km²) in 1947 pushed the city south to Eighty-fifth Street, but in 1950, 19.7 sq miles (51 km²) were annexed, jumping over North Kansas City and the village of Randolph, making them enclaves within the boundaries of Kansas City. The federal census in that year indicated a population of 456,622.

Between 1957 and 1963 the boundaries of Kansas City were extended to encompass 234.61 sq miles (607.8 km²), bringing the total area to 316.33 sq miles (819.3 km²). The U.S. Bureau of the Census estimated the city's population for 1980 at 446,865. When the Kansas City standard metro-

politan statistical area (SMSA) is included in the tally, the population rises to 1,322,156. The SMSA consists of five counties in Missouri (Jackson, Clay, Cass, Platte, Ray) and two in Kansas (Wyandotte, Johnson). The SMSA includes Kansas City, Kansas, with more than 175,000 people and Independence, Missouri, with a population of 111,760.

A map of Kansas City is complicated. Tentacles reach around Grandview, a separate city on the south. A 10-square-mile (25.9-square-kilometer) area stretches between Raytown and Lee's Summit. North of the Missouri River the city has surrounded Gladstone and Birmingham, pushed north of Liberty, and sprawled across thousands of acres of southern Platte County farmlands. In the end, the city has incorporated sufficient territory both to contain growth for some time to come and to extend its boundaries into raw farmland on a number of frontiers. It is unlikely that Kansas City will become landlocked by incorporated suburbs as is St. Louis; although, in recent years, several fringe suburbs have engaged in defensive annexation, that is, annexation of territory before Kansas City can incorporate the land within its boundaries. Examples of cities that have added land by annexation in the 1960s and 1970s are Liberty, Sugar Creek, Independence, Lee's Summit, Greenwood, and Grandview.

On the Kansas side, a shatter belt of residential suburbs has developed south of Kansas City, Kansas. Shawnee, Merriam, Lenexa, Mission, Roeland Park, Westwood, Westwood Hills, Prairie Village, Leawood, and Overland Park occupy a nearly contiguous block of land.

Business and Industry

Several factors have influenced the growth of Kansas City as an industrial city. Originally it was an outfitting point for the Santa Fe, Oregon, and California trails. A major advantage was its situation south of the Kansas River. Trails and later railroads leading southwest from St. Joseph, Atchison, or Leavenworth had to cross the Kansas River. Kansas City became the hub of a major rail network that tapped the grain- and cattle-producing regions of the Great Plains and western Corn Belt. It was an early leader in aircraft manufacture and air transportation. Trans World Airlines' (TWA) general headquarters are established in Kansas City. The city is admirably suited to tap the wholesale trade of the Great Plains and to serve as cultural and entertainment center for the central Great Plains. Kansas City football and baseball are fol-

lowed two-thirds of the way across Kansas and Nebraska, and the Kansas City newspapers are read in approximately the same areas.

Kansas City has been described as a city with manure on its feet and wheat in its jeans. Between 1868 and 1888 the great Texas drover trails brought 98 million cattle and 10 million horses north to central markets including Kansas City. The Kansas City Stock Yards Company, founded in 1871 and occupying 13.5 acres (5.5 ha) of pens on the east bank of the Kaw River,

PHOTO 12.9.   Truman Sports Complex in Kansas City. Courtesy Convention and Visitors' Bureau of Kansas City.

was the nexus of the large meat-packing industry. During its first year, the stockyards company received 120,827 cattle, 41,036 hogs, 4,527 sheep, and 809 mules through its gates. In the 1920s the market peaked with more than 2 million cattle received each year.

The first packing plant, which J. L. Mitchener built in Kansas City in 1859, did not last long. The boom in the meat-packing industry did not occur until the 1880s, when "the Big Four"—Armour and Company, Swift and Company, Cudahy Packing Company, and Wilson Packing Company—came to dominate the industry.

Throughout the 1800s and early 1900s, the landscape of Kansas City was controlled by its two major industries: meat and wheat. Total production of wheat in Kansas in 1889, just fifteen years after the Mennonites introduced the Turkey Red variety, the "miracle crop," was more than 30 million bu (10,563,380 hl) harvested from 1.5 million acres (607,500 ha). The wheat, which was freighted to Kansas City in thousands of grain cars, contributed to the growth of the Board of Trade, originally in the Armour Building. Much of the agribusiness for which Kansas City became famous centered on grain. Processors of all kinds were moving to where the raw agricultural products were collected. By 1929 the fledgling corn-products industry, which refined corn into sweeteners such as corn syrup, had spawned a $10 million confectionery manufacturing business.

As technological developments in agriculture spurred production, Kansas City became the world's largest hard-winter wheat market. The use of summer fallowing—planting a crop every other year in order to conserve moisture—fertilizers, improved seed varieties, and irrigation increased production per acre dramatically. In 1930 Kansas farmers harvested 186 million bu (5,061,000 t) of wheat; in 1980 Kansas farmers reaped a record 414 million bu (11,264,000 t).

By 1946 a major change was under way in major livestock terminals in the United States. Just as Kansas City and Omaha replaced Chicago and St. Louis as the largest livestock markets, they were, in turn, abandoned by the meat packers in favor of smaller, modern plants in smaller cities in the Corn Belt and Great Plains. Irrigated corn drew huge commercial feedlots to western Kansas. In 1979 the Kansas City yards received only 300,000 head of cattle and calves compared to the 1.2 million per year during the 1940s.

In Kansas City, the federal, state, and local governments employ over 80,000. Manufacturing employment accounts for 21 percent of the total labor force of 604,500. The City Development Department has identified fifteen economic categories that have comprised a fast development group over the past twenty years: construction; paper and allied products; printing and publishing; stone, clay, and glass products; machinery; electrical machinery; air transport; wholesale trade; insurance, finance, and real estate; personal and repair services; business and professional services; amusements; health services; and state and local government (Table 12.3).

The production of durable goods is increasing manufacturing employment in the Kansas City SMSA. Manufacturing employment is highest in printing and publishing (13,800), fabricated metal products, (13,000), electrical equipment (11,900), food and kindred products (9,200), nonelectrical machinery (8,600), and chemicals and allied products (7,300).

There are over seventy-five industrial areas in metropolitan Kansas City. Most of the manufacturing, however, can be grouped into seven main industrial districts: (1) Armourdale, (2) Kansas City Terminal, (3) North Kansas City, (4) Fairfax, (5) Riverside, (6) Blue Valley, and (7) the Kansas City International Airport (Figure 12.4).

The *Armourdale District*, also called the West Bottoms, is the oldest of Kansas City's manufacturing districts. Kansas City began there in the Kaw Valley. Saloon and liquor wholesalers lined Union Avenue, the site

TABLE 12.3

Kansas City Area Employment, April 1982

Employment Category	Number of Employees	(Percent of Total Work Force)
Manufacturing	109,600	(15%)
Wholesale trade	51,100	(7%)
Retail trade	111,900	(16%)
Finance, insurance, and real estate	44,100	(6%)
Services	131,200	(18%)
Federal government	22,900	(3%)
State and local government	68,800	(10%)
Transportation and public utilities	49,600	(7%)
Contract construction	20,400	(3%)
Other nonagricultural employment	49,242	(7%)
Agricultural employment	7,078	(1%)
Other work force	49,242	(7%)
Total	715,162	

Source: Kansas City Department of City Development, 1982.

of the train depot. Within smelling distance were the stockyards, packing plants, and agricultural equipment dealers. From the West Bottoms rose such industrial giants as the Armour Packing Company, the Moline Plow Company, Swift and Company, John Deere Plow Company, plus a host of grain elevator companies.

By 1886 the district had flour mills, foundries, a linseed-oil mill, soap factories, and a couple of brewing companies. It was dotted with lumberyards and bordered by industrial suburbs like Armstrong, Wyandotte, Rosedale, Argentine, and Turner on the Kansas side. Today stockyards, railroad switching yards, and an assemblage of agri-industries such as feed mills, flour mills, seed companies, packing houses, and other processors of grains and animal products are situated on the Missouri side. The Union Pacific Freight Depot and switching yards are on the near Kansas side. Most of the manufacturing and wholesale houses occupy two- to six-story buildings built around the turn of the century. Farther west in the Armourdale District, warehouses and switching yards of the Union

Pacific and the Atchison, Topeka, and Santa Fe are located. Oil refineries occupy the less built-up area along the Kansas River.

The *Kansas City Terminal District* forms an eastern appendage to the Armourdale District. This district of warehouses and light-manufacturing plants grew up along rail lines and switching yards in a narrow valley south of the central business district.

The *North Kansas City District* initially was developed in 1929 as an industrial suburb of Kansas City by the North Kansas City Development Company, a subsidiary of Armour and Company, Swift and Company, and the Burlington Northern Railroad. Although in the shadow of downtown Kansas City, the area had remained undeveloped because of the barrier effect of the Missouri River and the necessity to make ferry crossings. Construction of the North Kansas City Wagon and Railway Bridge in 1912 opened the way for development, but the Depression retarded the district's growth. Strikes were never a serious problem because the company-owned streets could be cleared of pickets.

The North Kansas City District, now

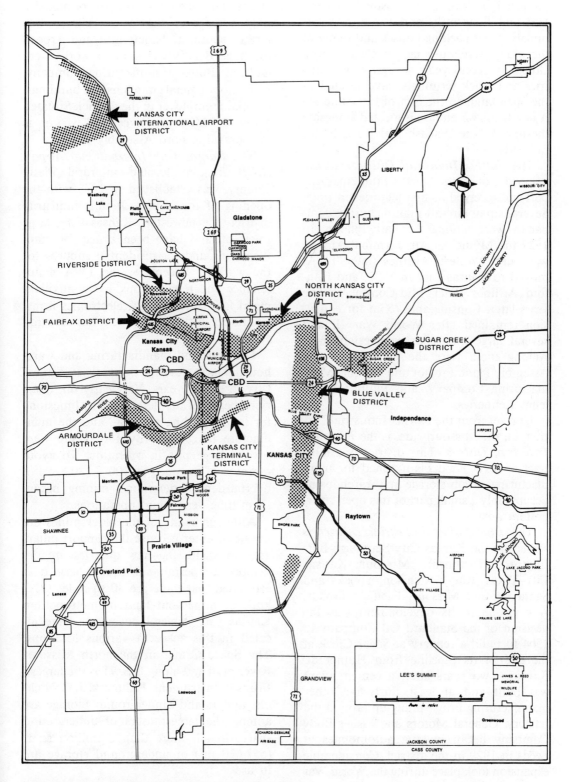

FIGURE 12.4. Industrial Districts in Kansas City.

protected by levees, is the site of several feed and flour mills and large grain terminals. Meat-packing houses and many of the older warehouse facilities have been closed. In recent years several new industries and truck terminals have located in the open lands to the east of Interstate 35. A new Sears warehouse is located alongside the lines of the Wabash and Rock Island railroads.

The *Fairfax Industrial District* was developed around the Fairfax Municipal Airport and received its first factories in 1925. Several small aircraft manufacturing companies were among the early plants. In 1929 the Municipal Air Terminal Airport was built. Western Airlines (later TWA) moved to Kansas City in 1931, and Hanford Airlines (later Mid-Continent) five years later. Considerable room for expansion remained after World War II, and several large industries were established. Among these were the General Motors Assembly Plant, Proctor and Gamble Manufacturing Company, and Phillips Petroleum Refineries.

Upriver from the Fairfax Industrial District, on the Missouri side, is the *Riverside Industrial District*. This district is a large tract of level flood plain zoned for manufacturing. Grain storage and warehousing occupy only a small part of this open river-bottom area.

The *Blue Valley Industrial District* is served by the Kansas City Southern; Burlington Northern; Missouri–Kansas City–Texas (Katy); Atchison, Topeka and Santa Fe; and Missouri Pacific railroads. A keystone in its development was the decision of the Standard Oil Company in 1904 to build a refinery at Sugar Creek at the end of its pipeline from Humboldt, Kansas. Two years later, a cement plant was built and at least thirty-five other manufacturing firms sprang up around the refinery. General Motors and Fisher Body Company began making automobiles at Leeds in 1929 in the district. Considerable expansion took place during the World War

II era. The huge Armco plant occupied a large acreage in the lower valley, while farther south, at Ninety-fifth and Troost, the huge Bendix Corporation works were laid out. Butler Manufacturing Company, fabricator of metal grain bins and buildings, is a major employer in the district. Situated across the Missouri River at Claycomo is the sprawling Ford Assembly Plant.

The *Kansas City International Airport (KCI) District,* located in rural Platte County, was established in 1973 with the opening of the airport. In this industrial district, the newest in Kansas City, large tracts of land have been zoned for manufacturing and for residential suburbs for the workers. Except for the TWA maintenance and repair shops, a few auxillary metal fabrication plants, electronics firms, and hotels, little development has occurred as yet.

Underground manufacturing and warehousing have developed rapidly in Kansas City in recent years. Very early on, quarrying began of the Bethany Falls limestone for lime, building material, and the manufacture of cement. By 1902 there were several large pits in operation. To avoid removal of as much as 100 ft (30.5 m) of overburden, underground mining began, permitting year-round operations.

Although many of the older mines are unsafe to enter because the support pillars are too small, the new quarries are developed to permit subsequent use. It is estimated that there are 30 sq miles (77.7 km²) of mined-out land in metropolitan Kansas City. Several businesses have located in this space at various locations. The Space Center in the north Missouri River bluff and along U.S. 71 is the largest. Brunson Instrument, Hallmark, J. C. Nichols, and Inland Underground Storage are among the largest users of underground space. In all, more than 6 million sq ft (557,620 m²) of underground storage are in use.

PHOTO 12.10.   General Motors Assembly Division Leeds Plant in Kansas City. Courtesy General Motors Corporation.

Commercial and Residential Patterns

Downtown Kansas City's skyscrapers are made more conspicuous by their location at the crest of the spur of hills where the Kansas River joins the Missouri River. The city's first skyscraper was the ten-story New York Life Building, which opened in 1889. During the 1890s, the skyline of the twelve-square-block business district expanded as Kansas City assumed its central banking role. Increased specialization of wholesalers and retailers was accompanied by the emergence of mail-order houses and traveling salespeople.

The 1920s were a time of great growth in the downtown area as new hotels, office buildings, and department stores were con-

structed. The 1920s also were a time of great residential growth, with construction moving at a pace not exhibited since the 1880s. The central city, its houses and apartments, achieved a look much like it has today.

The J. C. Nichols Company expanded its housing empire through the decade, laying out the Country Club Plaza in the Brushy Creek bottoms and adding several residential developments. Kansas City already had prosperous commercial centers outside of the downtown, which were natural outgrowths of the population's needs. They were located at bus and streetcar transfer points—at Thirty-first and Troost and Thirty-ninth and Main, for example.

The plaza was a harbinger of things to

PHOTO 12.11. Armco, Incorporated, Union Wire-Rope Facility in Kansas City. Electric Furnaces Convert Scrap for Production of Steel Rods, Wire, Nails, and Spikes. Courtesy Armco, Inc.

come as the residential belt expanded outward and automobile travel became the standard means of travel. The full development of the integrated shopping center with offstreet parking was delayed by the sluggish economic conditions of the 1930s and the wartime shortages of the 1940s.

The large decentralized, suburban retail malls blossomed during the 1960s and 1970s as the downtown area diminished as the chief shopping district. Ward Parkway, begun in 1961, was the first enclosed mall. Other, for the most part larger, malls followed, including Blue Ridge, Antioch, Metcalf South, Indian Springs, Independence Center, Oak Park, Metro North, and Bannister (Figure 12.5).

The downtown area became the focus of development and redevelopment during the 1960s as it naturally evolved into a center for banking, law, government, and conventions. Several new skyscrapers were added: the Trader's Bank Building and Commerce Tower, Ten Main Center, Executive Plaza, Mercantile Bank Building, and City Center Square. Hotel and motel growth began with the expansion of the Muehlebach in 1965 followed by construction of the Prom Sheraton, Holiday Inn, and Hyatt Regency. Crown Center and the Alameda Plaza were redeveloped in time to accommodate visitors for the 1976 Republican National Convention.

Neighborhoods and Suburbs

Greater Kansas City is made up of seventy-five neighborhoods and more than two-dozen fringe cities. Like many U.S.

PHOTO 12.12. Downtown Kansas City. Courtesy Convention and Visitors' Bureau of Kansas City.

cities it has a number of ethnic neighborhoods where immigrant groups settled. Many of these neighborhoods have been occupied in turn by new groups as the descendants of the older immigrants have moved up the economic ladder and out to the suburbs. Also, each of the fringing suburbs has developed its own unique character.

On the far north side of Kansas City proper is Little Italy. There, between the riverfront industries and the downtown, most of the Italian immigrants settled around the turn of the century. It has since then shrunk in size due to the outmigration of second- and third-generation families and the construction of Interstate 70 through part of the neighborhood. Nevertheless, some of the Italian cultural atmosphere remains in the Holy Rosary Catholic Church, in Italian restaurants, and in the Italian family names on storefronts.

The west side is a Spanish-American area situated on the hills bordering the central business district and extending several blocks farther south. Some 32 percent of Missouri's Spanish-origin population lives in Jackson County, predominantly on the west side. The strong first-generation ethnic character of the neighborhood is demonstrated by the frequent use of Spanish in conversations. Mexican restaurants and Spanish-language advertising are common features of the cultural landscape.

A large area southeast of downtown is made up of Black neighborhoods. The area east of downtown has been mainly Black for generations. Troost and Prospect avenues have been the main streets for Black migration to the south. Many of the migrant Black families were displaced from their close-in residences by the construction of freeways and urban renewal. The migration frontier of mixed neighborhoods

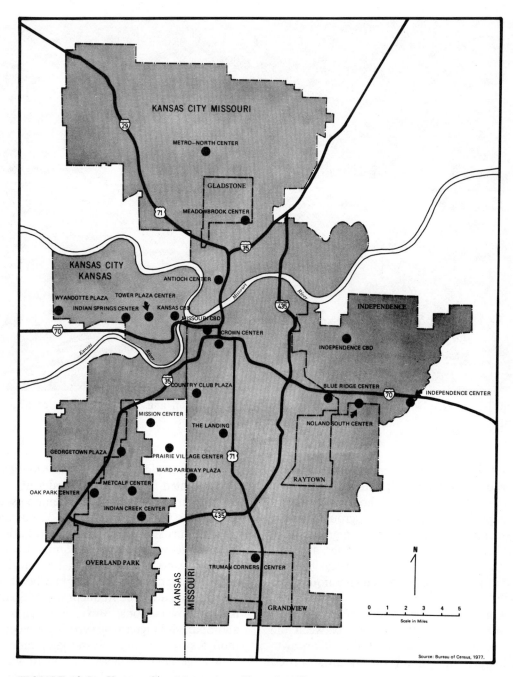

FIGURE 12.5. Kansas City Metro Area Shopping Centers.

has passed through the Blue Hills area, past Sixty-third Street, to well beyond Swope Park. The movement in the 1960s and 1970s was accelerated by antidiscrimination federal housing laws and federal financing programs such as the U.S. Department of Housing and Urban Development 235 program (HUD-235). It was further accelerated by blockbusting practices and the tendency of white families

PHOTO 12.13.   Crown Center in Kansas City. A Redevelopment Project of the Hallmark Company, Housing a Hotel, Convention Facilities, Offices, and Apartments. Courtesy Convention and Visitors' Bureau of Kansas City.

to sell property out of fear for declining real estate values as more Blacks moved into the area.

The neighborhoods near the intersections of Swope Parkway and Troost and Prospect avenues are strongly influenced by the University of Missouri (UMKC) and Rockhurst College. It is an area of faculty homes as well as of rooming houses and apartments for many of the 13,000 UMKC students and 1,500 Rockhurst students.

Northeast Kansas City comprises a large quadrant of the city made up of around two-dozen neighborhoods of predominantly white, Protestant, conservative, and working-class people. The voting pattern, although Democratic, is strongly conservative.

The southwest area, which encompasses the plaza, the Southwest High School neigh-

borhoods, and the state line region bordering the Kansas communities of Prairie Village and Overland Park, comprises upper-middle-class to upper-class neighborhoods. In general, the residents are professional people, college educated or technically trained, and the area is characterized by manicured lawns, tree-shaded boulevards, and elegant houses. Republican candidates run stronger there than in other parts of the central city.

The largest of the outlying towns is Kansas City, Kansas. KCK, as it is sometimes called, is much more of an industrial town than its sister city across the Kaw. The populace is an ethnic mixture, including Poles, Romanians, Hungarians, Croatians, Russians, Irish, Spanish Americans, and a large Black contingent. Downtown Kansas City, Kansas, is situated on the western hills, overlooking the junction of the Kansas and Missouri rivers. The city is hemmed in by the Missouri River on the north and by incorporated towns— Westwood, Roeland Park, Mission, Merriam, Edwardsville, and Bonner Springs— on the south and southwest. The northwest boundary has pushed all the way to the Leavenworth County line and to within a couple of miles of the city of Lansing.

Johnson County, Kansas, is a jigsaw puzzle of bedroom communities for greater Kansas City. In terms of the theoretical models of city structure, it illustrates nicely Homer Hoyt's pielike sector theory as a high-rent wedge. It ranks in the top five counties nationally in per family income. The incorporated towns are a variety of shapes and sizes from tiny Countryside, less than 1 sq mile (2.59 km²) in area, to sprawling Overland Park. Westwood, Fairway, Prairie Village, and Leawood crowd the Missouri line, whereas the western suburban frontier is comprised of Olathe, Lenexa, and Shawnee. These communities are for the most part commuter towns, and much of the money that supports the schools, the large churches, the winding landscaped streets and comfortable homes comes from wages earned in Missouri.

The suburbs to the north in Clay County are a mixed lot. North Kansas City was designed to be and is an industrial town, as is Riverside. There are old communities like Gladstone, Liberty, Oakview, Oakwood, Oakwood Park, Oaks, Claycomo, and Pleasant Valley, plus large acreages of residential neighborhoods in Kansas City proper.

Independence is the largest suburb of Kansas City on the Missouri side. The town is well named since it developed as an independent city and is even now the fourth largest city in Missouri with more than 110,000 residents. This old-fashioned courthouse-square town is the home of the Reorganized Church of Jesus Christ of Latter-Day Saints, a 207,000-member denomination that differs from the Mormons of Utah.

Raytown and Lee's Summit, located south of Independence, are the other large towns in eastern Jackson County. They are middle-class suburbs that have experienced substantial growth in population over the past twenty years.

Southtown, the area south of Raytown and Swope Park, is mostly a middle- to upper-middle-class residential area. Grandview is an older town that has been reshaped into a typical post–World War II residential suburb with curvilinear streets, cul de sacs, and neon-lighted string streets. The closing of the Richards-Gebaur Air Force Base in the late 1970s sapped some of the area's vitality. Nevertheless businesspeople and government executives from Southtown can be seen each morning fighting the traffic as they head northward for the downtown, the plaza, or other Kansas City business districts.

ST. JOSEPH

St. Joseph, Missouri's fifth largest city (with a city population of 76,691 and SMSA of 101,868 in 1980), covers the bottomlands and bluffs overlooking the Missouri River. Much of its early history is linked to the operations of the American Fur Company. The post was located at the mouth of Roy's Branch in the Blacksnake Hills. The stream is now enclosed by the St. Joseph storm-drainage system.

Roubidoux's Post, as it was called, was visited by local Indian tribes—the Blacksnake and Fox—who traded furs and cash from government gratuities for hardware, flour, guns, beads, and whiskey. In 1834, Roubidoux purchased the post from the fur company. The same year, Maximilian, Prince of Weid, visited the settlement, which consisted of a farm, two houses painted white, and the trading post. Roubidoux employed about twenty Creole traders in the Indian trade.

Three years later, on March 28, 1837, the federal government made the Platte Purchase, which added approximately 2 million acres (810,000 ha) to Missouri. The purchase helped to end the conflict between the resident Indians and the white settlers who were encroaching on Indian lands. By disposing of the Indian land claims, the way was open to establish six new Missouri counties—Buchanan, Platte, Atchison, Holt, and Nodaway. Settlement progressed rapidly as the country proved to be well suited to the crops familiar to Kentucky and Virginia immigrants. Corn, hemp, and tobacco were the main crops; cattle, hogs, sheep, and poultry provided meat for the table and produce for the market.

Buchanan County was organized in 1838 and Sparta was designated county seat. In 1846, when the seat was moved to St. Joseph, the settlement consisted of 350 houses, 2 churches, 1 city hall, and 1 jail. The *St. Joseph Gazette* was first published in 1845 and the town enjoyed a thriving business as the last river port on the trail to Oregon country.

Through the 1840s and 1850s, St. Joseph developed a prosperous trade exchanging staples, guns, and hardware from the east for the hides and furs brought in from the west by grizzled mountain men. When, in 1849, gold was discovered in California, the rush of immigrants generated an economic boom in St. Joseph. Because cholera had broken out at Independence and Westport, many immigrants were diverted to St. Joseph where they were provisioned with foodstuffs, harnesses, gear, guns, and guides.

St. Joseph was established as a livestock market at a very early date. In 1846, John Corby built a slaughtering house. The brisk market for cattle in California made St. Joseph a natural location for the sale of cattle to be herded west. Cows purchased in Missouri for $10 a head brought $150 in California. The Colorado gold rush in 1858 brought on another round of brisk outfitting trade and expanded the trail herd and slaughtering businesses. At the end of the Civil War in 1866, drovers from Texas attempted to herd some 260,000 longhorn cattle through southwest Missouri to the railhead at Sedalia, but were detoured west through Kansas to the railroad center of

St. Joseph. The lean and stringy meat from the longhorn cattle was suitable for canning purposes and a large industry was in the making. Stockyards were built in St. Joseph in 1887, but big-time livestock marketing and slaughtering did not occur until 1895, when Gustavis Swift purchased the stockyards and built a major packing house. By the 1920s half a million animals per year were butchered at the St. Joseph stockyards.

St. Joseph gained an advantage over competing cities on the western frontier in 1859, when the first train arrived on the Hannibal and St. Joseph Railroad. The railroad made connections in St. Joseph with two important transports to the West: the overland stage line that John M. Hockaday established to Salt Lake City in 1858 and the famed Pony Express. Mail service by daring riders was inaugurated April 3, 1860, with St. Joseph the eastern terminus and Sacramento, California, the western. Later, when railroads spanned the continent, mail cars were dispatched from St. Joseph and the mail sorted en route to California.

The Civil War caused a hiatus in the economic growth of St. Joseph, partly because Buchanan County was predominantly Southern in its sympathies. Even before the outbreak of war, conflicts erupted between abolitionists from across the Missouri River in "free Kansas" and the owners of the 2,000 slaves in the county. During the war the major battles were confined to central and southern Missouri, but guerrilla bands were active throughout Missouri. Nearly 2,000 men went south from Buchanan County to join Confederate forces.[1]

Following the war, St. Joseph shared in the general economic upsurge. A bridge was built to span the Missouri River in 1873 and five more railroads laid tracks to the city. By the turn of the century, St. Joseph had four major packing plants, several large flour mills, and major horse and mule market operations. It was supposedly the wealthiest city per capita in the nation. Large mansions were built on the hillside

PHOTO 12.14.   Pony Express Stables in St. Joseph. Courtesy Walker—Missouri Division of Tourism.

overlooking the commercial and industrial bottoms. By 1910 the population had reached 77,000 and manufacturing and commerce with its productive agricultural hinterland had replaced outfitting and western trade businesses.

St. Joseph has developed into a two-level city typical of Midwestern river towns. The Missouri River was the focal point for early commerce and industry and initially log and sawed-lumber buildings housed these activities close by the riverbank. Later, when railroads built up the valley, taking advantage of the lower cost of construction on the floodplain, the commercial and industrial area was expanded with many brick-and-mortar buildings. Tall buildings of four to eight stories came to dominate the downtown area. The east-

west streets in the downtown area the founder, Joseph Roubidoux, named for members of his family: Faroon, Jules, Francis, Felix, Edmond, Charles, Sylvania, Angelique, and Messanie. There the central business district grew up.

East of the retail section, the brick and stone mansions of St. Joseph's prosperous 1880s crowd the steep hillsides. Many of the gingerbread-trimmed homes with their turrets, dormer windows, and broad porches are listed in the National Register of Historic Places. The largest, oldest houses lie northeast of Frederick Avenue along Lover's Lane and in the vicinity of Twenty-eighth Street, where tree-shaded drives lead southwest from Krug Park on the north, through Corby Grove and Bartlett Park, past the Municipal Golf Course to Hyde

Park and King Hill. Newer residential sub-divisions lie at the city's periphery, particularly alongside the north-south belt highway (U.S. 169) and spreading beyond Interstate 29. The shopping mall and commercial development on the belt highway, coupled with the Interstate 29 employment centers at Missouri Western State College and the St. Joseph Industrial Park, are strong magnets for additional east side residential growth.

St. Joseph, once Missouri's third largest city, has now slipped to fifth place, behind St. Louis, Kansas City, Springfield, and Independence and may fall to sixth rank, behind Columbia, by the 1990 census. The city's population, which was 75,711 in 1940, increased to 79,673 in 1960, then declined to 72,691 by 1970. In 1980, it reached 76,691 with 101,868 in the SMSA.

Employment data from the Missouri Division of Employment Security show the following major categories of employment: manufacturing, wholesale and retail trade, services and miscellaneous, government, and construction and mining. St. Joseph's manufacturing is for the most part agriculturally related. According to the census Standard Industrial Classification (SIC), the highest-ranked industries are food and kindred products (twenty-eight firms); machinery (nine firms); and chemicals and allied products (ten firms).

Manufacturing in St. Joseph is located in three main districts: the Missouri River Bottoms, the St. Joseph Industrial Park, and the St. Joseph Industrial Airpark (Figure 12.6). The *Missouri River Bottoms* includes most of the older manufacturing plants located in the bottomlands bordering the Missouri River and adjacent to the central business district. All of the major rail lines focus on the riverfront. These include the Atchison, Topeka, and Santa Fe; the Burlington Northern; the Chicago and Northwestern; the Missouri Pacific; and the Union Pacific. Barge service is available on the riverfront, and the business route of Interstate 29 serves the downtown area.

Although a few plants are located north of the CBD along the Burlington Northern tracks, most of the district extends south of the main commercial establishments where the floodplain is broader. The Union Stockyards, rail switching yards, Armour and Company, and the Quaker Oats Company are conspicuous occupiers of space. General warehousing, wholesaling, and trucking firms are mixed among the manufacturers. Many of the buildings are two- to four-story brick structures that were built more than fifty years ago.

St. Joseph Industrial Park is a 200-acre (81-hectare) site, located in southeast St. Joseph. The park is served by the Chicago, Burlington, and Quincy Railroad and by three highways: Interstate 29, U.S. 169, and U.S. 36. Major manufacturers housed in modern buildings on landscaped grounds include Hoerners-Waldorf Corporation (paper products and boxes) and Globe Union (batteries).

St. Joseph Industrial Airpark, a 58-acre (23-hectare) site, is situated in the French Bottoms, a parcel of Missouri territory in an abandoned loop of the Missouri River 4 miles (6.4 km) west of the city. The site is zoned for light industry and is accessible via the Union Pacific Railroad, Missouri River, and Rosecrans Memorial Airport.

SPRINGFIELD

Because of its size, location, and importance as a regional center in Missouri, Springfield's historical geography merits examination. Springfield is sufficiently large to exhibit distinct land-use areas, but small enough to be easily described. Its growth and development mirror many, if not most, of the theoretical models of city structure.

Springfield is situated on the Springfield Plateau (Springfield Plain), which lies mainly on the western flanks and elevated portions of the Ozark Plateau. The city occupies the site of two large grassy uplands in pioneer times: Grand Prairie and Kickapoo Prairie. The urban fringes are spreading into adjacent Greene County uplands:

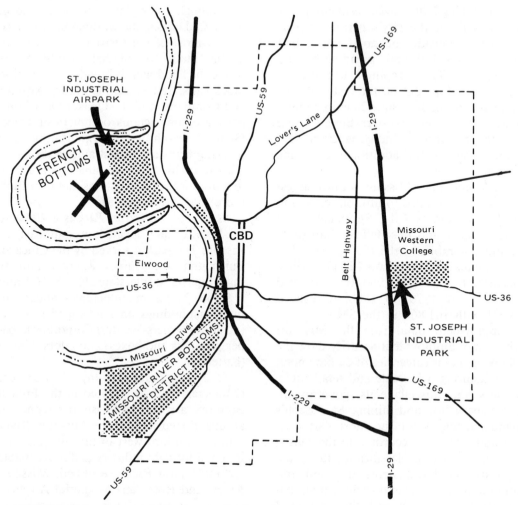

FIGURE 12.6.   Industrial Districts in St. Joseph.

Leeper Prairie, Whittenburg Prairie, and Robberson Prairie.

The uplands drain north to the Sac River and south to the James River. Within the city three main watercourses—Jordan Creek, Fassnight Creek, and South Creek—drain to Wilson's Creek, a tributary of the James River. The eastern subdivisions drain to Pearson Creek, another tributary of the James.

Springfield has had a record of continuous growth since its founding in 1830, except for a period during the Civil War, when the city was alternately in the hands of Confederate and federal troops. By 1910, it had grown to 35,210. At present it is

Missouri's third largest city, behind St. Louis and Kansas City. In 1980 the population of the city reached 133,016, while the SMSA, which included Greene and Christian counties, contained 207,704 people.

Because of its size and geographical location, Springfield claims the title "Queen of the Ozarks." St. Louis is 220 miles (354 km) to the northeast; Kansas City, 176 miles (283 km) to the northwest; Memphis, 283 miles (455 km) to the southeast; Tulsa, 182 miles (293 km) to the southwest; and Little Rock, 229 miles (368 km) to the south. Within this large territory, Springfield is the central supply point and market.

Thus, the city's geographical situation well suits its function.

According to H. J. Nelson's classification of U.S. cities, based on 1950 census data, Springfield is an important transportation and wholesaling center. In 1950 the chief city-forming industries were railroads, retailing, and wholesaling. As early as 1917 the wholesale houses of the city were doing a business of nearly $20 million annually, and more than 1,000 traveling representatives for these concerns made their homes in Springfield. The main shops of the St. Louis and San Francisco (Frisco) Railway were at that time Springfield's largest single employer.

In 1917, the city was already a manufacturing center of importance. In addition to the Frisco shops, there were ironworks, furniture manufacturers, stove companies, four large flour mills, several large cold-storage plants, packing plants, two or three firms handling poultry products and produce, cooperages, carriage factories, and the Springfield Wagon Company, which turned out 6,000 farm and logging wagons annually.

The 1980 *Missouri Directory of Manufacturing* shows Springfield to be a city of diverse manufacturers. Food products, printing, electrical machinery and supplies, and chemicals are especially important. Nearly two-thirds of the manufacturing firms listed in the directory have located in Springfield since 1940. Among the largest employers are Zenith Television (1,500), the Burlington Northern general offices and shops (2,000), Lily Tulip, Incorporated (1,250), Dayco Corporation (1,300), and Kraft Foods (1,000). These and other smaller plants employ many workers from surrounding towns and farms.

Springfield has been the leading cultural and religious center of the Ozarks since pioneer times. More than 150 churches are located in the city, among them the largest churches in the Ozarks with the largest membership. The worldwide church program and publishing house of the Assembly of God churches are centered in Springfield,

as well as the regional offices of several other denominations.

In the fall of 1980, the five colleges in Springfield had a total enrollment of more than 20,000. The largest is Southwest Missouri State University (14,500), followed by Drury College, Baptist Bible College, Evangel College, and Central Bible College. The Springfield Public Library and its branches hold approximately 210,000 volumes, constituting the largest municipal library system in the Ozarks. Nationally known performers are hosted at the several colleges and in the Shrine Mosque. The community is especially proud of the Springfield Symphony Orchestra and the Springfield Art Museum, where "Water Color U.S.A.," a juried show, is displayed annually. The attention of a large part of the Ozark population in both Missouri and Arkansas is focused on Springfield through its three television stations, eight radio stations, and the morning and evening editions of the Springfield newspaper.

Early Developments

From time to time various white men entered the region before the removal of the Indians, notably Henry Rowe Schoolcraft, who dug lead at a site on Pearson Creek in east Springfield in 1818. The first permanent white settlement was made in March 1830, when John P. Campbell, from Maury County, Tennessee, brought his family to the territory. He had previously explored the area and discovered its abundant resources—forest, wildlife, plentiful water, and wide expanses of prairie for cultivation.

The economic development of Springfield can be divided into three stages: pioneer, farming, and commercial. In the pioneer stage the area was almost completely isolated: communication with the outside world was difficult and infrequent. Consequently, the settlers were almost entirely self-supporting, depending upon the resources of the immediate vicinity. Because the area had many advantageous features, the number of inhabitants increased rapidly. John Campbell reportedly built thirteen cabins in one year, vacating one after another in order to provide new-comers with homes.

In 1835 Springfield was designated the county seat for Greene County and the courthouse was built on a 50-acre (20.25-hectare) tract donated by John Campbell. In 1838, when incorporated, the town was 132 acres (53 ha) and had several busi-nesses. By 1860 some mills and small factories had been built along Jordan Creek to take advantage of water power. By that time roads had been marked to Boonville, St. Louis (Ridge Road), and to Forsyth on the White River (Ozark Road).

As Springfield increased in size and im-portance, it became the commercial center for the entire region. Farmers within a radius of 50 (80 km) to 75 miles (121 km) brought their products to the town and traded them for goods transported from St. Louis or Boonville. The traffic that converged on Springfield required many supplies; as a consequence, a large number of warehouses and wholesale stores were established to meet the increasing demand. Future development of the town was very favorable to the wholesale business.

To meet the needs of the growing pop-ulation of Greene County, stagecoaches were run between Springfield, St. Louis, Boonville, and Jefferson City, Missouri, and Fayetteville, Arkansas. In 1858 the Butterfield Overland Mail Company started its line of stagecoaches for California from St. Louis through Springfield, and the ar-rival of the first regular stage in the town was an eventful occasion. This line ac-commodated both passenger and express traffic until the disruption of the Civil War, after which the line was discontinued. This loss of regular stages accentuated the need for transportation facilities—a need the railroads soon filled.

Three railroads were built to Springfield. The first, the Atlantic and Pacific, was completed in 1870. The Kansas City, Fort Scott, and Memphis Railroad and the Mis-souri Pacific Railroad provided additional connections to points north and south. Later the Frisco system consolidated sev-eral lines in the region, providing additional railroad connections for Springfield resi-dents.

The manufacturing stage developed mainly after World War I. Springfield's early-day gristmills, sawmills, woolen mills, and tanneries were supplanted by modern lumber companies, furniture factories, flour mills, and foundries. World War I furnished a stimulus that focused attention upon manufacturing; after the war, however, many plants that had sprung up "over-night" went out of existence.

The manufacturing the city of Spring-field engages in is a reflection of its agri-cultural background. From its earliest days Springfield was an agricultural community, and this phase was carried throughout its history until major changes in economic development occurred during and follow-ing World War I. Today, there are several grain elevators and flour mills within the city. Packing companies handle stock from the farms, and milk processors and produce companies utilize the abundant supply of dairy and poultry products.

The retail and wholesale functions of the city during the 1930s provide an in-teresting contrast with its present com-mercial structure. During the 1930s, Spring-field was the largest city in southwest Missouri and its retail trade area was ex-tensive, about 75 miles (120 km) in radius. In 1934, there were approximately 592 retail stores and 55 wholesale firms in the city (Table 12.4). The Missouri Pacific and Frisco railways provided distribution by rail, and the network of highways facilitated motor transportation.

Changes in City Structure Since 1935

The downtown area, formerly called the Public Square and now known as Park Central Square, has undergone important changes in form and function. Most of the buildings are three to five stories in height and the few higher buildings are accen-

TABLE 12.4

Retail and Wholesale Firms in Springfield, 1934

Retail

Books	3	Confectioneries	17
Cigars and tobacco	4	Coal dealers	25
Department stores	8	Druggists	37
Dry goods	24	Electrical	8
Florists	10	Flour and feed	14
Fruit stores	11	Furniture	35
Grocers	294	Hardware	19
Household appliances	11	Jewelers	11
Lumber supplies	19	Meats	26
Men's clothing	14	Millinery	8
Office supplies	6	Ready-to-wear	10
Shoes	25	Tailors	9
Variety goods	21		

Wholesale

Agricultural implements	2	Automobile equipment	5
Bakers	6	Candy	1
Cigars	1	Drugs	2
Dry goods	3	Feed	4
Flour	1	Fruits	5
Furniture	2	Grocers	6
Hardware	2	Lumber	2
Packing houses	4	Plumbing	1
Produce	5	Radios	1
Seeds	2		

Source: Virginia Hogg. "Urban Pattern of Springfield, Missouri." Master's thesis, Washington University, 1934, pp. 18-19.

tuated because of their location on the upland. Formerly, Park Central Square was the location for the larger retail establishments of the city, including department stores, shoe stores, and office buildings. The four streets that entered the square prior to 1974 showed how diverse the development of products was in both quality and type. St. Louis Street was noted for specialty shops dealing in men's and women's clothing. Automobile agencies and repair shops, which formerly lined St. Louis Street, Jefferson Street, and McDaniel Street east of the core, have moved to new "automobile rows," notably on St. Louis Street between National and Glenstone, along Glenstone south of St. Louis Street, and on Campbell Street south of Battlefield Road.

Many of the low-rent establishments west of the square have been cleared and the land has been developed as parking lots under urban renewal programs. In this district on Campbell Street and College Street, there were once small cafés, shoe stores, dry good stores, taverns, and secondhand shops. Space above the ground floor was rented out as living quarters for low-wage earners.

In recent years, several businesses in the downtown area have built branch offices at other locations, notably at the Battlefield

Mall. J. C. Penney Company was the largest retailer to vacate multistory space on the square in favor of new facilities completed on the Battlefield Mall in 1972. In 1974, the four radiating streets were blocked to create a pedestrian mall. Recent construction and expansion have been mainly by banking and financial firms. Extending from Olive north to Chestnut Expressway, between National and Grant avenues, lies a heavy commercial district. Wholesale grocers, lumber dealers, agricultural business houses, and wholesale hardware outlets occupy much of the area. Formerly coal and fuel dealers were situated in the area. A central location with rail connections was essential to these concerns in earlier years; but with the development of rapid truck service to larger cities, many of the businesses have moved to new buildings outside the central section of the city.

In former times, there were several businesses in the Jordan Creek Bottoms that shipped hides, wool, and fur. Only one such company remains. Produce companies, feed companies, flour dealers, and seed companies, however, continue to operate in the Jordan Creek Bottoms north of Park Central Square. Originally, their location was influenced by the existing railroad lines and the proximity to the "trading center" of the city. Feed dealers were attracted to the area because the major mills were close by in the Jordan valley and the railroads facilitated handling feed shipped from the city. Fruit dealers both received fruits from distant sources to be sold in the Springfield trade area and collected and shipped homegrown strawberries, tomatoes, apples, and fruits. The latter group has largely disappeared except for the Hammons Product Company, which collects walnuts for shipment from its plant on North Campbell.

After the turn of the century, commercial dairying grew rapidly. In the mid-1930s, Springfield supposedly ranked fourth in the nation in butter churning. There were eleven creameries, with 650 employees. Seven creameries—including Armour and Company, Swift and Company, and Borden—were located in the valley adjacent to the Public Square. A major change in the industrial geography of southwest Missouri since World War II has been the centralization of dairy production. Many small plants have closed in the towns surrounding Springfield, and their production has subsequently been concentrated in Springfield's huge Kraft Foods plant and the Mid-America Dairymen Incorporated and Highland dairies. More emphasis is placed on the production of fresh whole milk since bulk handling and trucking have been developed. The Mid-America Dairymen Incorporated now handles the largest volume.

The retail district between Washington and Lyon avenues, along Commercial Street, is an expansion of the area that originally comprised the business district of North Springfield, a separate incorporated city until annexed in 1886. The volume of traffic on Commercial Street is increased because several streets are discontinued at their Commercial Street intersections. In this district, the dry goods stores, jewelry shops, shoe stores, furniture stores, banking concerns, hotels and drug stores are fairly evenly distributed, with no concentrations of particular concerns as in the Park Central Square core. Most of the stores are home owned in buildings more than fifty years old.

Between Park Central Square and Commercial Street, an area of government and public service employment is situated. The main trolley line connecting Springfield and North Springfield was built on Boonville Avenue in 1871. Soon business houses grew up along the main line. Trolleys were also routed along Central (Center) Street to Washington. Today this section has developed into a governmental core including the city hall, city utilities, the federal post office, the Social Security office, the police station and jail, the county court house, Central High School, the Springfield schools administrative offices, and the main city library. Drury College, Springfield Newspapers, and KGBX radio are close by.

Numerous small retail stores serve the public administration core.

The concentration of civic functions in this area is due partially to a controversy that arose over the location of the present courthouse. After the old courthouse on the northwest corner of the Public Square was vacated in 1912, the county court voted to build it near the geographical center of the city—midway between the competing businesses on the square and on Commercial Street. Other services were similarly located.

Farther north on Boonville, the Assemblies of God Publishing House and the Cox Medical Center form a major employment node. Many residences in the area have been torn down and removed for the expansion of commercial buildings and the construction of parking lots. On either side of Boonville Avenue, there are many apartments and rooming houses, occupied principally by low-wage earners from the adjacent business districts. The southeastern section of the area is a Black residential section. Near the upper Jordan area and along the east belt line, Blacks occupy a dozen or so square blocks of mainly low-rent houses. The area is small since the 2,858 Blacks comprise only 2 percent of the population.

Outlying Commercial Districts

Rapid increase in use of the automobile has reshaped the geography of U.S. cities, and Springfield is no exception. Earlier, small retail centers developed at transfer points and terminals along the streetcar lines. Several of these small clusters of grocery stores, drug stores, and cleaners have continued in business, partly because the bus lines follow the same routes as the streetcars, which ceased operations in 1937.

Commercial development along heavily traveled thoroughfares has become ubiquitous in U.S. cities. These "string-street" developments serve the people moving through the city and to and from work. Clusters of offstreet shopping centers develop where major thoroughfares were for-

PHOTO 12.15.   Downtown Springfield and the Jordan Creek Industrial District Viewed from the West, 1972. Photograph by the author.

merly the main bypass highways. Glenstone Avenue is the most maturely developed string street—11 miles (17.6 km) of service stations, restaurants, motels, grocery stores, discount stores, insurance agencies, automobile dealerships, and so on. One major node is the motel, restaurant, and service station cluster on Glenstone Avenue between Kearney Street and Interstate 44. In the late 1970s, the North Town Mall was built at the northeast corner of Glenstone and Kearney.

A second major node is the group of offstreet shopping centers developed at the intersection of Sunshine Street and Glenstone (said to be the fourth or fifth busiest intersection in Missouri) and north on Glenstone to Bennett. The plaza on the southeast corner of Sunshine and Glenstone is the oldest; a Ramey supermarket was built there in the early 1950s. The Katz City, Glen Isle, and Country Club shopping centers were developed in the late 1950s and early 1960s. Construction of the University Plaza—a hotel, convention center, shopping mall, and apartment complex, conceived and financed by developer John Q. Hammons—was under way in 1982 on a tract in the center city

PHOTO 12.16. The Battlefield Mall Vicinity in Springfield, 1972. Mall Under Construction. Photograph by the Author.

north of Southwest Missouri State University and east of the central business district. The 17-acre (6.8-hectare) tract, cleared by the Land Clearance for Redevelopment Authority, will be a planned development district.

The most recent and rapid development on Glenstone is in the vicinity of the Battlefield Mall. The mall, after opening in 1970 as a regional shopping center, immediately became the largest node on the Glenstone commercial complex and shifted the center of gravity of Springfield's commercial structure and traffic pattern to the southeast. After a major expansion in 1982, 150 businesses operated in the Battlefield Mall including Sears, Montgomery Ward, J. C. Penney Company, Dillards, and Famous Barr. Several "satellite" retail establishments are located close to the mall to take advantage of the high automobile-traffic flow. Between 1975 and 1980, Battlefield Street from Glenstone Avenue to Campbell Avenue experienced frenzied development and was converted from a hedge-bordered country road to a traffic-jammed commercial street. Other string-street developments on business-route highways include East Sunshine Street, Kearney Street, and South Campbell Street.

Developments in Manufacturing in Springfield Since 1934

The Bureau of Census classification of manufacturing according to the Standard Industrial Classification (SIC) shows Springfield to be high in food and kindred products; fabricated metals; printing, publishing, and allied industries; and chemicals and allied products. Most of Springfield's older manufacturing plants are located in the *Jordan Creek Industrial District;* notably feed mills and food wholesale houses, furniture and fixture manufacturers, and printers and publishers (Figure 12.7). In the 1960s new plants were constructed in the *Northeast Industrial District* and at other scattered outlying locations. Recently, several of the long-established industries have vacated old buildings with obsolete equipment and built more modern facilities in the new industrial parks, taking advantage of cheaper land, better accessibility, and the lack of congestion.

Many of the industries that were important in the 1930s have closed their doors and many others have moved to new locations. The Marblehead Lime Quarry is being used again as a landfill after a fire on the site burned persistently for several months in 1972. The Springfield Wagon and Tractor Company works have been abandoned and the buildings razed. The stockyards on Mill Street have been torn down and new facilities are now located on Division Street east of Kansas Avenue.

The 1980 *Missouri Directory of Manufacturing* lists manufacturers by the number of employees. Those in the "over-1,000" category include Zenith Corporation (televisions); the Burlington Northern Railroad; Fasco Industries, Incorporated (electric motors); Dayco (V-belts); and Lily Tulip Corporation (paper cups and food containers). Manufacturing companies employing 250 to 999 employees are Foremost Foods Company (dairy products); the R. T. French Company (mustard); General Electric (electric motors); Gospel Publishing House (religious literature); Hiland

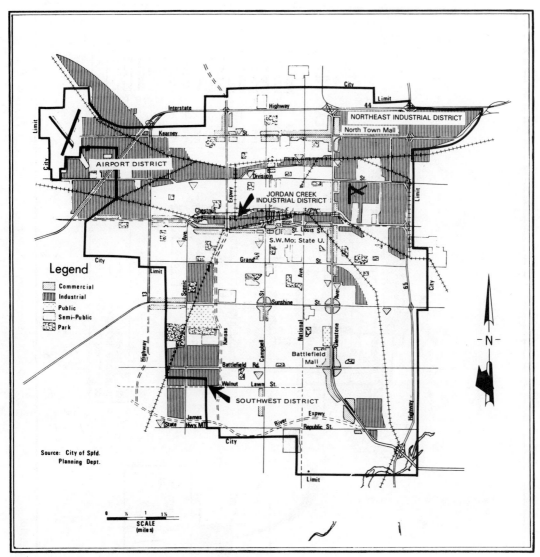

FIGURE 12.7. Industrial Districts in Springfield.

Dairy; Kraft Foods Corporation (cheese); Litton Industries (printed electrical circuits); Mid-America Dairymen, Incorporated (milk products); Paul Mueller Company (dairy equipment); and Springfield Newspapers.

Springfield and the Theoretical City

Although the internal pattern of each city is unique, all U.S. cities have business, industrial, and residential districts. Three theoretical models, based on concentric zones, sectors, and multiple nuclei, can be used to describe the geography of individual cities and to illustrate the similarities and differences between various cities in one given state or in the United States as a whole.

According to the concentric zone theory, as proposed by Ernest W. Burgess, the pattern of growth of cities can best be understood in terms of five concentric zones from the city center to the periphery: (1) the central business district; (2) the zone in transition, an area of light manufacturing

194

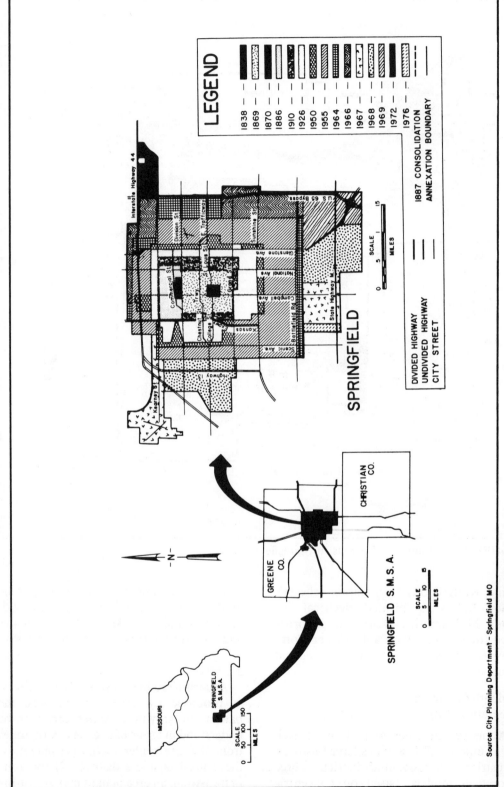

Source: City Planning Department - Springfield MO

FIGURE 12.8.   Annexation History of Springfield.

and warehousing mixed with low-quality multiple-family housing; (3) the zone of independent workers' homes; (4) the zone of better residences; and (5) a commuters' zone, made up of a discontinuous belt of suburban subdivisions and satellite cities. Burgess devised this model of city growth and development in the 1920s when the automobile had as yet made only a small impact on the geography of cities and streetcars and commuter trains were still the chief means of mass transportation.

Homer Hoyt outlined a second model of city structure in the 1930s. Hoyt maintained that residential growth takes place along main transportation routes or along lines of least resistance to form star-shaped cities made up of sectors of high- , medium- , and low-rent neighborhoods.

Chauncy Harris and Edward Ullman devised a third, more complicated model in the late 1940s. According to this model, cities comprise several commercial and industrial nuclei surrounded by geographically discrete residential neighborhoods arranged in a hierarchy of low- , medium- , and high-quality housing. This model of city structure incorporates the string commercial streets, outlying business centers, industrial satellite cities, and bedroom suburbs, which have developed as the two- and three-car family has replaced the one-car family and the individual driver, and the mass-transit commuter. The number of nuclei that form and the operation of localization forces vary greatly from city to city. The larger the city, the more numerous and specialized the nuclei.

Springfield, like most cities, exhibits aspects of the three models of urban land use (Figure 12.8). Although subject to modification because of topography, transportation, and previous land use, concentric zones do exist. The city of Springfield has a recognizable central business district with light manufacturing and wholesaling nearby, albeit the CBD is not completely ringed by these activities. Also, there are recognizable elements of the zone in transition, particularly to the south and east of the

CBD in an area roughly bounded by National Avenue and Grand Street, where older, large, single-family dwellings have been converted to rooming houses and apartments. In the vicinity of Southwest Missouri State University, the demand for student housing has pushed the zone in transition east of National Avenue and south of Grand Street. On the city's periphery, there is a recognizable commuters' zone, but the zones of workers' homes and of better residences are not clearly concentric.

The sector model can be applied especially to the outward movement of residential districts. The high-rent district extending southeast of Park Central Square toward Southwest Missouri State University, and the Country Club addition (southeast of SMSU), beyond the intersection of Glenstone Avenue and Sunshine Street, and into the Brentwood and Southern Hills additions, illustrates a persistent growth trend in the city. Various high-rent areas were established north of the CBD between Springfield and North Springfield in the days of the trolley lines, but the rail lines and switching yards served as barriers to further outward growth of these sectors.

Because the multiple-nuclei model is the most recent and incorporates characteristics of land-use geography associated with automobile transportation, it seems to fit Springfield best. Nearly all the land-use components can be identified except for heavy manufacturing, of which there is none. There are the CBD, and outlying commercial centers such as Commercial Street (North Springfield), the North Town Mall, and the Battlefield Mall. String-street developments are easily recognized on Glenstone Avenue, Campbell Avenue, Sunshine Street, St. Louis Street, and Kearney Street. Light manufacturing districts are well defined in the Jordan Creek and the Upper Jordan Creek districts. Low- , medium- , and high-rent districts are fairly easily identified, and the commuters' zone radiates out along Highways 65, 60, 13, and Interstate 44. There are no industrial suburbs, but Republic, Strafford, Nixa, and Ozark exemplify developing residential suburbs.

NOTES

1. Missouri State Highway Department and Writers' Program of the Works Progress Administration, *Missouri: A Guide to the "Show-Me" State,* American Guide Series (New York: Duell, Sloan and Pearce, 1941), p. 287.

SELECTED REFERENCES

Adams, John Q. "The North Kansas City Urban District." *Economic Geography,* vol. 8, pp. 409–425. 1932.

"Bicentennial: 200 Years in Mid-America." *Star.* Magazine of the *Kansas City Star,* July 4, 1976.

Boehm, Richard G., and William B. Wagner. *Principal Interaction Fields of Missouri Regional Centers.* Columbia: Extension Division, University of Missouri, 1976.

Boyce, Ronald R. *Changing Industrial Patterns in Metropolitan St. Louis and the Demand and Supply of Industrial Land to 1980.* Meramec Basin Research Project, Washington University, St. Louis, 1961.

Boyer, Mary J. *The Old Gravois Coal Diggings.* 1952. Reprint. Cape Girardeau, Mo.: Ramfre Press, 1968.

Brenner, Velma R. "Webster Groves, Missouri: Residential Satellite of St. Louis." Master's thesis, Washington University (St. Louis), 1950.

Brown, S. Theodore. *Frontier Community: Kansas City of 1870.* Columbia: University of Missouri Press, 1963.

Burghardt, Andrew F. "The Location of River Towns in the Central Lowland of the United States." *Annals of the Association of American Geographers,* vol. 49, pp. 305–323. 1959.

Charlton, Thomas L. "The Development of St. Louis as a Southwestern Commercial Depot, 1870–1920." Ph.D. dissertation, University of Texas (Austin), 1969.

Charvat, Arthur. "The Growth and Development of the Kansas City Stockyards: A History, 1871–1947." Master's thesis, University of Missouri (Columbia), 1948.

Collier, James E. *Trends in Manufacturing in*

Missouri. Missouri Economic Study no. 11. Business and Public Administration Center, University of Missouri (Columbia), 1965.

Dodds, Charles. "Description and Analysis of Residential Location Changes Originating in Independence, Missouri." Ph.D. dissertation, University of Kansas (Lawrence), 1975.

Douglas, Harlem P. *The St. Louis Church Survey.* New York: Arno Press and New York Times, 1970.

Dry, Camille N. *Pictorial St. Louis, The Great Metropolis of the Mississippi Valley: A Topographical Survey Drawn in Perspective* A.D. *1875.* Republished. St. Louis: Knight Publishing Company, 1979.

Dunlop, Richard. *St. Louis.* Rev. ed. American Geographical Society Know Your America Program. New York: Nelson, Doubleday, 1963.

Harris, Chauncy D., and Edward L. Ullman. "The Nature of Cities." *Annals of the American Academy of Political and Social Science,* vol. 242, pp. 7–17. 1945.

Hogg, Virginia. "Urban Pattern of Springfield, Missouri." Master's thesis, Washington University (St. Louis), 1934.

Holt, Glen E. "St. Louis's Transitional Decade, 1819–1830." *Missouri Historical Review,* vol. 76, no. 4, pp. 365–381. July 1982.

Howe, Gary C. "The Negro Ghetto: The Dynamics of Its Spatial Distribution in St. Louis: 1940, 1950, 1960." Master's thesis, Southern Illinois University (Carbondale), 1968.

Jenner, J. S. "Areal Expansion of the City of St. Louis." Master's thesis, Washington University (St. Louis), 1939.

Jordan, Robert P. "St. Louis: A New Spirit Soars in Mid-America's Proud Old City," *National Geographic,* vol. 128, pp. 605–641. 1965.

Kansas City Star, Special Centennial Section, September 14, 1980.

Kerschten, Ernest. *Catfish and Crystal.* Garden City, N.Y.: Doubleday, 1960.

Kersten, Earl W., Jr., and D. Reid Ross. "Clayton: A New Metropolitan Focus in the St. Louis Area." *Annals of the Association of American Geographers,* vol. 58, pp. 637–649. 1968.

Koepke, Robert L. "Industry in the Saint Louis Metropolitan Area: A Guidebook for the Industrial Field Trip, St. Louis Meeting, Association of American Geographers." Mimeographed. Edwardsville: Southern Illinois University, 1967.

Korsak, Albert Joseph. "Residential Structure of East St. Louis, Illinois." Master's thesis, University of Illinois, 1959.

Lusk, Charles B. "The Location of Manufacturing Establishments in the Kansas City Metropolitan Area." Master's thesis, University of Oklahoma, 1967.

Midwest Research Institute. *Economic Development of the Kansas City Metropolitan Area.* Kansas City: Midwest Research Institute, 1961.

Mills, Anna C. "An Historical Interpretation of the Geography of Nuclei of St. Louis." Master's thesis, Washington University (St. Louis), 1933.

Missouri Directory of Manufacturing, Mining, Industrial Services, Industrial Supplies, 1980. St. Louis: Informative Data Co., 1980.

Missouri State Highway Department and Writers' Program of the Works Progress Administration. *Missouri: A Guide to the "Show-Me" State.* American Guide Series. New York: Duell, Sloan and Pearce, 1941.

Rafferty, Milton D. "Springfield's Golden Age of Mass Transportation." *Springfield Magazine,* vol. 3, nos. 10–11. March–April 1982.

Riley, Marianna. "The Rise and Fall . . . of Urban Mass Transit." *Midwest Motorist,* vol. 46, pp. 3–7. December 1968.

St. Joseph Area Transportation Study. St. Joseph, Mo.: Metropolitan Planning Commission of Greater St. Joseph and Buchanan County and the Missouri State Highway Commission, 1972.

St. Joseph–Buchanan County, Missouri Business District Plans. Comprehensive Plan. St. Joseph, Mo.: Department of Zoning and Planning, Greater St. Joseph and Buchanan County, 1972.

Thomas, Lewis F. "Decline of St. Louis as Midwest Metropolis." *Economic Geography,* vol. 25, pp. 118–127. 1949.

———. "A Geographic Study of Greene County, Missouri." Master's thesis, University of Missouri (Columbia), 1917.

———. *The Localization of Business Activities in Metropolitan St. Louis.* Washington University Studies, Social and Political Sciences, n.s. no. 1. St. Louis, 1927.

Thomas, Tracy, and Walt Bodine. *Right Here in River City: A Portrait of Kansas City.* New York: Doubleday and Company, Inc., 1976.

Troen, Selwyn K., and Glen E. Holt, eds. *St. Louis.* New York: New Viewpoints, 1977.

CHAPTER 13

THE GEOGRAPHIC REGIONS

Missouri's geographic regions are based mainly on physical features—especially relief and slope—but land use, crop production, numbers of livestock, and population density are also criteria. In this description of Missouri's regions additional elements of human geography are included. The data—population, crop production, numbers of livestock—are calculated on the basis of the percentage of total area of a given county that lies within a given region.

Four major sections of Missouri are recognized: the Ozark Upland, the Western Plains, the Northern (glaciated) Plains, and the Southeast Lowlands (Figure 1.1, page 2, and Figure 13.1). Variations within each of these large sections, or provinces, are generally more striking than the differences among their subdivisions, or regions.

The four provinces differ greatly in topography, soils, land use, systems of agriculture, standards of living, and degree of urbanization. Contrasts between the Ozarks on the one hand and each of the plains areas on the other are greater than the differences among the plains provinces, particularly between the Northern Plains and the Western Plains. Compared to the Ozarks each of the other provinces is flatter, its soils more productive, and its land better adapted to agriculture. In these aspects,

the Northern Plains and the Southeast Lowlands are superior to the Western Plains.

The Northern Plains province can be broadly distinguished from adjacent provinces on the occurrence of glacial till and loess. Most of the other characteristic features (soils, terrain, agriculture, for example) are greatly influenced by glacial features. The dominantly alluvial material of the Southeast Lowlands province, together with its longer growing season (200 or more frost-free days) and distinctive agriculture, forms the chief basis for its differentiation from the upland provinces. Likewise, dissection and steep slopes, poor soils, and distinctive economies set the Ozarks apart from the plains sections. The Western Plains province is probably the least distinctive, but its topography still differs from that of the adjacent provinces.

The boundaries of the provinces also serve as regional boundaries. The southern boundary of the Northern Plains in the east is the approximate southern limit of glacial till, whereas the southern boundary of the western portion of the Northern Plains is at the southern extent of deep loess (8 ft [243.8 cm] or more). The loess extends as a thin mantle into the Ozarks and Western Plains, but it is not deep enough to affect the topography.

The boundary of the Ozark province is

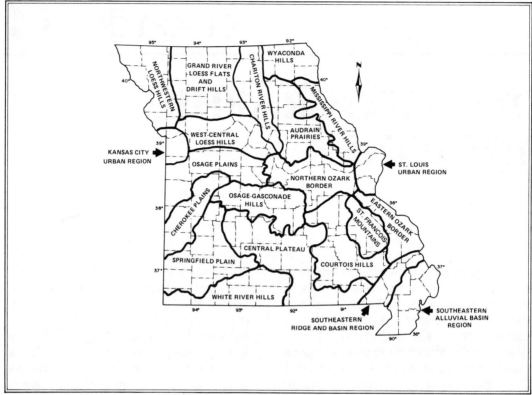

FIGURE 13.1. Geographic Regions of Missouri.

relatively distinct throughout its length. It is most obvious in the southeast where the Ozark Escarpment stands clearly above the alluvial lowland. Other portions of the boundary are less sharply distinguished. In the vicinity of St. Louis, many Ozark features (such as karst terrain, entrenched streams) are present; and on the western border, the Springfield Plain lies between the rugged interior Ozarks and the Western Plains province. The western boundary has traditionally been placed at the contact between Mississippian and Pennsylvanian period rocks, but some students of Ozark landforms place the western boundary at the topographically prominent Eureka Springs (Burlington) Escarpment, thereby excluding the Springfield Plain from the Ozarks. However, local usage places the Springfield Plain within the Ozarks.

REGIONS OF THE NORTHERN PLAINS

The *Northwestern Loess Hills,* the westernmost subdivision of the Northern Plains province, encompass approximately 3,600 sq miles (9,324 km²), placing it seventh in size among Missouri's geographic regions. The region includes the counties of Atchison, Nodaway, Holt, Andrew, Buchanan, Platte, and small portions of adjacent counties. Its population, based on the 1980 census estimates, is calculated at 217,692, a decrease of 14,531 from the 1970 population.

The Northwestern Loess Hills have the deepest loess soils in the state. The upland is rolling, particularly along the "breaks" of the Missouri River, but the deep, porous soils tend to reduce the effects of steep slopes. The agricultural land is rivaled only by the fertile lands of the Southeast Lowlands. The region includes some of the state's highest values of land and the greatest value of crops per acre. The landscape is dominated by agriculture with a very high percentage of land in crops. Corn normally comprises about two-fifths of the cropland and soybeans account for another 25 percent. Wheat and grain sorghums are also important. The loess soils are excellent for plantings of deciduous fruits, particularly apples. Some apple orchards persist, but fruit growing is much reduced from former times.

Atchison and Nodaway counties are normally among the top five counties in the state in corn production. Relatively little corn, however, is marketed, as it is used primarily as livestock feed. Soybean production is increasing in importance all across northern Missouri and is challenging corn as the major crop. Already the number-one cash crop north of the Missouri River, soybeans are fast becoming a leader in crop acreage. A small amount of truck farming is done along the Missouri River bottomlands, primarily for sale in the larger metropolitan areas.

The agricultural economy focuses on meat production—primarily beef and pork. Feeder hogs and cattle are the main livestock; the ratio of the former to the latter is about 1.3. The 316,730 head of cattle in 1980 was 1.5 times the human population, whereas hogs numbered 424,290. The combined number of cattle and hogs exceeds the human population nearly 4 times. The feedlots and fields of northwest Missouri drain to the Missouri River by way of the Nishnabotna, Platte, and One Hundred and Two rivers and their tributaries. All of these streams carry much more fecal waste than the streams of any other region of the state.

About 1 percent of the nation's bright burley tobacco is grown in Missouri, mainly in Platte and Buchanan counties. There are three tobacco warehouses in Weston where the tobacco, which has cured through the fall months in specially ventilated barns, is brought to be auctioned during the late fall and winter months. In 1979, tobacco valued at $10 million sold at the three warehouses.

Tobacco growing, from planting to stripping and curing, requires tedious labor mostly by hand. Yields often run between 2,500 lbs (1,135 kg) and 3,500 lbs (1,583 kg) per acre (.405 ha), which at 1979 prices might gross $4,000 on the average. But after paying the bills, a farmer most likely will net 30 to 50 percent of that figure.

Historically, northern Missouri has been a major supplier of labor for the state's large metropolitan centers. Kansas City and St. Joseph are the chief industrial cities and the major trade centers for the Northwestern Loess Hills region. Interstate 29, which runs north-south, links the farms and towns of the region with these two large Missouri cities. There is a well-developed railroad network to haul the huge cargoes of grain and meat and to bring in the necessary machinery, fertilizer, and farm supplies. The rail lines tend to follow the river valleys—the Burlington Northern Railroad in the valleys of the Missouri, Nishnabotna, Tarkio, and Nodaway rivers; the Chicago and North Western in the One Hundred and Two and Platte valleys.

The towns of the Northwestern Loess Hills have been affected by highway transportation in several ways. Some towns formerly outside reasonable commuting distance have been brought into range by new or improved highways. Small villages and towns, however, have suffered economic stagnation as the rural population has declined and the remaining residents have bypassed the small places to shop in St. Joseph and Kansas City. Very often the county seat, and possibly one other larger town, captures most of the retail and service trade of the county. For example, Maryville is by far the dominant retail center in Nodaway County. Operating as a service

PHOTO 13.1.   Field of Corn in Early Summer. Courtesy Missouri Department of Agriculture.

center and retail outlet, Maryville's influence covers the entire county. Moreover, since Maryville is the site of Northwest Missouri State University, the town provides many urban services not offered by the rural villages in Nodaway County.

The decline in the number of persons engaged in agriculture, the loss of professional people (doctors, dentists, lawyers), and the increase in the average age of the population are all indications of the plight of the small village, but none is so striking to the visitor as the extent of business abandonment. The cultural landscape of small agricultural towns all across Missouri is much the same. A windshield survey would show the familiar scene of paint-peeled signs and gaping windows of abandoned banks, restaurants, movie theatres, service stations, drugstores, clothing stores, barber shops, newspapers, hotels, lumberyards, railroad depots, high schools, and doctors' and lawyers' offices.

Many of the residents of hamlets and villages are reluctant to leave even when their standard of living must suffer. Because of close social and family ties, they are willing to maintain several jobs in order to earn a living. An intensive study of Nodaway County in the early 1970s found one rural villager engaged in the sale of grave monuments, used cars, salvaged auto parts, and real estate, while serving as a carpenter, electrician, concrete finisher, bricklayer, and grave digger. Another owned and operated a service station, general store, café, feed store, and auto garage all under one roof.

Aside from Kansas City and St. Joseph, the major trading center of the Northwestern Loess Hills is Maryville. The town was selected for the seat of newly organized Nodaway County in 1845 and named in honor of Mary Graham, the wife of one

PHOTO 13.2. Tobacco Drying in a Tobacco Barn at Weston, Platte County. Courtesy Walker—Missouri Division of Tourism.

of the town's leaders for many years. The State Normal School (now Northwest Missouri State University) was founded in 1905. The university is the single most important employer in Maryville. Other major employers include Riegle Textile Corporation (baby diapers) with 150 employees, Union Carbide (flashlight batteries) with 100, and Uniroyal Incorporated (rubber hose), with 190.

All the other towns in the region have populations of less than 3,000. Most of these towns have experienced little population change for the past ninety years. Nevertheless, as with most farm trade centers, there has been much migration to and from these towns. As the younger people have moved away to seek education and jobs in larger places, they have been replaced by farmers and returnees seeking to retire in their home communities.

Savannah, Tarkio, Plattsburg, and Mound City have had remarkably stable populations. Savannah is the seat of Andrew County. On the west side of town is an extensive, well-platted residential section, which was developed about 1911 by St. Joseph commuters. Since about 1960 the growth of commuter population in Savannah has contributed to an upturn in the town's growth. There is little manufacturing employment in the town even today.

Plattsburg is a typical county seat, with low, flat-roofed commercial buildings forming a square around the Clinton County courthouse. Plattsburg profited as the locale of the U.S. Land Office (1843–1859). In this office the government lands in northwest Missouri were sold and squatters' claims filed. Only a little manufacturing employment supplements the main service and trade functions of the town.

Mound City, the largest town in Holt County, has survived four fires and many floods on Davis Creek. The name of the town is derived from a low hill or mound on which it was founded in 1840. The largest manufacturer in the town is the weekly newspaper, which employs approximately ten people.

Northwest Missouri is rich in tourist and recreational attractions. In St. Joseph, they include the Pony Express Stables, the St. Joseph Museum, the Patee House Museum, the Albrecht Art Museum, the scenic drive along Lovers' Lane (immortalized by poet Eugene Field), and the Hall Street and Roubidoux Row historic districts. Big Lake State Park, Squaw Creek National Wildlife Area, and Honey Creek Wildlife Area are popular with outdoor enthusiasts. The beauty of windblown loess bluffs and fertile plains makes this a land to be seen and enjoyed.

The *Grand River region* consists of some 5,856 sq miles (15,167 km²) of loess flatlands and glacial drift hills. Although the soils and terrain support prosperous farms, it is a fairly sparsely settled section of the state. Population densities are lower only in the interior Ozarks. The population, which has declined steadily for the past eighty years or more, increased slightly to 106,747 by the 1980 census.

The land is the chief resource and the economy predominantly agricultural. Corn, the chief crop, occupies slightly less than a third of the cultivated land, but it is closely rivaled by soybeans. Most of the corn and grain sorghums are fed to hogs and cattle. The Grand River basin is truly feeder cattle country—the combined number of cattle and hogs approaches 2 million, more than seventeen times the number of human inhabitants. Land values are among the highest in the state and the value of crops per acre is nearly twice that of the poorer parts of the Ozark province.

The Grand River country is made up of hamlets, villages, and small towns. There are a half-dozen towns, mainly county seats, which have had stable populations over the past several decades. Bethany, the seat of Harrison County, derives its principal

income from agricultural trade and services. Settled on an upland prairie in 1840, Bethany soon became the leading trading town for surrounding farms. Its long-standing function as a livestock and grain market is still important. Grain is shipped over the Burlington Northern Railroad, but most livestock is trucked to slaughtering plants. The largest manufacturing plant is the Lambert Manufacturing Company (baseball caps) with 156 employees. Cameron was platted in 1855. Its leading employer is the Ithaca Gun Company (wood gun stocks) with 132 employees. Maysville, in DeKalb County, has experienced only minor fluctuations in population over the past three-quarters of a century. The largest employer is the Lambert Manufacturing Company (head gear) with 100 employees. Similar trade and service centers that have experienced little population change since 1900 include Unionville, Princeton, Trenton, Kingston, and Gallatin. These towns are typical of northern Missouri. Brick business buildings are built around a courthouse square or along business streets related to the railroad; and one or two clusters of businesses, such as service stations, cafés, motels, and farm implement dealers are situated along state or federal highways. The city water tower and cylindrical-tube grain elevators are the most prominent landmarks.

Chillicothe, the largest town in the Grand River country, was platted in 1837 and named for Chillicothe, Ohio. It became the seat of Livingson County in 1839, but remained a small place until the completion of the Hannibal and St. Joseph Railroad in 1859, which brought settlers and economic development to the area. In addition to conducting a prosperous business in retailing and services for residents of surrounding farms and small towns, Chillicothe has attracted a number of industries.

Visitors to the Grand River country find a surprising number of recreational and historical attractions. They include the very popular Crowder State Park, Wallace State Park, the Amish Farms near Jamesport,

PHOTO 13.3. Quail Hunting near Breckenridge, Caldwell County. Courtesy Walker—Missouri Division of Tourism.

the Mormon Shrine near Gallatin, and a half-dozen large community lakes.

The *Chariton River Hills* comprise the most rugged region of the Northern Plains. The steep-sided and closely spaced hills contrast sharply with the Grand River country to the west and the flat Audrain Prairies on the east. The Chariton River Hills encompass 2,723 sq miles (7,053 km²) with a population of 100,468 as of 1980. This section is one of the most sparsely populated of the state.

Because the slopes are steep, most of the loess has been removed and the soils are correspondingly less fertile, making much of the area unsuited for cultivation. In some areas half to two-thirds of the land produces timber, mainly oak. Half or more of the open land produces forage

crops or pasture, and the sale of livestock provides 80 to 90 percent of farm income. Of the cultivated acres, corn and soybeans each comprise a fourth, but in a given year one may exceed the other, depending on weather conditions. As in the remainder of the Northern Plains province, cattle and hogs are the chief animals raised, but unlike in other sections, there are more cattle than hogs. The area is better suited to forage crops, and the raising of stocker and feeder cattle and the production of dairy cattle are more important than in other parts of northern Missouri. Sullivan, Linn, and Adair counties are ranked second as a dairy area after the Springfield vicinity. More sheep are raised in the northern section of the Chariton River Hills than in any other section of Missouri. Schuyler County produces more than twice the number of sheep than any other Missouri county.

Most of the towns in the Chariton River Hills have less than 2,000 population. Kirksville, Macon, and Moberly are situated on the upland to the east of the hilly belt, and on the western flank of the hills are smaller trade towns—Brookfield and Marceline. Columbia serves as the large shopping town for the southern half of the region, whereas Kirksville is the major retail and service center for the residents of the northern part.

Kirksville, seat of Adair County and home of Missouri's first normal school for teacher training, is one of the largest towns in northeastern Missouri. The town was founded in 1841 when Adair County was formed. Coal mining was of some importance until about 1930, when the larger mines located to the west in Putnam and Sullivan counties were closed because of low prices and reduced demand. Northeast Missouri State University is the chief employer in Kirksville. There are also a half dozen manufacturing plants that employ more than 100 workers. The larger plants are Florsheim Shoe Company with 570 employees; Burroughs Corporation (business forms), 325 employees; Donaldson Company Incorporated (engine air cleaners), 184; Hollister Incorporated (plastic hospital supplies), 550; Lambert Manufacturing Company (work gloves), 107; and McGraw-Edison Company (electrical appliances), 500.

Macon, an important farm service and trading center, is located between two quite different geographical regions—the Chariton River Hills and the Audrain Prairies. Livestock sales at the barn draw livestock from surrounding farms and buyers from an even larger area. The largest manufacturing employer is Banquet Foods Corporation with 448 employees, producers of frozen foods and frozen prepared dinners and pies. Two other manufacturing plants employ more than 100 people: the McGraw-Edison Company (electrical appliances) with 443 employees and Peabody Coal Com-

pany's Bee Veer Mine with 155 employees, where bituminous coal is mined.

Columbia, one of several medium-sized cities in central Missouri that historically shared centralized functions for surrounding farms and communities, is beginning to gain ascendency over its competitors. The construction of Interstate 70 as the mid-state transportation corridor between St. Louis and Kansas City extended Columbia's trade hinterland, drawing business from a larger area of farms and small towns. Because of competition among the several central Missouri cities—Columbia, Jefferson City, Moberly, Fulton, and Sedalia—none could gain overall leadership and grow to be the dominant city of productive and well-populated central Missouri. Since about 1960 Columbia has begun to move ahead of the others.

Columbia, now a standard metropolitan statistical area, is the site of the main campus of the University of Missouri and two other colleges. The university professional schools, professional meetings, and the University of Missouri Tiger football and basketball teams attract many visitors to the city. It is the seat of Boone County and a popular shopping town. Although Columbia is primarily a university town, there is some manufacturing. The largest manufacturing employers are American Press, Minnesota Mining and Manufacturing Corporation, Ribeck Pipe and Steel, and Kelly Press.

The Chariton River country offers a variety of recreation attractions. Fishing for catfish on the Chariton River and its tributaries is considered good. Thomas Hill Lake, one of the largest impoundments in northern Missouri, provides opportunity for fishing, camping, and water sports. Thousand Hills State Park, located 4 miles (6.436 km) west of Kirksville, has rental cabins, campgrounds, and a large lake and swimming beach. Finger Lakes State Park, just north of Columbia, offers similar attractions.

The *Audrain Prairies region* consists of the wide, flat remnants of the upland plain

PHOTO 13.4. Student Union Building at the University of Missouri, Columbia. Courtesy Walker—Missouri Division of Tourism.

lying in the wedge of territory along the Mississippi-Missouri-Chariton drainage divide. To the east, south, west, and north, the stream valleys are deeper and slopes steeper. The change in landscape is most striking in the west, and the boundary is the most distinct there. Local relief is usually less than 100 ft (30.4 m) and the broad uplands are covered with loess, the basis for the region's fertile soils.

The region, 3,486 sq miles (9,029 km²) in area, contained 140,658 people in 1980. This region typifies the Corn Belt landscape perhaps better than any of Missouri's other regions. The towns are laid out uniformly with grid-pattern streets, red-brick business buildings focusing on a courthouse square

or along a railroad right-of-way, and white one- and two-story frame houses set back on tree-shaded lawns. Contemporary bungalows and ranch-style homes occupy small new subdivisions on the outskirts. The countryside is a larger grid pattern of 40-acre (16-hectare), 80-acre (32-hectare), and 160-acre (64.8-hectare) fields bordered by roads on the mile (1.6 km) line, following the U.S. Land Survey. Farmsteads are laid out alongside section-line roads and typically include a wood-frame, two-story house—clapboard sided, and well painted. Outbuildings include a loft barn, either red or white, two to four silos or Harvestors, and a half dozen to a dozen outbuildings for the storage and repair of machinery and the housing of grain, feed, and livestock. Many of the houses were built in the great development period following the Civil War and reflect the elegant Victorian, gingerbread, and steamboat Gothic styles of the period. From time to time one may see the substantial, severe but classic federal-style house that was popular with well-to-do antebellum settlers.

The economy rests on meat production—cattle and hogs—with emphasis on the latter. The feeder hog and cattle industry is supported by high per acre yields of high-calorie feeds, especially corn. Soybean production is more important here and two-fifths of the cultivated land is planted in this legume crop.

Although there are no large towns in this section of Missouri, several medium-sized towns are prosperous trade centers. Four county-seat towns—Fulton, Mexico, Paris, Edina—lie from south to north along Missouri Highway 15 in the middle of the Audrain Prairies region. Columbia, Moberly, and Kirksville lie on the western border near the Chariton River country.

Fulton, the seat of Calloway County, is built about a public square, occupied by a red-brick and limestone courthouse. The State Lunatic Asylum opened there in 1849, the first hospital for mental patients west of the Mississippi River. Another longtime employer of Fulton residents is the

State School for the Deaf, which was founded in 1851. Westminster College was founded in 1849 under the auspices of the Presbyterian Church. In 1946, on the campus of Westminster College, Prime Minister Winston Churchill delivered the famous "Iron Curtain" address. Last among the institutional employers is William Woods College, a junior college for girls. There are more than a dozen small manufacturing plants in Fulton and one large manufacturer—Harbison-Walker Company—which employs more than 330 workers in its three plants.

Mexico, located in the midst of what was known as the Salt River settlements, was settled by southerners. Audrain County was founded in 1836 and Mexico was laid out as the county seat in 1837. By the time of the Civil War, Mexico had grown into a sizable county seat town. Most of the residents wished to preserve the Union, but when forced to choose sides, they supported the Confederacy. Because of activity of Confederate recruiters and bushwhacking incidents, federal troops were quartered in the town.

Mexico is in the heart of Little Dixie, a region characterized by southern sympathies, slavery, and Democratic politics. There, in the northern part of the state bordering the Missouri River, a rural aristocracy flourished. The love of fine horses was a tradition among the people and racetracks were laid out even before the Civil War. By the 1890s, George and William Lee and other Mexico horsemen had established well-equipped stables. Trotting and pacing races became a part of the Mexico fair, and the saddle-horse auctions became traditional in the spring and fall.

About the turn of the century, an important deposit of fireclay was discovered directly under the town. Clay refractories were established and today Mexico is the center of one of the most important fireclay manufacturing districts in the United States. Many of the city's workers find employment in the clay refractories or on one of the three railroads—the Gulf, Mobile, and

Ohio; the Norfolk and Western; and the Burlington Northern. Major manufacturing employers are A. P. Green Refractories (1,200 employees), Kaiser Refractories (604), and Florsheim Shoe Company (338).

Paris, a farm trade and service center, was founded as the seat of Monroe County in 1831. Very soon the area was heavily settled by families from Kentucky and Tennessee. The region became part of Missouri's "South up North"—Little Dixie. Breeding of saddle horses, draft horses, and mules became important. The opening of the Santa Fe trade created a ready market for mules, and Missouri mules were considered the best for stamina and intelligence. Following the Civil War, a larger market for mules was created as cotton growing spread into the Mississippi valley and beyond to Arkansas, Louisiana, and eastern Texas. Buyers from the cotton country traveled to Missouri's bluegrass country and drove thousands of mules south to the cotton country.

Paris is primarily a farm market and service center. The livestock sales pavilion, grain elevators, feed stores, farm implement dealers, and automobile and truck agencies are important businesses. Only a small number of people are employed by eight or nine small plants of such diverse commodities as wood fixtures, boats, anhydrous ammonia, and custom slaughtering. The largest plant—American Cyanamid Company—produces nitrogen fertilizers, a product liberally applied to the lush fields of corn in the region.

Shelbyville, seat of Shelby County, and Edina, seat of Knox County, do not have important manufacturing plants. Their largest plants employ less than fifty people and are mainly repair shops and machine shops for farm equipment service or small sand-, gravel-, or stone-quarrying operations for local use.

Centralia, located on the southwestern fringe of the Audrain Prairie, is a manufacturing town based on one industry. By far the largest employer is the A. B. Chance Company, manufacturer of telephone and electrical line supplies and hardware. The 1980 *Missouri Directory of Manufacturing* lists 2,241 employees in the company's two plants. Workers are engaged in fabricating pole-line hardware and helical-coil products for utility construction, anchors for petroleum-communications and electrical-utility industries, and hand tools for the electric-utility industry. The half-dozen other manufacturing plants in Centralia employ about 115 people.

Centralia, so named because it was half-

way between St. Louis and Ottumwa, Iowa, was founded in 1859 when the North Missouri Railroad reached that point. It was at Centralia, in September 1864, that eighty Confederate guerrillas under the command of "Bloody" Bill Anderson robbed and burned a North Missouri passenger train and murdered twenty-three or twenty-four unarmed Union soldiers who were on the train.

The Audrain Prairies region is farm country; its recreational and cultural at-

PHOTO 13.5.   A. B. Chance Company Engineering Research Laboratory in Centralia. The Plant Produces Electric Power Tools, Hardware, and Equipment. Courtesy A. B. Chance Company.

tractions are not well known. Nevertheless, there are a number of important sites that local residents use. At Mark Twain State Park is the two-room cabin where Sam Clemens was born in 1835. Rental cabins, nature trails, picnicking, and camping are available. Near the park, 19,000-acre (7,695-hectare) Mark Twain Lake is the largest lake in northern Missouri as of 1982. The Audrain County Museum at Mexico, one of the best of its kind, features memorabilia of the champion saddle horses grown in the area. One of Missouri's few remaining covered bridges—Union Bridge—is located in Paris just three blocks north of the courthouse on Salt River. It was constructed in 1857 of braced arches of quarter-sawed oak. At Bethel there are some thirty buildings built by the successful communal colony Dr. William Keil established in 1844. Public hunting and fishing are available at wildlife areas—Deer Ridge, Redman, Hunnewell, Marshall Diggs, and Wellsville. Nineteenth-century historic homes, many built prior to the Civil War, reflect a degree of elegant living not found in most other parts of Missouri. The grain fields and wooded creeks provide excellent habitat for pheasant, quail, and deer.

The *Mississippi River Hills region* is comprised of the gently rolling to steep-bluffed land along the margins of the Missouri till plain bordering the Mississippi River. Near the Mississippi, relief is 200 ft (60.9 m) to 300 ft (91.44 m), and at one locale it reaches a maximum of 520 ft (156 m). The relief and degree of slope decrease toward the west, gradually merging with the Audrain Prairies. The alluvial plain of the Mississippi is mainly on the Illinois side, but fairly wide bands of alluvium extend up the larger tributary streams, namely the Fabius, North, and Salt rivers.

With 2,738 sq miles (7,091 km²) and a population of 116,385, the density is 43 people per sq mile (2.59 km²), well below Missouri's average density of 70. The region gained moderately in population during the 1970s due to growth of some of the larger towns. Corn, soybeans, and wheat

account for 80 percent of the cultivated acreage. Unlike any other region of Missouri, the number of hogs raised is more than twice the number of cattle, which is in keeping with the general emphasis on hogs in the eastern Corn Belt.

The most important towns in the region are located along U.S. 61—Bowling Green, New London, Hannibal, Palmyra, and Canton. Hannibal, with a population of 18,811, is the largest. Abraham Bird of New Madrid acquired the site of Hannibal in 1818 in exchange for property destroyed by the New Madrid earthquake of 1811. The following year, a group of land speculators platted a town at the mouth of Bear Creek. The business of the town focused on shipping and receiving goods at the waterfront. Flatboats loaded with grain and hemp were tied up at the waterfront, hogs fattened in the back country were loaded on boats for shipment down-river, and logs were floated down from Wisconsin and Minnesota and converted into boards. Prior to the Civil War, a pork-packing plant was built; tobacco factories, flour mills, and sawmills also flourished.[1]

In 1856 construction of the Hannibal and St. Joseph Railroad began, and three years later it was completed across the state. New business and manufacturing were attracted to Hannibal. In 1871, the Hannibal Bridge was completed—the second bridge across the Mississippi River to touch Missouri shores. As the lumber boom wound down and flour mills closed, new industries were established. The towering bluffs of Burlington limestone attracted one of the largest cement manufacturing plants in the nation.

A Currier and Ives print of Hannibal in 1869 shows the town located on a narrow floodplain near the water's edge. Business houses were built along Main Street paralleling the river and along Broadway, which extends westward. When railroads were built to the city, a substantial industrial district grew up south of the business district. Extending across the remaining bottoms and up the lower slopes of surround-

PHOTO 13.6.   Packet Boat at Hannibal. Courtesy Walker—Missouri Division of Tourism.

ing hills are modest frame houses. Westward on the hillsides and perched on the tops of hills are the homes of Hannibal's original well-to-do families. On the outer edges near the highway bypasses are post–World War II subdivisions of low, contemporary-style houses. The Black population, which once comprised 40 percent of the total, now amounts to only a few hundred, residing near the south-side industrial area.

Although Hannibal is most famous as the locale for Mark Twain's tales of Tom Sawyer and Huck Finn, its industries and businesses serve a large and growing market area in northeastern Missouri and western Illinois. Major manufacturing employers are Atlantic Building Systems, Huntington Rubber Company, William Underwood Company, and Watlow Industries, Incorporated.

Bowling Green, the seat of Pike County, was platted in 1826 and named for the Kentucky home of many of the town's early residents. The courthouse lawn is graced by a sculpture of the U.S. House of Representatives. Bowling Green is in the heart of Little Dixie. Today, Bowling Green is a farm trade center with less than a dozen small manufacturing plants. The largest is Bridal Originals, Incorporated, where about 100 workers manufacture bridal gowns.

Monroe City is a product of the pre–Civil War railroad-building era. Platted in 1857 as a shipping point on the Hannibal and St. Joseph Railroad, it developed as a grain and livestock market for settlers who planted the surrounding prairie in bluegrass and began raising horses. The poultry industry was promoted by the Henderson Produce Company around the turn of the century. Vestiges of the horse farm and foxhounds era remain, but the main support of the town stems from trade and service with surrounding grain, poultry, and livestock farms. This trade is supple-

PHOTO 13.7. Mark Twain Home and Museum in Hannibal. Courtesy Walker—Missouri Division of Tourism.

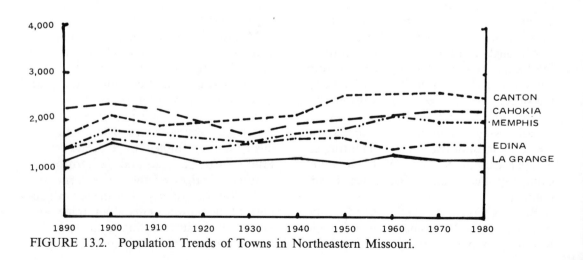

FIGURE 13.2. Population Trends of Towns in Northeastern Missouri.

mented by several small manufacturing plants producing plastic molds, tools and dies, and processed poultry and eggs.

Palmyra, the seat of Marion County, was platted in 1819 around a large spring in the middle of the village. The agricultural economic base of Palmyra is reflected in the small manufacturing plants that produce materials for local farms. The largest plant, American Cyanamid Company, employs about 100 workers in the manufacture of nitrogen fertilizers.

The largest town between Hannibal and St. Louis, along the Mississippi River, is Louisiana. One of the earliest settlements in Missouri north of St. Louis, Louisiana has always been a stable commercial town. Two fairly large manufacturers are located there. Hercules Incorporated–Missouri Chemical Works, a manufacturer of agricultural chemicals and fertilizer, is the largest (409 workers). Louisiana Plastics Incorporated (215 workers), manufactures plastic containers.

Recreational and cultural attractions in the region are plentiful. The Mississippi River provides abundant opportunities for boating, fishing, and camping. The most important tourist attractions are in Hannibal where there are numerous reminders of Mark Twain. The historic district on the waterfront includes the boyhood home of Sam Clemens (208 Hill Street), the adjacent Mark Twain Museum, the Becky Thatcher House, and Grant's Drug Store. More reminders of Twain are nearby at Cardiff Hill. At its foot are statues of Tom Sawyer and Huck Finn, and at the crest stands a lighthouse built in 1935 on the hundredth anniversary of Twain's birth. South of town is Mark Twain Cave, Missouri's oldest commercially used cave, which is open for tours year-round. Also south of town is the Clemens Amphitheatre, where an outdoor pageant, *The Life and Times of Mark Twain,* is presented during the summer months. Elsewhere in the city there are a number of restored old homes, such as the Garth

Woodside Mansion, Rockcliffe Mansion, and Stonecraft House.

The *Wyaconda Hills,* encompassing 2,023 sq miles (5,240 km²) comprise one of the smallest geographic regions in the state. The region includes all of Clark and Scotland counties and parts of Lewis, Knox, Adair, and Schuyler counties. Its population of 60,180, the smallest among Missouri's regions, averages 21 persons per sq mile, a density only slightly greater than that of the rugged sections of the Ozark Uplands.

Physically the Wyaconda Hills region shares the qualities of adjacent regions. Level lands with dark, loam-textured prairie soils occupy elongate, tabular divides similar to those of the Audrain Prairies. A road map illustrates the strikingly parallel southeast-trending valleys. They have relatively wide alluvial floors as do the rivers of the Mississippi River Hills. When viewed on aerial photographs the land-use pattern is strikingly linear—long strips of checkerboard-patterned, bottomland corn-and-soybean fields separated by a less uniform texture of woodland and pasture.

Soybeans and corn are the chief crops; hogs and cattle are the chief livestock. The combined number of cattle and hogs is more than nine times the number of human inhabitants, one of the highest ratios of animals to people in the state.

There are no large towns in the region; the closest large-town trade centers are out of state at Keokuk, Iowa, and Quincy, Illinois. Canton, the oldest town (founded in 1830) in Lewis County, is the site of Culver-Stockton College, a small liberal arts school. The town has always served primarily as a farm trade center. The 1980 *Missouri Directory of Manufacturing* lists only five manufacturers, the largest of which employs 30 people. La Grange, at the confluence of the Wyaconda and Mississippi rivers, was platted in 1830. As with many river towns, the business district faces the river and the residential section spreads back across the adjacent hills. The largest employer is the Gardner Denver Company plant, manufacturer of mining equipment, oil-drilling equipment, and air tools. Cahokia, the seat of Clark County, has no large manufacturing plants; the town relies on service and trade generated from surrounding farms. Memphis has only one important manufacturing plant, the National Garment Company, which employs 113 workers. The half-dozen other plants employ less than 50 people and are mainly repair shops, machine shops, or small sand-, gravel-, or stone-quarrying operations for local use.

Recreation and cultural attractions in extreme northeastern Missouri focus on the Mississippi River and the state parks. Past and present merge gracefully in this part of the state, with nineteenth-century homes overlooking the modern locks and dams that make river navigation possible. The river bluffs provide magnificent panoramic views of the river, the barge traffic, and the bordering belts of forested hills. At Wakonda State Park, just south of Canton, there are cabins, campgrounds, and boating, swimming, and fishing on any of the several lakes. Near the Iowa-Missouri border the Battle of Athens State Park is located, the site of the northernmost Civil War battle fought in the state. Boating, fishing, hiking, and camping are available on the 355-acre (143.7-hectare) grounds.

The *West-Central Loess Hills* encompass the hilly deep-loess belt bordering the Missouri River between Boone County and the Kansas City metropolitan area. Included in the region are most of Ray, Lafayette, Saline, Carroll, Howard, and Cooper counties and small parts of Boone and Moniteau counties. The region covers 3,486 sq miles (9,029 km²) with a population of 98,573. During the 1970s the region increased in population by 4,500, mainly because of population growth in towns within commuting distance of Kansas City.

The region consists of the Missouri River floodplain and the rolling, loess hills extending 5 miles (8.04 km) to 25 miles (40.22 km) from the plain on either side.

The limits of the region both north and south correspond to the deepest and most complete coverage of loess. The hills stand 200 ft (60.96 m) to 300 ft (91.44 m) above the Missouri River floodplain, which attains its maximum width in this section, averaging between 5 miles (8.04 km) and 10 miles (16.09 km).

This region is Missouri's second-ranking agricultural region in value of crops and livestock. Corn occupies nearly two-fifths of the cultivated acreage, soybeans another fourth, and wheat about one-tenth. Milo (grain sorghum) and oats are also widely grown. The value of crops per acre (.405 ha) corresponds closely to that in the remainder of northern Missouri, but the main source of income is from the sale of hogs and cattle from feedlots.

The location of trade centers—hamlets, villages, towns, and cities—is influenced by transportation and major technological changes. Towns such as Boonville, Franklin, Arrow Rock, Glasgow, and Lexington were founded on the banks of the Missouri River to take advantage of favorable sites for wharfage or crossing or to command a productive hinterland. Towns such as Higginsville, Marshall, Richmond, Carrollton, and Fayette owe their prosperity to a later time when railroads brought manufacturing, trade, new settlers, and modern technology. Dozens of small hamlets and villages were founded during the time when the population was mainly engaged in agriculture and was dispersed throughout the countryside. Because the principal transportation beyond the railroad was either horseback, wagon, or shank's mare, the centers for essential services were necessarily close spaced. So many small towns were founded throughout Missouri during the 1850–1910 railroad construction era that very few have been founded since.

Since then, the percentage of population engaged in agriculture has declined continuously. A second significant change has been in transportation. *Time distance* is a convenient term to use as a measure of the distance a person travels in one hour. On foot, people can travel 4 miles (6.43 km) or 5 miles (8.04 km), on horseback 10 (16.09 km) or 12 (19.3 km). With today's system of highways and the development of motor-vehicle transportation, it is easy to travel 50 miles (80.45 km) in an hour. Thus today, an hour's time distance is about 50 miles (80.45 km). In recent years, population growth in the medium-sized and larger towns has been stimulated by industrialization. Because of improved transportation, rural shoppers often bypass small hamlets to travel to larger towns. As a result, many of the original communities have become functionally obsolete, and at the same time a few have grown into important centers of industry and population.

Some of the towns in the central part of the state, in the Boon's Lick region, are among the oldest in Missouri. One such town, Boonville, built on the bluffs overlooking the Missouri River where the western prairie meets the Ozarks, became the main river port for southwestern Missouri. Two- to four-story brick and frame warehouses were built along Main Street and the waterfront. Surrounding the core area of commercial and warehousing structures is the older residential section, which comprises an unusually well-preserved assemblage of antebellum brick residences with generous rooms, wide halls, and modest classic-revival details as well as flamboyant houses of the gingerbread era. Several of these fine old houses are in the National Register of Historic Places.

Boonville was first settled in 1810 by a widow, Hannah Cole, who, with the assistance of her nine children, built cabins on the bluffs overlooking the river. During the War of 1812 the settlement was palisaded and named Cole's Fort. When Cooper County was organized in 1818, Boonville became the county seat.

Boonville is served by two railroads— the Missouri, Kansas, and Texas (Katy) and the Missouri Pacific—and by three highways—U.S. Highway 40 and Missouri

Highways 5 and 87. It is primarily a farm market and service town. There are about twenty manufacturing establishments, but only five employ more than 100 workers— Certex Manufacturing Company (shirts), Boben Manufacturing Company (shoes), Fuqua Homes of Missouri, Incorporated (mobile homes), Holsum Bakers, and Intertherm Incorporated (baseboard heaters).

Marshall, seat of Saline County, was settled in 1839 by immigrants from Virginia, Kentucky, and Tennessee. The town grew slowly until the Chicago and Alton Railroad arrived in 1878. Over the past century it has experienced slow but fairly steady growth.

The town is served by two railroads— the Missouri Pacific and the Gulf, Mobile, and Ohio—and by three state highways— 20, 65, and 41. There are more than a dozen manufacturing plants and food processing is important. The largest plants are Banquet Foods with 840 employees, International Shoe Company with 414, Quinn Concrete Company with 150, and Wilson Food Corporation (hog killing and meat packing) with 500 employees.

Lexington, established at William Jack's Ferry in 1819, became the seat of Lafayette County in 1823. It is named for Lexington, Kentucky, the former home of many of its early residents. The town is built around the Lafayette County Courthouse, a two-story, white-painted brick structure of classic-revival design. Embedded in one of the columns in the Ionic portico is a cannonball fired during the Battle of Lexington in 1861. Surrounding the public square is the business district, which includes numerous red-brick structures from the nineteenth century. Many of the houses are old with architectural details reminiscent of the South.

Over the years Lexington has been the home of five colleges: Baptist Female College, Elizabeth Aull Seminary, Masonic College, Central Female College, and Wentworth Military Academy. The town is served by the Missouri Pacific Railroad, Missouri Highway 13, and U.S. 24. Only eight manufacturers are listed in the 1980 *Missouri Directory of Manufacturing,* three of which employ between 100 and 200 workers. Plastics, clothing, wood products, electrical equipment, agricultural lime, and printing are manufactured.

Richmond, seat of Ray County, was platted in 1827 and named for Richmond, Virginia. In 1829 it became the county seat. Richmond is served by the Atchison, Topeka, and Santa Fe Railroad and by Missouri Highways 10, 13, and 210. It is primarily a shopping and market town for the smaller towns and farms in the county. Banks, insurance brokers, real estate offices, grain elevators, a livestock market, farm implement dealerships, professional services, and the usual array of business houses and courthouse-town services provide most of the jobs. There is a small amount of manufacturing: printing, agricultural lime, ready-mix concrete, candy, and aluminum windows. The largest company, Ferguson Manufacturing Company (rubber moldings), employs 150 workers.

Carrollton, seat of Carroll County, was first settled in 1819 by John Trotter. The town site occupies a high bluff overlooking the Missouri River valley. The town grew slowly until the Wabash, St. Louis, and Pacific Railroad arrived after the Civil War. Today Carrollton is served by three railroads: the Burlington Northern, the Norfolk and Western, and the Atchison, Topeka, and Santa Fe. It is at the junction of two federal highways: U.S. 24 and U.S. 65. Most of the working population is occupied in retail trade and services for customers from farms and small towns in the county. Nevertheless, there are more than 1,000 workers, many from surrounding farms and villages, employed in manufacturing plants in Carrollton. The small plants are engaged in printing, alfalfa dehydration, welding, meat packing, and the manufacture of ready-mix concrete, sportswear, and cattle feeders. There are three large plants: Banquet Foods Corporation (prepared frozen foods) with 502 employ-

ees; Formel Baking Company (packaged cookies) with 171; and Green Quarries, Incorporated (crushed stone, ready-mix concrete, and agricultural lime), with 210.

It is remarkable that a town such as Carrollton has manufacturing jobs equivalent to one-fourth its total population, whereas the total manufacturing employment in St. Louis amounts to only 20 percent of the total population. Such high ratios are not uncommon in outstate Missouri towns and reflect a dependence on manufacturing in rural Missouri not ordinarily recognized. The closing of a single plant of 150 to 200 employees can have a devastating effect on the local economy of such small communities.

Fayette, seat of Howard County, was so designated in 1823. The town grew slowly until the 1880s, when Glasgow declined as a river port and a railroad was built to Fayette.

Today, Fayette is served by the Missouri, Kansas, and Texas Railroad (Katy) and by Missouri Highways 5, 240, and 124. Its chief function is as a retail trade, service, and farm market center. Fewer than 200 workers are engaged in manufacturing. The largest plant, the National Garment Company, employs 124 workers in the manufacture of sportswear.

The West-Central Loess Hills reveal the beauty of a productive agricultural landscape—where fields of corn, soybeans, milo, and wheat are well-cultivated; where the fields are solidly fenced; and where the farm buildings are in good repair, well painted, and substantial. The landscape reflects more than 150 years of occupancy by people concerned with the stewardship of the land. The panoramic views from the Missouri River bluffs across the bottoms and to the opposite wooded bluff 8 miles (12.9 km) to 10 miles (16.1 km) distant are truly spectacular. At early morning sunrise or at sunset, the scene is enhanced by the reflection of the sun from the waters of the wide Missouri.

The mid-Missouri region, particularly

the Boon's Lick country, is rich in history and cultural attractions. At Fayette is Central College, which traces its history to the establishment of Franklin Academy in 1820. The Kemper Military School at Boonville attracts young men from across the nation. At Marshall is Missouri Valley College, a coeducational school affiliated with the Presbyterian Church.

The mid-Missouri area was the site of many of the key confrontations during the Civil War, and these events are memorialized with markers and reenactments. The first land battle of the Civil War was fought 4 miles (6.4 km) below Boonville June 17, 1861. State troops under the command of the Confederate Colonel John S. Marmaduke were defeated by federal forces under Captain Nathaniel Lyon. Military historians consider that this victory was important in preserving Missouri for the Union. The Battle of Lexington was fought in September 1861, when General Sterling Price moved his Confederate troops north into the Missouri valley after the Battle of Wilson's Creek and the fall of Springfield. The Confederate forces advanced under cover of hemp bales, and the Union forces under command of Colonel James A. Mulligan surrendered after running short on supplies. A state historic site preserves memories of the Battle of the Hemp Bales at the red-brick Anderson House. Just south at Higginsville, Confederate Memorial State Park is another reminder of the war.

At historic Arrow Rock, in Saline County, more than forty original buildings remain in the little town where pioneers stopped on their way west. Arrow Rock has been a Santa Fe Trail town, a river port for overland commerce, a county seat, and a meeting place for persons who helped shape the history of the West. The Old Tavern and the Lyceum Theatre are popular with visitors. Community lakes, wildlife areas, rivers for boating, and open countryside are some of the other attractions of the West-Central Loess Hills of Missouri.

REGIONS OF THE WESTERN PLAINS

The Western Plains province is a transitional area between the Ozarks and the Northern Plains. Much of it is actually smoother than the Northern Plains, but the soils are generally of lower quality than the glacial and loessal soils of northern Missouri. In a general way the agricultural productivity, level of living, and the cultural landscape are intermediate between the two adjacent provinces. The Western Plains province is divided into two regions.

The Osage Plains region, the larger of the two regions, encompasses 4,390 sq miles (11,770 km²). It is a region of limestone, sandstones, and shale strata containing beds of coal. Resistant limestones and sandstones form linear northeast- to southwest-trending cuestas with intervening lowlands formed on shales. The region is alternatively known as the Scarped Plains and the Osage Cuestas. It is differentiated from the Cherokee Plains to the south and the east by the greater relief and more prominent escarpments.

Feed grains and livestock are the main products of agriculture, but on the whole production is below that of the Northern Plains. About one-fourth of the cultivated acreage is planted in soybeans; corn comprises about one-fifth. Grain sorghums and wheat are more important than in northern Missouri. These dry-land crops are widely grown to the west and southwest in Kansas, Oklahoma, and Texas. Cattle ranching and feedlot operations are more important than hog farms.

Sedalia is the largest trade center in the Western Plains. It was founded in 1857, when General George R. Smith purchased land and laid out the town along the proposed route of the Pacific Railroad. The first train arrived in January 1861, and merchants from the surrounding hamlets moved to Sedalia and reestablished their businesses. During the Civil War Sedalia benefited by the protection and trade of a military post established there. Later the railroad shops were built and the Missouri State Fair grounds were laid out.

Sedalia is situated in the midst of the triangle formed by Kansas City, Springfield, and Jefferson City. Its early growth was connected with its position as a railroad junction and the employment afforded by the railroad repair yards located there (Missouri, Kansas, and Texas; Atchison, Topeka, and Santa Fe; Missouri Pacific). In recent years Sedalia's growth has abated because the closing of the railroad repair shops offset employment increases in other industries. The population declined in the 1970s from 22,847 to 20,927.

Sedalia's largest manufacturing plants produce electrical appliances, disinfectants, wax, aluminum ware, conductors, clothing, small power tools, special railroad cars, shoes, and insulators. Its hinterland is agricultural and recreational.

Butler, seat of Bates County, is an important trade and service center in the western Osage Plains. Its location on four-lane U.S. 71 has attracted small industries that serve the Kansas City market. The largest company, Keller Perfection Aluminum Products of Missouri, employs about 100 workers in fabricating storm windows and doors.

Warrensburg, seat of Johnson County, is a service and trade center of considerable importance. Central Missouri State University is the most important employer and landmark in the town. The largest manufacturing plants produce circuit boards, women's uniforms, and men's work clothes.

Residents of the Osage Plains region are located midway between the natural attractions of the Ozarks and the cultural attractions and entertainment and shopping offered in Kansas City. Local attractions include Knob Knoster and Bothwell state parks and the Museum of Pioneer History at Butler.

The Cherokee Plains, with an area of 2,552 sq miles (6610 km²) and a population of 55,121, is one of the smallest and more sparsely populated regions in the state. Weak shales with interbedded coal deposits form broad valleys between low limestone and sandstone buttes.

Mixed crop and livestock farming is typical. Grain sorghums and wheat occupy nearly as much acreage as corn and soybeans. Feeder calves sold off pastures and steers and heifers fattened in feedlots provide the main source of income.

Nevada and Clinton are the chief trade centers. Both of these towns, as highway and railroad junctions, have better access to goods and services. Nevada is the site of the State Mental Hospital and has several medium-sized and small manufacturers. The largest plants manufacture plumbing fixtures, oil filters, clothing, and decorative film. In Clinton the largest manufacturers are Clearfield Cheese Company, Incorporated, and the Rival Manufacturing Company (electrical appliances).

Lamar and El Dorado Springs are smaller service and trade centers. Lamar's three major manufacturers produce television cabinets, clothing, and metal office furniture. El Dorado Springs, once a health spa of some importance, now relies on light manufacturing and farm trade. The largest manufacturing plants produce shoes, sportswear, and register forms.

Residents of the Cherokee Plains have easy access to the fine outdoor recreational and cultural attractions of the western Ozarks. Nevertheless, the region has several attractions of its own. The better known are the Harry S Truman birthplace at Lamar and the upper reaches of the Harry S Truman Reservoir at Osceola and Clinton. Hundreds of acres have been strip-mined to recover coal. The abandoned strip pits, long a burden to local governments because of delinquent taxes, have regained economic importance for fishing and wildlife habitat.

REGIONS OF THE OZARK PROVINCE

Because of its rugged landforms, heavy forest cover, clear spring-fed streams, and limited agricultural resources, the Ozarks constitute a most distinctive section of Missouri. Although these factors distinguish the Ozark province as a whole, there is sufficient diversity within the Ozarks so that no less than eight geographic subdivisions may be recognized.

The *Springfield Plain* forms the western Ozark border. It is physically and culturally much like the Western Plains province, but traditionally it has been a part of the Ozarks. This is partly because the people who live there regard themselves as Ozarkers. Also, even though the Springfield Plain region is relatively smooth and fairly fertile by Ozark standards, the landscape has considerable Ozark character. Streams are deeply entrenched, as much as 200 ft (61 m) to 300 ft (91 m) along the southern border; cherty limestones are predominant; and sinkholes, caverns, springs and other karst features are ubiquitous.

Encompassing 4,855 sq miles (12,585 km^2), the Springfield Plain is the second largest region of the state. Its population in 1980 was 387,639 for an average density of 80 people per sq mile, more than the state's average density. However, more than one-third of the population (133,166) lives in the corporate limits of the city of Springfield and another 38,893 people live in the city of Joplin.

Farm income is based largely on production of feeder cattle and dairy farming. Grain growing assumes a much less important role compared to farming in the Western Plains and Northern Plains. Wheat occupies one-sixth of cultivated acreage. Small acreages of corn, milo, and soybeans are also grown. Most of the cleared land is in pasture or forage crops. This results in a substantially lower value of crops per acre than in the Western Plains and Northern Plains. Hog raising is unimportant compared to northern Missouri, but production of feeder pigs for the Corn Belt is increasing in importance. About four times as many cattle as hogs are raised. Dairying is important in the vicinity of Springfield. The eight counties surrounding Greene

County form the most important dairy region in Missouri, encompassing nearly half the dairy cattle in the state.

The hierarchy and spacing of central locales in the Springfield Plain come close to the theoretical models that geographers have devised. Grocery stores, elementary schools, churches, service stations, and taverns are the typical services found in hamlets. These unplanned settlements occur as crossroads clusters and as sparse strings of assorted buildings. Spaced at somewhat greater distances are villages with greater numbers of businesses and more elaborate services. Grocery stores, taverns, service stations, elementary schools, lumberyards, auto dealers, farm implement dealers, hardware stores, and livestock feed dealers are typical retail outlets. Banks, veterinarians, attorneys, and post offices are the usual services. Even more specialized are the towns of 1,000 to 7,000 population, which usually have extensive commercial districts with at least fifty retail units. Represented are all types of public schools and professional services, medical, legal, and veterinary. The seats of county governments are most frequently (but not always) located in towns rather than in hamlets or villages.

The two places of true city status are Springfield and Joplin. Springfield's geography and history are discussed in Chapter 12. Joplin's development is intimately connected with lead and zinc mining. Much of its history Thomas Hart Benton, a native son of the Tri-State District, captured in a mural, which decorates the new municipal building in Joplin. In it are scenes of the mines and miners and the gaudy saloons, dance halls, and gambling halls that once were strung out along Main Street. The city was built, literally, upon the mines, straddling the boundary of Jasper and Newton counties.

Joplin's first settler, John C. Cox, built a home on Turkey Creek near the end of what is now Mineral Avenue. Shortly after that, the Reverend Harris C. Joplin, a Methodist minister from Greene County, settled on an 80-acre (32.3-hectare) tract.

Lead is reported to have been discovered in 1849, but only a few diggings were opened before the Civil War. After the war the Atlantic and Pacific Railroad was extended to Joplin, and the mining boom was on. Two towns grew up on either side of Joplin Creek: Murphysburg to the west and Joplin City to the east. In 1873 they were incorporated as the city of Joplin. As additional ore bodies were discovered, more mining camps were established so that by the turn of the century Joplin was surrounded by small mining towns.

As the mines in Joplin were worked out, the city turned to other businesses: buying and selling lead and zinc, processing and smelting ores, manufacturing explosives and mining equipment, providing services for mining companies and workers. Joplin became the largest city of the Tri-State Mining District; but, as the ores gradually petered out, the city relied increasingly on other manufactures and commerce. The abandoned tailing piles and mine shafts scattered about the town and the elegant homes just west of the downtown are reminders of the mining era. Range Line Road, a 5-mile (8.04-kilometer) commercial strip extending north from Interstate 44 through the east edge of the city, is a manifestation of the new Joplin. The large North Park Mall and the usual assortment of restaurants, motels, service stations, and fast-food outlets indicate the city has recovered its commercial vitality. Within a 50-mile (80-kilometer) radius of Joplin is a population of more than 350,000. Joplin has long been the marketing, commercial, and transportation hub of this area, which covers parts of Missouri, Kansas, and Oklahoma.

Joplin's excellent rail facilities and location at the junction of U.S. 71 and Interstate 44 are advantageous for the assembly of materials and the distribution of manufactured goods. The 1980 *Missouri Directory of Manufacturers* lists ninety-four manufacturing firms in Joplin. Those employing more than 300 workers are Atlas Powder Company (explosives), Eagle Picher

Industries, Incorporated (batteries), FAG Bearing Company, and Motorola Display Systems (electronics).

The growth patterns of towns in the Joplin area are some of the most distinctive in Missouri. This is in keeping with the development of the Tri-State Mining District and its subsequent decline. Only two large towns, Carthage and Neosho, both outside the main mining district, show a normal development pattern (Figure 13.3). The population trends of Webb City, Carterville, and Granby reflect the fact that these towns originated as mining camps and relied heavily on the mines. They grew fast about the turn of the century, but experienced a rapid population decline between 1920 and 1940.

As is the case in most other outlying towns in the Ozarks, the chief functions are those providing goods and services to people who live in the surrounding countryside. Nevertheless, manufacturing is of considerable importance. As in other sections of the Ozarks, it is mainly food processing, clothing and shoes, electronics, and light-metal fabrication.

The eastern section of the Springfield Plain is in the trade area of Springfield. Monett, the largest town between Springfield and Joplin, was incorporated in 1887 as a railroad town. Until the mid-1930s, Monett was the center of a strawberry- and tomato-growing area in southwest Missouri, and each summer the sheds along the railroad south of the business district were a beehive of activity. Much of the industry of Monett is related to the regional agricultural economy, which emphasized dairying and poultry raising. Leading manufacturing employers include Armour and Company (turkey processing), Tyson's of Missouri, Incorporated (poultry processing), the U.S. Shoe Corporation–Jumping Jacks Division (children's shoes), and Wells Aluminum, Incorporated (aluminum extrusions).

Several towns show abnormal growth curves. Aurora and Pierce City were mining camps that followed the boom-and-bust

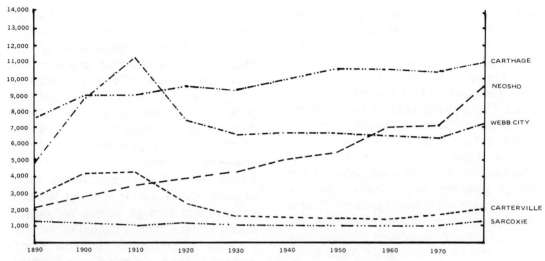

FIGURE 13.3. Population Trends of Towns in Southwestern Missouri.

growth so typical in the Joplin area. Republic and Ozark experienced abnormally sharp upturns in the 1960s because of overspill from Springfield. In the 1970s additional towns in Springfield's orbit—Nixa, Strafford, and Fair Grove—experienced sharp upturns in population.

As in other sections of the Ozarks, manufacturing employment in the outlying towns is of considerable importance. Even though the plants are small by the standards of large cities, the opening or closing of an industry that employs as many as 300 workers can have a marked impact on a town of 1,000 or 2,000 people. For example, the closing of a shoe manufacturing plant at Cassville in Barry County in 1980 threw more than 200 people out of work and depressed the local economy.

The 1980 *Missouri Directory of Manufacturing* lists the following types of plants employing 100 workers or more in outlying towns in the Springfield trade area: turkey processing, children's shoes, aluminum extrusions, prepared feeds, printing, gas and electrical furnaces, women's uniforms, hospital supplies and laboratory instruments, evaporated milk, boys' clothing, electric motors, men's and women's clothing, automotive fans, bread production, camping trailers, machine tools, white-oak barrels, aluminum boats, electric controls, men's and women's shoes, truck bodies and suspensions, custom woodcarving, artificial flowers, and charcoal briquettes. Not only is the list of manufacturers surprisingly diverse, but there is an interesting pattern of industry clustering. Several manufacturing companies operate plants that are close enough together to share warehousing and technically trained personnel.

The rural landscape of the Springfield Plain is one of the most attractive in Missouri. The combination of rock outcrops, forests, and free running water with farmsteads has resulted in a landscape reminiscent of the bluegrass region of Kentucky. Level uplands have been cleared and planted in lespedezas, orchard grass, and fescue. Many river and creek bottoms, which formerly grew fields of corn and wheat, are now hayfields and bluegrass pastures. Herefords and Black Angus are the main beef animals, but Charolais, Simmental, and other breeds are raised. Holsteins and Guernseys are the main dairy stock. Set back behind well-made barbed-wire fences, the typical farmstead is comprised of a dwelling and five or six outbuildings. Large dairy barns and silos built around the turn of the century are still in use, but they are being replaced by low, insulated, sheet-metal milking sheds and the popular sheet-metal Harvestor feed storage bins.

The Springfield Plain is rich in recreational and cultural attractions. Just 10 miles (16.1 km) southwest of Springfield is Wilson's Creek Battlefield National Park. Northwest of the city is Fantastic Caverns, which features a tour by vehicle. To the east on Interstate 44 is Exotic Animal Paradise, which features automobile tours of the property, where various animals from all parts of the world are kept. Within the city are several major attractions: the national cemetery; Southwest Missouri State University; Drury, Evangel, Central Bible, and Baptist Bible colleges; the federal medical center; and the national headquarters of the Assemblies of God Church. In addition to a number of historic homes and commercial buildings, there are shopping centers, good hospitals, a wide range of motel and convention accommodations, a selection of movies, a symphony orchestra, dozens of restaurants to suit varied tastes, and many evening-entertainment and cultural attractions.

Joplin is likewise rich in historical and cultural attractions, particularly for history buffs and mineral collectors. It is built upon the now-abandoned lead and zinc mines, and mineral collectors are attracted to the abandoned mine dumps and chat piles. The mineral museum in Schifferdecker Park is perhaps the best of its kind in Missouri. Some of the most elegant houses in the Ozarks were built by mining tycoons west of downtown Joplin. Many of these homes, which included servants' quarters and carriage houses, are opened during a house tour in the fall of the year.

Other attractions in extreme southwestern Missouri include Geoge Washington Carver National Monument near Diamond, Truitt's Cave at Lanagan, Ozark Wonder Cave at Noel, Rockhound Paradise at Anderson, the tiff mines near Seneca, and the Carthage marble quarry at Carthage. Pineville, the county seat of McDonald County, is an undisturbed and picturesque town built around the courthouse square. Here, under storefront canopies, Vance Randolph collected from res-

PHOTO 13.8.   Camping Area at Pomme de Terre Lake. Courtesy U.S. Army Corps of Engineers, Kansas City.

idents many of the stories he incorporated into several books on Ozark folklore.

The *Northern Ozark Border region* manifests characteristics of the rugged hill districts of the Ozarks and the fertile Northern Plains province. More fertile and topographically less rugged, the region's agricultural production is greater than in the Osage-Gasconade Hills and Courtois Hills regions adjoining it on the south.

The population density, about sixty-eight people per square mile, is substantially greater than in the interior Ozarks. The higher rural density is in part due to the larger number of medium-sized towns and in part to greater rural densities, especially in the German communities where small family farms are still numerous.

The largest city in the Northern Ozark Border is Jefferson City, the capital of Missouri and the seat of Cole County. Known locally as Jeff or Jeff City, it is built on the steep southern bluffs of the Missouri River. Although it has attracted a number of industries, it is primarily a political city; state government, for which it was created, is its principal business.

Jefferson City was only one of several areas—"within 40 miles (64.36 km) of the mouth of the Osage"—that vied for selection as Missouri's capital. In December 1821, Jefferson City was selected as the site, but growth was slow until the state penitentiary and the new capitol were built in the 1830s.

The focal point of Jefferson City is the state capitol built on the bluff overlooking the Missouri River. High Street, following the first of the ridges east and west, forms the axis of the downtown business district. The business buildings are two- to four-story brick and stone structures. The governor's mansion, a red-brick Italianate structure, is a block north of High Street overlooking the capitol. A cluster of office buildings scattered about the capitol rises above the business district. The residential districts fan out east, south, and west of the central business district. Several blocks east of the capitol, the massive state penitentiary dominates the river bluff. Blacks, comprising 11 percent of the population, live mainly in the southeastern portion of the city in the vicinity of Lincoln University, formerly a state-supported Black college but now open to all.

Over the past twenty-five years a large residential area has spread west following the river bluff mainly north of U.S. 50. The new Capitol Mall built alongside U.S. 50 accentuated the westward growth trend of the city in the 1970s.

Compared to most state capitals, Jefferson City is small; its population was 33,619 according to the census of 1980. It is not served directly by an interstate highway, but Interstate 70 is only 30 miles (48 km) north via U.S. 63. Commercial airlines serve the Columbia-Jefferson City Regional Airport, located between the two cities. Government and finance continue to play the largest role in the city's economy.

California, Owensville, Belle, Hermann, and Washington are the largest of the outlying towns. California is a long rambling town, disjointed during the 1850s by construction of the Missouri Pacific Railroad almost a mile south of the square. The focus of the town is the square and the two-story brick courthouse, built in 1867. Small-paned windows and the original interior woodwork make the building one of the most interesting of the surviving early Missouri courthouses.

Owensville, the principal town in southern Gasconade County, is situated on one of the small upland "prairies." The town is located in the middle of a district where many people of German ancestry settled. Belle is more than twice the size of Vienna, the seat of Maries County. Belle's largest employer is the International Shoe Company. The Kingsford Company, a manufacturer of charcoal briquettes, employs more than 100 workers in the plant. It is one of the largest charcoal-briquette manufacturers in Missouri, and bulk charcoal is shipped to the briquette plant at Belle from charcoal ovens throughout the central Missouri Ozarks. Linn, seat of Osage

County, serves as the focus for politics, county government, trade, and services for people from surrounding farms, hamlets, and villages.

Washington, located west of St. Louis on the bluffs of the Missouri, is the major trade center for Franklin County and adjacent parts of Warren and St. Charles counties. One of the most unusual manufacturing plants in the state is located at Hermann. The Missouri Meerschaum Company is the world's largest manufacturer of corncob pipes. Several automotive parts and light-metal manufacturing plants have located in Washington where they can readily serve the St. Louis market.

Hermann, the seat of Gasconade County, was founded by the German Settlement Society of Philadelphia in 1837. Educa-

tional, cultural, and social institutions, which nurtured German traditions, were founded that made Hermann the cultural capital of the mid-state Missouri Rhineland. German architecture, furniture, and mementos are preserved in many fine old residences in the town.

The towns of the Northern Ozark Border have attracted a variety of firms engaged in manufacturing. A 1980 directory listed the following types of manufacturers employing more than 100 in the outlying towns: saddlery, poultry processing, shoe manufacture, clothing, charcoal briquettes, electric motors, fishing boats, wooden novelties, and aluminum and copper tubular parts. Shoe and clothing manufacturing combined make up more than half the total employment in manufacturing in the

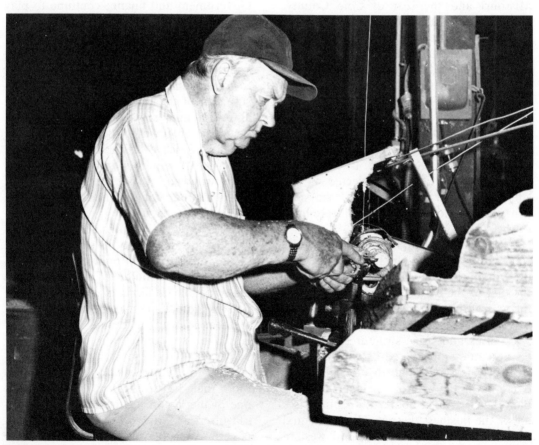

PHOTO 13.9. Hand Turning a Corncob Pipe Bowl at the Missouri Meerschaum Company in Washington. Courtesy Missouri Meerschaum Company.

towns in the region. The pattern from town to town is similar to that of other rural trade centers: several small manufacturers or service companies supply the needs of local or regional farms and agribusinesses, and one or two large manufacturers of products distribute on a larger regional or national market. The latter are usually of the footloose type taking advantage of less-expensive land and low-cost labor in rural communities.

The Ozarks' northern border has many physical and cultural attractions. The territory is rich in German heritage and culture. The old-world tradition and heritage are perhaps best preserved in Hermann. Tours of the old homes (more than 100 are in the National Register of Historic Places) or of the town's two wineries are held year-round. At Jefferson City there is the State Capitol Building, the Executive Mansion, the Jefferson Landing State Historic Site, and the Cole County Historical Museum.

The rural landscape presents considerable variety. The broken lands bordering the larger streams are steeply sloping and heavily forested. River-bottom alluvial soils and rich yellow loess soils on the uplands support more corn and wheat than in any other section of the Ozarks. Farms in the areas of better soils appear prosperous with tightly fenced fields and pastures.

The *Eastern Ozark Border region* includes the hilly belt bordering the Mississippi River from Cape Girardeau to the St. Louis urban area and extending west to the St. Francois Mountains. It is the lowest in elevation among the regions of the Ozarks. Its soils are less cherty and more fertile, being in large part derived from loess, and its topography is less rugged than adjacent parts of the Ozarks. To the south, in Perry and Cape Girardeau counties, the region flattens into a rolling karst plain.

The accessibility of the Eastern Ozark Border from its earliest period of settlement to the present has been one of its outstanding characteristics. In density of population, it is exceeded only by the Springfield Plain among the geographic regions of the Ozarks. Even so, there are no large cities within the region. The rural population densities are among the highest in the state, and, as in the Northern Ozark Border region, many small farms continue to be operated by conservative German farm families.

The percentage of cleared land is comparable or slightly higher than in the other border regions of the Ozarks. The combination of crops and livestock is similar to that of the Northern Ozark Border; corn (29 percent), soybeans (15 percent), and wheat (14 percent) are the leading crops. As in the Northern Ozark Border region, hog and cattle feeding is more important than in other sections of the Ozarks.

Because of excellent north-south highways—U.S. 61 and Interstate 55—much of the region lies in the trade hinterland of St. Louis. Several of the larger towns have experienced steady growth. Each is unique in its development. Crystal City is a company town that grew up around the Pittsburgh Plate Glass Company plant. Ste. Genevieve, the old cultural capital of French settlement, now serves as the main trade center and seat of government for Ste. Genevieve County. Large limestone quarries and kilns operate near the town and are major employers for Ste. Genevieve. The Mississippi Lime Company employs more than 750 workers. The dust plume from the quarries and kilns located west of the town may be seen for many miles. Festus, located within easy commuting distance of St. Louis, has experienced slow but steady growth since about 1900.

The history and culture of the Eastern Ozark Border are centered on the Mississippi River and a heritage of French, American, and German settlement. Missouri's oldest town, Ste. Genevieve, is rich in historical attractions. The old eighteenth-century homes are the best-preserved examples of French architecture between Louisiana and Quebec. These fine old homes, which were built when Ste. Genevieve was the headquarters for lead mining and fur trading, are open for tours.

Farther south along the river is scenic "East Perry," the Lutheran German settlements in eastern Perry County. These unique string towns—Altenburg, Frohna, Wittenburg—are laid out along a winding Ozark ridge road. Just south of Wittenburg is the ferry across the river, a striking natural gas pipeline bridging the Mississippi River, and the unusual Tower Rock, rising dramatically from the river. In Perryville there are fascinating museums to visit at the St. Mary's of the Barrens Seminary, founded in 1818. Farther south are other attractions: historic Jackson; Cape Rock, site of the early trading post that became Cape Girardeau; Trail of Tears State Park, where towering limestone bluffs front the river; and the scenic Bollinger Mill and Covered Bridge on the Whitewater River.

The *St. Francois Mountains region* is the smallest (1,711 sq miles [4,431 km²]) and most distinctive section of the Ozark province. Most of the hills are formed of granite or porphyry that has been carved into relief because of its greater resistance to erosion than the sedimentary rocks. The latter form basins between the knobs. The hills rise as much as 1,000 ft (304.8 m) above the basin floors although most are around 750 ft (228 m) high. No other region of Missouri can claim as much elevation and relief. The summit of Taum Sauk Mountain, located in Iron County a few miles southwest of Ironton, is the highest elevation in the state (1,778 ft [541.93 m] above mean sea level). Most of the inhabitants live in villages and on farms in the sedimentary lowlands where soils are deeper and of better quality. Certain of the lowlands—Fredericktown, Farmington, Potosi, Richwoods, Belleview, and Arcadia basins—form picturesque and productive "islands" in an otherwise forested landscape. Streams such as the St. Francis River, Stout's Creek, and Black River have cut narrow water gaps through the resistant

igneous rocks. Johnson's Shut-ins on the Black River are a notable example.

Crop agriculture is relatively unimportant. The value of crops per acre on the small amount of cultivated acreage is only slightly more than half that in northern Missouri. Only 68,607 acres (27,786 ha) were cultivated in 1980, of which the combined acreage of corn, wheat, and soybeans accounted for only 7,327 acres (2,967 ha). Cattle outnumber hogs by more than two to one, but even the raising of cattle is limited because of the large amount of land that is heavily forested. All in all the St. Francois Mountains region is the least productive of Missouri's regions.

The history of the St. Francois Mountains region is closely connected to mining of lead, zinc, and iron. Extensive deposits of lead were discovered in Washington, St. Francois, and Madison counties and the great Old Lead Belt (mineral district) developed there. Bonne Terre, a community of 3,622 on the northeastern border of the St. Francois Mountains, lies in the heart of the so-called Mineral Area. The last active mining ceased in the district in 1973, but mining had been declining throughout the 1950s and the 1960s. As ores were depleted, the St. Joe Minerals Corporation shifted operations and management offices to Viburnum in the extreme western part of Iron County in order to be close to their New Lead Belt operations.

Other towns in the Old Lead Belt—Elvins, Festus, Flat River, and Desloge, to name the larger ones—also suffered economic decline as the mines closed. They are slowly beginning to regain their vitality. Many residents commute to jobs in St. Louis via U.S. 67. Also, various small manufacturers—toys, small engines, light-metal products, clothing, shoes—have located in the Mineral Area to serve the St. Louis market.

Potosi, the seat of Washington County, is a farm trade center and the focus of the barite-mining district. Major employers include a company that manufactures oil-well driller's mud from barite and a shoe-

PHOTO 13.10. Bollinger Mill and Covered Bridge at Burfordville, Cape Girardeau County. Courtesy Walker—Missouri Division of Tourism.

manufacturing plant. Farmington, seat of St. Francois County, is an important town for retailing and services. The largest industries are manufacturers of shoes and clothing. Ironton, the seat of Iron County, is the chief town in the Arcadia Valley. The largest employer is the Brown Shoe Company. The southeastern section of the mountain area is served by Fredericktown, the seat of Madison County.

For generations the region has been a summer retreat and sometime retirement residence for St. Louisans. It is a favorite area for landscape painters who find the scenes elusive; the brooding purple mountains and intricate valley patchworks in virescent hues are fleeting under clouds, wind, rain, and lingering daybreak fog. The greenery, outcrops of pink granites and

purple-red porphyries, and turquoise-blue headwaters crashing through rugged gorges provide scenes splendid and fascinating. Six generations of human habitation have resulted in farmsteads, villages, and towns rendered in rust-red brick, distinctive Missouri Red granites, rough field stones, and milled lumber in whites, greens, and contemporary hues of blue and gray. The combination is altogether pleasing to the eye.

Shortly after the Civil War, the Arcadia Valley became a popular summer place for wealthy St. Louis families. Great summer homes were built in the valley in the shingle and gingerbread styles so popular in the late 1800s. These great estates—the Maples, the O'Fallon Estate, the Langdon Estate, the General John Turner Estate, to name a few—served the wealthy of St. Louis as the great cottages at Cape May served the wealthy families of Philadelphia. Many of the large homes in the valley have burned, but a few remain in and near the town of Ironton.

The irregularly shaped *Courtois Hills region* lies across the major Ozark drainage divide and extends well down both north and south slopes of the dome. It is the most hilly and most isolated section of the Missouri Ozarks and can therefore be regarded as a core area. The region is a wilderness of steep-sloped forested ridges separated by headwaters of the Black, Current, Big, and Meramec rivers. Relief of 300 ft (91 m) to 600 ft (182 m) is typical.

Production focuses on feeder cattle and a few dairy animals, but many of the farms operate near the subsistence level. As in most of Missouri, farms are increasing in size through abandonment and consolidation. Many of the farmers of the Courtois Hills support themselves in part through employment in sawmills or in the new lead mines that have opened in Iron and Reynolds counties. The small amount of cropland is used mainly for production of forage.

There are no large towns in the Courtois Hills, and the average population density is only about 10 per square mile (2.59 km²). The settlement pattern, both rural and village, is of two types—valley and ridge. The valley settlement came first when pioneers from Tennessee and Kentucky entered the region and selected river-bottom sites usually close by free-flowing springs. Later, when railroads were built into the area, small ridge-top settlements grew up alongside railroad sidings where railroad ties, and oak and pine timber were shipped. Both upland and valley settlements have declined since about 1920, but the valley settlements have fared somewhat better. Certain river towns, Van Buren and Eminence for example, have experienced a modicum of economic well-being from the tourist-recreation industry and the new

enthusiasm for canoeing and river float-fishing trips. The county seats are often small villages. Centerville, seat of Reynolds County, is a community of 241 residents. The dozen or so businesses are in one-story canopied buildings extending around three sides of the courthouse square. Very often communities are strung out along a valley road—a cemetery, a mobile home, a house or two, a farmstead, a general store, and occasionally a sawmill.

After the shortleaf pine and oak timber was cut, milled, and shipped, the railroads had little to haul and many miles of railroad were abandoned. The small ridge-top hamlets that had grown up along the tie-yard sidings soon declined and many were abandoned entirely. One exception to the established pattern was the new town of Viburnum. When the deep lead ores were discovered in western Iron County in the 1960s, the old timber shipping hamlet experienced a rebirth. St. Joe Minerals Corporation employed Harlan Bartholomew and Company to plan a new town, and in a few years the settlement of two stores and a half-dozen houses had grown to 842 people. The town of mine workers and their families now has a new shopping center, a large new school, modern suburban-style houses, and five new churches.

The tourist-recreation resources of the region are truly superb, and in recent years the revenues from that sector have increased substantially. The heavily forested area is drained by a number of clear streams that are fed by large springs. There are three state parks as well as the National Scenic Riverways on the Current, Jack's Fork, and Eleven Point rivers. Big Spring Recreation Area contains supposedly the biggest spring in the United States. Three other camping areas—Montauk, Alley Spring, and Round Spring—also are noted for large springs, whereas Sam A. Baker State Park is known for encompassing some of the wildest country in Missouri. There are numerous caves in the area, but few have been developed commercially because of their remoteness from major highways.

The establishment of the Ozark National Scenic Riverways has attracted national attention to the formerly isolated region. As a result, considerable development is taking place in the form of motels, camping areas, canoe rentals, and supply stores. Development along the riverways is controlled by the federal government in order to preserve the riverfront.

Included in the area are large acreages of the Mark Twain National Forest. These lands and private property support some of the largest deer herds in Missouri. Texas and Shannon counties are usually among the leading counties in number of deer killed during the autumn hunting season.

The two medium-size reservoirs—Lake Wappapello and Clearwater Lake—attract a large number of visitors from nearby counties in the Ozarks and from the lowlands to the southeast.

The Central Plateau, encompassing 7,286 sq miles (18,871 km²) in the interior Ozarks, is the largest of Missouri's geographical regions. This large area, inhabited by only 161,161 people, has an average density of 22 people per square mile (2.59 km²), approximately one-third the state's average density. It is bordered by hill regions, but the upland "prairies" are remarkably level. Slopes are moderate except along the major stream courses. Economically the region has suffered from isolation.

The agricultural produce is similar to

PHOTO 13.11.   Canoeing on the Current River. Courtesy Walker—Missouri Division of Tourism.

that of the other regions of the interior Ozarks—hay crops and livestock, particularly feeder cattle. Corn and wheat combined occupy only 11 percent of the cultivated land. Hog raising is much less important than in the intensively tilled areas of northern Missouri, but feeder-pig production is increasing and is locally significant in Howell and Oregon counties.

The best agricultural land is on the uplands, which are extensive in some areas. The larger upland tracts were named at an early date and have always been known as productive agricultural islands in the forested interior Ozarks. The larger tracts are the Salem, Licking, and Summersville uplands; the Lebanon and West Plains prairies; and the Buffalo Head Prairie in Dallas County. These prairies, mainly long narrow strips with wood and water at short distances, historically provided excellent grazing, and their sod was not so difficult to break as that of larger prairies. Moreover, the principal roads and railroads followed these ridge lands. They therefore did not repel settlement as did the large prairies of the northern and western parts of the state.

Most of the larger towns in the Missouri Ozarks are situated in prairies of the Central Plateau. Lebanon has profited from its location on Interstate 44, one of Missouri's growth corridors. It is the chief town between Rolla and Springfield. It had its beginning when Laclede County was formed in 1849. When the railroad reached Lebanon in 1868, the depot was built a mile from the village center, but Lebanon picked itself up and moved to the new site.

Lebanon's location on the Burlington Northern and Interstate 44 is advantageous to manufacturing. The largest plants are Appleby Manufacturing Company, a manufacturer of boat trailers and tents; Detroit Tool and Engineering Company; Independent Stave Company, a manufacturer of whiskey barrels; and Lowe Industries, manufacturer of aluminum boats.

Salem, which bills itself as the gateway to the Big Springs country, was founded in 1851 as the seat of newly formed Dent County. The construction of the St. Louis and San Francisco Railroad made possible the opening of large iron deposits south of town in Simmons Mountain in 1872. The town has had a long and steady growth as a mining and shipping center.

The seat of Howell County, West Plains, is the only town of size for many miles. It has a long tradition as a regional livestock market as well as a retail trade and service center for Howell and Oregon counties and parts of Texas, Shannon, and Carter counties. The Southwest Missouri State University Residence Center offers college courses for students from south-central Missouri.

As in other sections of the Ozarks, manufacturing is of considerable importance in the economy of the towns of the region. The main manufacturers are familiar: clothing, shoes, food processing, light-metal products, plastics, and electronics. On the northern border, in the drainage basin of the Piney River, Fort Leonard Wood is an important source of employment for workers from surrounding farms and towns.

In the Ozarks in the years since World War II, there has been a marked shift from crop farming to a livestock economy based on the production of unfinished feeder cattle. During the 1960s and 1970s, the shift in emphasis reached major proportions, constituting one of the most significant economic changes in the Ozarks. The shift has been especially dramatic in the rolling uplands of the Central Plateau. Here, land-use and landscape patterns have been altered significantly and will continue to change. Thousands of acres of wooded land have been converted to pasture, either by aerial spraying with herbicides or by bulldozing. The cleared land is planted with fescue, lespedeza, and mixed grasses. Fescue, a drought-resistant grass that provides winter forage, has earned the title "the miracle grass" because of its influence on the livestock industry over the past twenty-five years.

Outside capital has been attracted by a

PHOTO 13.12.   Specker Barracks at Fort Leonard Wood. World War II Barracks in the Right Foreground. Courtesy of U.S. Department of the Army.

strong demand for beef and relatively low land prices. For example, the 5,000-acre (2,024-hectare) RCT Ranch near Mountain View founded by St. Louis entrepreneur Claude Treaman produces registered polled Herefords using embryo transplants and computer management of breeding and business records.

The *Osage-Gasconade Hills* region is in the northwestern Ozarks. The surface, thoroughly dissected by streams, forms a maze of hills separated by deeply entrenched valleys. The most rugged land lies along the Osage and Gasconade rivers where local relief is 300 ft (91.44 m) to 400 ft (121.92 m). The average population density of 22 per sq mile (2.59 km²) is comparable to other Ozark hill regions.

Farm income is derived mainly from feeder cattle and to a lesser extent from dairying. Somewhat more corn is grown in this hilly region mainly because of the better soils in the floodplains of the Osage and Gasconade rivers. Nevertheless, most of the land is forested and cleared land is mainly used for pasture or forage crops.

The core counties—Camden, Morgan, Miller, and Maries—exhibit some of the more extreme traits of isolation so frequently associated with the Ozarks. Here, in the shadow of the state capital and only a short distance from Kansas City, hill-country heritage and traditional life-styles, mannerisms, and dialect persist to a remarkable degree.

Towns are small and many have passed their zenith. The larger and more prosperous are either county seats or have profited from the tourism-recreation business connected with Lake of the Ozarks. Eldon, the largest town, was platted in 1882 as a division point on the Rock Island Railroad. With the erection of Bagnell Dam in 1929, Eldon experienced a short-lived boom before the depressed economic conditions of the 1930s temporarily ended the expected prosperity connected with tourism and recreation around Lake of the Ozarks.

Beginning in the 1950s and accelerating in the 1960s and 1970s, the tourism and recreation industry has grown to be a major business for Eldon. The town has recovered the population lost in the 1930s, when the railroad shops were closed. Two manufacturing plants—Fasco Industries (fractional horsepower motors) and Fisher Footwear (women's shoes)—have helped to restore economic stability.

Two other towns—Camdenton and Osage Beach—are intimately connected with the tourism-recreation industry. Camdenton, founded in 1929, is a new town by Ozark standards. It was built as a service center for the expected tourist trade when Bagnell Dam was built forming the Lake of the Ozarks. The town is laid out about a large landscaped circle. The business buildings are of the modern pseudo-English half-timber design.

Osage Beach began as a tiny resort village planned and promoted by real estate developers in connection with the lake. A town was platted and a few lots sold when Bagnell Dam was first proposed in 1928. The economic depression halted development after 1930, however, and many lots were unsold until the economic recovery during and following World War II. At the foot of the steep hillside is an artificial sand beach. The economy of Osage Beach is based almost wholly on providing lodging, food, entertainment, and recreation and in selling recreation equipment and supplies to tourists.

The rural landscape of the Osage-Gasconade Hills is similar to that of the other Ozark hill districts. There is the familiar pattern of ridge and valley settlement with humble farmsteads comprised of a small house and two to five outbuildings. Some houses are simple shacks built by unskilled workers using oak lumber cut and sawed on the property. The exterior walls of these houses are sometimes of rough, unpainted, vertically placed boards, but more frequently the walls have been covered with tar paper or composition shingles. The houses are set on simple foundations, sometimes unmortared native stone.

There are more log cabins in use there than in any other section in Missouri. There are good reasons for this. In other hilly and isolated sections of the state, pine forests attracted sawmills. In these areas many of the original log houses were replaced by houses built from sawed and milled lumber; and as new settlers arrived, the houses were built of the readily available lumber. Because there were no large pine forests to attract large sawmills to the Osage-Gasconade Hills, the traditional log cabins remained.

In the middle of this rugged rural region is a burgeoning resort and recreation economy developed around Lake of the Ozarks. Lake of the Ozarks, with its 1,300 miles (2,091.7 km) of shoreline plus the hills, creeks, bluffs, natural bridges, caves, and springs, is one of the outstanding recreation attractions of the Ozarks. Visitors come not only from the large urban centers of St. Louis, Kansas City, and Chicago, but also from other areas, especially Missouri, Illinois, Iowa, and Kansas. Major attractions in the region include Bagnell Dam, Lake of the Ozarks State Park, Bridal Cave, Jacob's Cave, Hahatonka "Castle," and Marriott's Tan-Tar-A resort.

The Lake of the Ozarks tourism-recreation economy is perhaps the most maturely developed in the Ozarks. The stretch of U.S. 54 from Camdenton to Eldon is a rather fully developed strip of motels, restaurants, fast-food establishments, children's rides, boat docks, resorts, country-

PHOTO 13.13.   Tan-Tar-A Resort, Lake of the Ozarks. Courtesy Walker—Missouri Division of Tourism.

music halls, antique shops and bric-a-brac stores, realty offices, and assorted other commercial activities that cater to both transients and residents.

The White River Hills region is one of the most scenic parts of the Ozarks. In Missouri, only the St. Francois Mountains and the Courtois Hills exceed it in relief and slope. Ridges tend to be elongate and of a uniform height, standing 400 ft (121.92 m) to 500 ft (152.4 m) above the valley floors. With an average density of 25 people per sq mile (2.59 km²), it is one of the most sparsely populated sections of Missouri.

Very little land is cultivated; cropland has always been confined to narrow stream valleys and to the small amount of level land on ridge tops. Today, most of the cropland has been abandoned or converted to pasture or hay. The small amount of corn and wheat is planted on the best quality soils. Some 70 to 80 percent of the land is forested and most of the cleared land is in pasture. Some natural forage for cattle is afforded by the grassy glades. Beef and dairy cattle are the main livestock. Small herds of milking goats and Angora goats are raised.

The scenery in the White River country is truly superlative. Forested slopes, bold limestone cliffs, and parklike cedar glades combine with fertile bottomlands. The region has some of the largest caves in the Ozarks, and streams and springs abound. Several large lakes—Table Rock, Taneycomo, Bull Shoals, and Norfork—have been impounded along the White River. The regional landscape has great variety and charm.

The pattern of settlement along ridge roads and in fertile bottomlands is similar to that of other Ozark hill districts. The chief business is livestock farming; thus the array of farm buildings is simple. Since little grain is raised there are no storage bins, corncribs, or farm grain elevators. A few farms, where dairy herds are kept, have silos and milking sheds. In Barry and McDonald counties the long, low poultry

PHOTO 13.14.   Table Rock Dam. Courtesy Walker—Missouri Division of Tourism.

barn is fairly common. The few barns are generally in poor condition. Mild winters make barns unnecessary for the protection of stock.

Many farms have been abandoned and some of the active farms appear run down. On these farms, buildings are unpainted and dilapidated, front porches hold an assortment of cast-off furniture and appliances, and often there is an assemblage of old abandoned automobiles scattered about the farmyard. On the whole, however, farmsteads are well tended. Lawns are mowed, and flowers and shubbery grow around the houses.

The lakes, caves, streams, and rugged forested hills form the basis for a highly developed resort economy, especially around Lake Taneycomo and Table Rock Lake. The area surrounding Branson, Hollister, and Silver Dollar City has come to be known as the Shepherd of the Hills

Area. The name derives from the popularity of Harold Bell Wright's book, *The Shepherd of the Hills,* and the much-visited Shepherd of the Hills Farm and Theatre. The attraction that draws the greatest number of visitors is Silver Dollar City. A stretch of Missouri Highway 76 west of Branson has become known as the Branson Strip. Included in the 13-mile (20.91-kilometer) section between Branson and Missouri Highway 13 are motels, inns, restaurants, antique shops, more than twenty gift and souvenir shops, a shopping center, a dozen country-music theaters, Shepherd of the Hills Farm, Silver Dollar City, and a collection of lesser attractions.

Rockaway Beach, Branson, and Hollister provide several different types of attractions for visitors. The area adjacent to the lakes is especially desirable as a location for retirement and second homes. As seen

PHOTO 13.15.   School of the Ozarks at Point Lookout on Lake Taneycomo. Courtesy Walker—Missouri Division of Tourism.

at night from a prominence, the lake district resembles a sparsely settled city.

THE SOUTHEAST LOWLANDS PROVINCE

The lowlands formed by the ancient and present floodplains of the Mississippi and St. Francis rivers contrast sharply with the Ozark Upland, which lies immediately to the north. The Ozark Escarpment, a line of ragged hills cut by streams leaving the Ozarks, forms the sharpest landscape boundary in Missouri. To the south of the escarpment is the great Gulf Coastal Plain Province of the United States with its dark rich alluvial soils supporting bumper crops of corn, soybeans, cotton, and rice; to the

north are the forested Ozarks. In the Southeast Lowlands of Missouri there are two subdivisions: the Southeastern Ridge and Basin region, which borders the Ozark Escarpment, and to the south, the Southeastern Alluvial Basin region.

The settlement of southeastern Missouri progressed in waves. First farmers from Tennessee and Kentucky settled on the small areas of better-drained land. Second, when railroads penetrated the areas, large lumber companies purchased extensive acreages and began clearing the land with the help of timber workers from these two states immediately east of the Mississippi River.

The lumber workers were a rough lot, and it seemed that lumber camps were a

PHOTO 13.16.   Basket Weaving at Silver Dollar City near Branson. Courtesy Walker—Missouri Division of Tourism.

refuge for the maladjusted from every quarter, as sheriffs from adjoining states seldom sought out a fugitive working in a lumber camp. Most of the workers were poor people who came from the hill country where the going was hard and were used to the hard work their employers demanded. A few of the large landowners imported Blacks from cotton-growing areas of the South to help in clearing land, but most of this work was done by people from the hill country.

When the large lumber tracts were depleted, in the early 1900s, many of the lumber workers stayed on to clear-cut for the plow. At this time, drainage operations were just getting under way. As the lowlands were drained, timber that once stood in shallow water was removed. The lumber workers were employed mainly by large landowners who wished to clear more of their land for cultivation and by local lumbering interests. By 1915 these workers had cleared thousands of acres of timber, making new lands available for cultivation.

Although small-scale drainage had begun prior to 1900, the most important project of this kind was undertaken in the Little River Drainage District, a political subdivision of the state organized in the circuit court of Butler County in 1907 (Figure 13.4). The costs of reclamation were assessed against the lands benefited. Prior to drainage, cutover lands within the wet area could be bought for a few dollars per acre (.405 ha), but by 1925 drained lands within

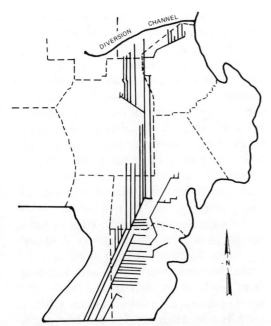

FIGURE 13.4.   The Little River Drainage Project.

the district were selling for $50 to $150 per acre. By 1980 agricultural land in southeastern Missouri was selling for $2,000 to $3,000 per acre, if it could be bought at all.

The development of farm lands resulted in a notable increase in the population of the district. One landholding company sold nearly 84,000 acres (33,600 ha) of the newly drained land from 1915 to 1924. Much of the immigration prior to 1920 came from areas in the East. From 1905 to 1915 settlers from the northern sections of the United States began to arrive in the delta area. This influx of farmers is termed *Yankee settlement,* because they came from Indiana, Illinois, and Ohio. Interested in speculating in the lands being drained, many had come into southeast Missouri as a result of glorified reports from land agents. These "Yankee" settlers were not cotton growers when they first arrived; they had neither the labor supply to grow cotton, nor the knowledge. Their crops of corn and wheat were the most important farm products of the delta region prior to 1922.

From 1922 through 1925, cotton acreage expanded tremendously. The expansion in southeast Missouri was brought on by the high prices from cotton, problems with the boll weevil in the deep South, and the efforts of the large landowners to induce settlement on their recently cleared lands. Large numbers of poor whites and Blacks from Mississippi and Arkansas were brought in by the landowners and land companies to farm on a sharecropper basis.

When cotton workers moved up from areas in the cotton south, delta-area cotton production expanded rapidly. Cotton acreage in 1921 was about 95,000 (38,475 ha) acres but in 1922 the total had risen to nearly 200,000 acres (81,000 ha). By 1924 total acreage had increased to 446,000 acres (180,630 ha) in the delta area. On January 3, 1923, an article in the Cape Girardeau newspaper, *The Southeast Missourian,* described the immigration of cotton workers. "'Cotton Negroes' from the South began to arrive in Cape Girardeau, having been driven north by the boll weevil. . . . Negroes by the hundreds are coming to Southeast Missouri from the southern States, and the indications are that there will be no trouble for farmers to get cotton labor for next spring." As land drainage progressed over the following two decades, more land was planted in cotton and the sharecropping system used throughout most of the South became established. Large landholders leased their land and sometimes provided seed, tools, mules, or other production inputs for a share of the crop. The tenants or sharecroppers provided the labor for planting, chopping (thinning and weeding), and harvesting the crop in return for a share. Very often sharecroppers were heavily in debt to landowners for food and necessities.

The *Southeast Ridge and Basin region* is a belt of land bordering the Ozark Escarpment that includes flat, poorly drained bottomlands and several loess-capped hills that escaped destruction by the ancient Mississippi and St. Francis rivers. The larger bottoms—the Drum, Advance, and

Morehouse lowlands—were former pathways of the Mississippi River when it followed a more westerly course after leaving the Ozark Border. The largest hills or ridges, formed of bedrock, are as much as 100 ft (30.4 m) above the bottomland. The most conspicuous hills are the Commerce Hills (Scott County Hills), Crowley's Ridge, and Hickory Ridge. Sikeston Ridge is much lower, a sandy swell rather than a ridge. It is an ancient alluvial terrace formed when the Mississippi River lay farther to the west. Except for the urban areas, the Southeastern Ridge and Basin region is the smallest in the state (1,379 sq miles [3,572 km²]). The population, 68,450 in 1980, was up by 14 percent from the 1970 figure.

Cropland occupies more than one-third of the area, and most of it is intensively cultivated. Soybeans, which have wrested the throne from the "king" (corn) in the state, occupy 70 percent of the cultivated land. Wheat occupies 12 percent of the cultivated land, corn another 11 percent, and cotton approximately 8 percent. Wheat and corn are the preferred upland crops. The region is well suited for cash-crop farming because of the availability of cheap rail and water transportation. Much of the farm produce is barged down the Mississippi River to New Orleans where it is shipped to world markets. Cattle and hog raising is small compared to that of northern Missouri, although feeds are plentiful.

The region has few large towns. The three main shopping and service towns—Cape Girardeau, Poplar Bluff, and Sikeston—are on the margins of the region. There are a half-dozen towns that exceed 1,000 in population. The largest, Dexter, is perched on top of Crowley's Ridge at a place where small streams have cut a gap, which provided a convenient route for passage of the Missouri Pacific Railroad. Dexter was laid out in 1873 and quickly became a railroad shipping point, first for timber and later for wheat, corn, soybeans, and cotton. There are about twenty-five manufacturing establishments. The five largest plants each employ between 100 and 500 workers in the manufacture of automotive supplies and clothing and in the dressing and packing of poultry.

The remaining towns in the region are typical farm-market communities. The commercial districts, usually clustered near the railroad, consist of one- and two-story brick buildings with false facades, sometimes remodeled with newer building materials such as metal or composition siding. The residential neighborhoods are mainly one-story frame structures with wood siding. Typically, one or two newer subdivisions are located near the edge of town, usually close by a main highway. Although the main business of each town is retail trade, services, marketing, and shipping, farm products are important as well. Each town has attracted a few industries. Chaffee, on Missouri Highway 77, has five manufacturers. The two largest—Florsheim Shoe Company and Thorngate Limited—employ more than 300 workers each. Scott City, located on Interstate 55 just south of Cape Girardeau, has only one manufacturer, a precast concrete company that employs about 25 workers. Bernie has only one large manufacturing plant, the Brown Shoe Company. Bloomfield, built around the yellow-brick Stoddard County courthouse, was platted in 1835 and lumbering and milling developed after the railroad arrived in the late 1800s. The Elder Manufacturing Company employs approximately 235 workers in the manufacture of clothing. Illmo, so named because of its location near the Missouri-Illinois boundary, is a railroad town. The business and residential districts are strung out along the switching yards where trains are made up before crossing the bridge over the Mississippi River at Thebes, Illinois. The largest manufacturing employer is E and W of Illmo, Incorporated, manufacturer of men's clothing.

The rural landscape of the Southeastern Ridge and Basin region is one of the most distinctive in the state. Striking features are the numerous drainage ditches, aligned north-south approximately every mile (1.6

km), which made possible the drainage of the swamps and the development of a productive agriculture. In the winter months, the monotonous flatlands present a rather bleak appearance with corn stalks, harvested cotton and milo, and dormant winter wheat. In the spring, summer, and fall, the land comes to life in shades of green, gold, and white as the fields of corn, wheat, soybeans, and cotton grow and mature. The uplands with their forested slopes appear as islands of greenery.

Hunting and fishing opportunities are good. The Mississippi and St. Francis rivers and the numerous drainage canals provide excellent habitat for catfish. The Mingo Wildlife Area, near Puxico, offers good fishing and waterfowl hunting in a natural swampland setting. The nature trails and the visitors' center provide excellent interpretation of the flora and fauna and a glimpse into the natural history of the area.

The *Southeastern Alluvial Basin region* consists of the Bootheel counties: Mississippi, New Madrid, Dunklin, and Pemiscot. There the broad lowland of the Mississippi and St. Francis rivers is broken only by Crowley's Ridge and the low sandy terrace known as Sikeston Ridge. Crowley's Ridge, one of Missouri's truly unique landforms, is a narrow, serpentine upland that begins near Dexter, Missouri, and extends to Helena, Arkansas. The ridge top, which is covered with wind-deposited loess, is nearly as fertile as the alluvial lowlands. Sikeston Ridge is barely perceptible (10 ft [3.04 m] to 20 ft [6.09 m] in relief), but its soils are sandy and well drained. Much of the lowland lies in the New Madrid floodway, an area the U.S. Army Corps of Engineers set aside as a safety valve to relieve flooding downriver. When flood levels threaten the larger downstream cities and agricultural land, the floodgates can be opened to the New Madrid floodway to help lower river levels downstream. Ditching and draining carry most of the runoff to the Little River drainage system.

Farm tenancy is higher in southeast Missouri than in other sections of the state and, because of farm mechanization and consolidation, there has been a surplus of agricultural labor for the past thirty years. Population in the region declined by 39,201 (23 percent) during the 1960s. In the 1970s population increased by 6 percent to a figure of 135,459 in 1980.

The Southeastern Alluvial Basin area is characterized by cash-crop farming and neoplantations. "Forty acres and a mule" describes the agricultural system that developed in the first half of the twentieth century. A farm tenant, many of whom were Black, with his family and a mule could tend about 40 acres (16.2 ha) of cotton. A 2,000-acre (810-hectare) plantation sometimes supported as many as thirty families. The rent was customarily paid as a share of the crop produced. Since about 1950, cotton production and growing of the cash grain crops—wheat, corn, soybeans, rice—have been mechanized, thereby reducing the need for tenant labor. As Black and white tenant farmers and their families moved away to find employment in area towns and large cities in the Midwest, the rows of simple two- and three-room "shotgun" cabins were demolished.

A modern 3,000-acre (1,214-hectare) neoplantation might entail an investment in land of $4 million to $5 million and an investment in buildings and machinery amounting to another $1 million. The main farmstead typically is set in a copse of trees. The array of buildings includes a two-story frame house (if not replaced by one of contemporary design), several machine sheds, a half-dozen or more grain storage bins, and one or two buildings for general storage and repair work. Hired hands sometimes live in remodeled sharecropper cabins. Many of the outbuildings are of pole construction covered by galvanized sheet metal. Barns and cattle lots are scarce. The investment in machinery is substantial: large four-wheel-drive industrial tractors and smaller row-crop tractors, disks, plows, field harrows, planters, cultivators, fertilizer applicators, combines, cotton pickers, and trucks and pickups to plant, cultivate, harvest, and haul farm produce to market. Trucks and tractors are often equipped with citizens-band radios so that operations, maintenance, and repairs can be promptly executed.

Cash-crop farming dominates the landscape. About two-fifths of the cultivated acreage is planted in soybeans, a fourth in cotton, a fifth in wheat, and a tenth in corn. Because the growing season normally exceeds 200 days, some land is double-cropped. Wheat is the winter crop, whereas soybeans, corn, and milo are grown in the summer. Cotton occupies the better-drained sandy tracts, whereas soybeans are planted on the dark heavier soils. Since most of the grains are shipped to New Orelans for entry into the world market, cattle and hog raising are relatively unimportant. The combined number of hogs and cattle only equals the number of human inhabitants, whereas in northern Missouri hogs and cattle exceed the human population by as much as eighteen times.

Cape Girardeau, Sikeston, Poplar Bluff, and Kennett are the main regional trade centers for the Southeast Lowlands. Cape Girardeau, situated behind the Mississippi River floodwall and on the bluff overlooking the river, is the largest city in the region. Its main business section has shifted from Water Street, behind the levee, to Main Street and Broadway. To the northwest, on the heights near Southeast Missouri State University, is a wealthier residential area.

Cape Girardeau was first settled by American families from North Carolina, Tennessee, and Kentucky; later the community attracted many German settlers. However, the town's growth was halted when the U.S. Land Commission rejected early Spanish land titles. With city lots in Cape Girardeau under clouded title, the county seat was moved to Jackson. After 1836 when land titles were confirmed, "Cape" again began to develop and in growth and commerce outstripped Jackson to become the leading city in Cape Girardeau County. Cape Girardeau has

profited from river trade, Bootheel agriculture—particularly wheat for its flour mills—education, and industry.

In 1880 Louis Houck organized the Cape Girardeau Railway Company. The new railroad stimulated growth, and soon other lines were extended to tap Cape Girardeau's traditional wagon trade area and to capture new trade and commerce. Today, Cape Girardeau is served by Interstate 55 and U.S. 61. Barge traffic on the Mississippi River is of some importance and the city is now served by Delta Airlines.

A 1980 manufacturing directory listed seventy-seven establishments of which nine employed more than 100 workers. Two plants employed more than 500 workers: Charmin Paper Products Company and Florsheim Shoe Company. Smaller manufacturing firms produce household electrical appliances, men's clothing, cement and concrete blocks, polyethylene, and beef and sausage.

Poplar Bluff has a geographic site similar to that of Cape Girardeau. It is built on the Ozark Escarpment where the Black River exits from the Ozarks onto the Southeastern Alluvial Plain. The older business district occupies a dozen blocks on the floodplain and the better residential districts stretch back across the upland to the north. A new commercial district has grown up along the stretch of U.S. 60–62 leading north through the west part of the city.

Founded in 1850 as the seat of Butler County, Poplar Bluff grew slowly until 1873 when the St. Louis and Iron Mountain Railroad linked its trade area with St. Louis and points east. The economy of the town has been supported at various times by the lumbering industry, mining of sink-fill iron deposits, trade with farms and smaller towns, employment in the Missouri Pacific and Frisco (Burlington Northern) switching yards and shops, and an assortment of manufacturing plants. In recent years Poplar Bluff has profited as the site of Three-Rivers Junior College. Major manufacturing plants in 1980 included Florsheim Shoe Company (men's shoes) with 400 employees; H. W. Gossard Company (ladies lingerie), 226; Reinell Boats Incorporated (boats), 250; Rowe Furniture Corporation (upholstered furniture), 350; and Smiley Container Corporation (candy boxes), 235.

Sikeston, at the junction of Interstate 55 and U.S. 60, is well located to capitalize on modern truck transportation. It has a long history as a railroad junction and shipping point and as a major farm trade center. Settlement was made in the vicinity prior to the Louisiana Purchase in 1803, but earlier attempts to build a town were not successful. Sikeston was platted by John Sikes in 1860. Like other communities in southeastern Missouri, it experienced a period of activity during the lumbering era that followed the Civil War. Cheap lands bred large plantations, which, with the drainage of lowland areas, brought rapid agricultural development. This wealth was expressed in gingerbread mansions with fenced lawns and cast-iron fountains, in the trim columns of grain elevators, and in the low corrugated-metal sheds of cotton gins and compresses.

A 1980 manufacturing directory lists twenty-six establishments in Sikeston. A half-dozen larger plants employ between 100 and 600 workers in the fabrication of such diverse products as athletic equipment, bakery goods, locks, men's shoes, polyethylene milk cartons, and electrical cords. Sikeston is considered to be a good shopping town, and its function as a grain and cotton market remains strong. The main commercial district is located close by the railroad tracks near the city center. A new commercial strip has grown up along U.S. 61 on the south side.

Kennett has been the business and governmental center for Dunklin County since the county was organized. Kennett was until recently a "cotton town." Its economy continues to rest on an agricultural base, but recently there is less emphasis on cotton and more emphasis on such crops as soybeans, wheat, and corn. Nevertheless cotton is still the recognized "money crop." Cotton paid for the substantial houses and

the rows of corrugated-iron cotton gins and brick and frame warehouses. Banks continue to lend money in the spring at "planting time" and collect at "harvest time" in the fall, when roads are lined with trucks and wagons on the way to the gins. There are about a dozen manufacturing plants, the largest of which include Ely and Walker of Kennett, Incorporated (men's shirts) with 338 employees; Emerson Electric (electric motors), 1,150; and Uniroyal Incorporated (industrial rubber hose), 180.

Ten smaller towns have populations in excess of 1,000. They are located on low, well-drained sandy ridges that were consequently settled early. In the days before the swamps were drained, these towns were isolated and their trade areas extended mainly north-south along the ridges; travel across the intervening swamps to another sandy swell was difficult and sometimes impossible. When railroads were built through the area, lumber mills were built; and later when the swamps were drained they became farm marketing and service centers. As in other sections of Missouri, the smaller towns have attracted a few industries. An inventory of manufacturers in the small towns in southeastern Missouri shows that shoes, clothing, light-metal products, lumber products, and food processing are important.

The rural landscape of the Southeastern Alluvial Basin region is stikingly different from that of any other section of Missouri. Crop farming dominates the scene. Little land is reserved for pasture, and fields are usually unfenced. Levees for flood control are planted in grass to provide some pasture. Because few livestock are kept, there are few barns, feedlots, or corrals.

Most of the sharecropper shacks have been demolished, although a few, usually unpainted and in dilapidated condition, still remain. Many new farmhouses have been built and old ones remodeled and enlarged. Household furnishings are much improved over those prevalent forty or fifty years ago. Houses are better painted, better furnished, better heated; and more than half are air-conditioned. Carpeting, paneling, and draperies are liberally used. Rural electrification has made the material culture—in the form of televisions, washers, driers, dishwashers, and vacuum sweepers—equivalent to that of town and city dwellers.

SELECTED REFERENCES

Augustin, Byron, and Kenneth E. Reger. "Rural Villages in Decline: Nodaway County, Missouri." *Transactions of the Missouri Academy of Science,* vol. 6, pp. 11–18. 1972.

Barber, Melvin C., III. "Change in the System of Central Places of the St. Francis Region." Ph.D. dissertation, Southern Illinois University (Carbondale), 1971.

Bird, Ronald. *Contributions of Tourist Trade to Incomes of People in the Missouri Ozarks.* University of Missouri Agricultural Experiment Station, bulletin 799. Columbia: University of Missouri Press, 1962.

Bird, Ronald, and R. D. Fenley. *Contribution of Part-Time Residents to the Local Economy of a County in the Missouri Ozarks, 1960.* University of Missouri Agricultural Experiment Station, bulletin 814. Columbia: University of Missouri Press, 1962.

Bird, Ronald, and Frank Miller. *Where Ozark Tourists Come From and Their Impact on Local Economy.* University of Missouri Agricultural Experiment Station, bulletin 798. Columbia: University of Missouri Press, 1962.

Bratton, Samuel T. *The Geography of the St. Francis Basin.* University of Missouri Studies, vol. 1, pp. 1–54. Columbia, 1926.

Carpenter, Rawlin M. "Geography of the Southeast Missouri Lowlands." Master's thesis, University of Missouri (Columbia), 1949.

Christensen, David E., and Robert A. Harper, eds. *The Mississippi-Ohio Confluence Area. A Geographic Interpretation of the Paducah 1:250,000 Topographic Map.* National Council for Geographic Education Special Publication no. 12. Normal: Illinois State University, 1967.

Collier, James E. "Geographic Regions of Missouri." *Annals of the Association of American Geographers,* vol. 45, pp. 368–392. 1955.

Conoyer, John W. *The St. Louis Gateway. A Geographic Interpretation of the St. Louis 1:250,000 Topographic Map.* National Council for Geographic Education Special Publication no. 14. Normal: Illinois State University, 1967.

Cralle, Waldo O. "Social Change and Isolation in the Ozark Mountain Region of Missouri." Ph.D. dissertation, University of Minnesota, 1934.

Crisler, Robert M. "Cities of Central Missouri." *Economic Geography,* vol. 23, pp. 72–75. 1947.

Duffield, Benny. "Comparisons of Float Trip Recreation Opportunities by Visitors to the Eleven Point River." Master's thesis, University of Missouri (Columbia), 1972.

Dulles, Foster Rhea. *A History of Recreation: America Learns to Play.* New York: Meredith Publishing Co., 1965.

Garland, John, ed. *The North American Midwest.* New York: John Wiley and Sons, 1955.

Gerstaker, Friedrich. *Wild Sports in the Far West.* Durham, N.C.: Duke University Press, 1968.

Gist, Noel P., ed. *Missouri: Its Resources, People and Institutions.* Columbia, Mo.: Curators of the University of Missouri, 1950.

Hall, Leonard. *Stars Upstream.* Columbia: University of Missouri Press, 1958.

Hawksley, Oscar. *Missouri Ozark Waterways.* Jefferson City, Mo.: Missouri Department of Conservation, 1965.

Kersten, Earl W., Jr. "Changing Economy and Landscape in a Missouri Ozarks Area." *Annals of the Association of American Geographers,* vol. 48, pp. 398–418. 1958.

Missouri Directory of Manufacturing, Mining, Industrial Services, Industrial Supplies, 1980. St. Louis: Informative Data Co., 1980.

Missouri Farm Facts, 1980. Compiled by the Missouri Crop and Livestock Reporting Service, Missouri Department of Agriculture, Jefferson City, Mo.: 1980.

Missouri State Highway Commission and Writers' Program of the Works Progress Administration. *Missouri: A Guide to the "Show Me" State.* American Guide Series. New York: Duell, Sloan and Pearce, 1941.

Rafferty, Milton D. *Historical Atlas of Missouri.* Norman: University of Oklahoma Press, 1982.

————. *The Ozarks: Land and Life.* Norman: University of Oklahoma Press, 1980.

————. "Persistence Versus Change in the Land Use and Landscape in the Springfield, Missouri, Vicinity of the Ozarks." Ph.D. dissertation, University of Nebraska, 1970.

Sauer, Carl O. *The Geography of the Ozark Highland of Missouri.* Geographic Society of Chicago Bulletin no. 7. Chicago: University of Chicago Press, 1920.

Schoolcraft, Henry Rowe. "Journal of a Tour into the Interior of Missouri and Arkansas in 1818 and 1819." In *Schoolcraft in the Ozarks,* ed. by Hugh Parks. Van Buren, Ark.: Press-Argus, 1955.

Schroeder, Walter A. *The Eastern Ozarks.* National Council for Geographic Education Special Publication no. 13. Normal: Illinois State University, 1967.

Shaner, Dolph. *The Story of Joplin.* New York: Stratford House, 1948.

Snider, Felix E., and Earl A. Collins. *Cape Girardeau, Biography of a City.* Cape Girardeau, Mo.: Ramfre Press, 1956.

U.S. Department of Commerce, Bureau of the Census. *Census of Population, 1980.* vol. 1, chapter A, pt. 27, "Missouri." Washington, D.C.: Government Printing Office, 1982.

Vogel, Robert S. "The Lake of the Ozarks Region, Missouri: A Study in Recreational Geography." Master's thesis, Michigan State University, 1957.

APPENDIXES

Appendix A

Selected Economic and Social Statistics

Total enrollment in universities and senior colleges, 1977	122,866
Total enrollment in public schools, grades K through 12, 1977	1,008,186
Total personal income, 1978	$35,538,000,000
Per capita personal income, 1978	$7,313
Total labor force, 1978	2,262,000
Total employed in manufacturing, 1978	454,000
Total employed in government, 1978	335,700
Total employed in federal government, 1978	67,600
Average hourly earnings in manufacturing, 1978	$6.21
Total motor vehicle registrations, 1978 (excluding military)	3,125,000
Total passenger car registrations, 1978	2,345,000
Tons of waterborne freight handled in Missouri's ports, 1977	1,956 (1,774 t)
Total number of farms, 1978	118,000
Average size of farms, 1978 (acres)	274 (111 ha)
Total land in farms, 1978 (acres) 32,300,000	(13,081,500 ha)
Cash receipts from farming, 1978	$2,911,660,000
Cash receipts from sale of livestock, 1978	$1,667,339,000
Cash receipts from sale of crops, 1978	$1,244,321,000
Total value of mineral production, 1976	$785,160,000
Value of lead production, 1976	$231,458,000
Rank of Missouri in Mineral production, 1976	21
Total tax revenues, 1978	$1,784,396,000
Revenues from sales and gross receipts taxes, 1978 . .	$1,050,310,000
Revenues from licenses, 1978	$160,326,000
Revenues from individual income taxes, 1978	$438,604,000
Assessed value of real estate, 1978	$7,463,800,000
Assessed value of tangible personal property, 1978 . .	$1,852,100,000
Assessed value of total public utilities	$1,277,200,000
Assessed value of merchants and manufacturers	$746,100,000
Total assessed value	$11,339,100,000

Source: Statistical Abstract for Missouri. College of Business and Public Administration, University of Missouri, Columbia, 1980.

APPENDIX B

Agricultural Statistics for Missouri's Geographic Regions (hectares shown in parentheses)

	Corn Acres (ha)		Percentage of Cropland in Corn	Wheat Acres (ha)		Percentage of Cropland in Wheat	Soybeans Acres (ha)		Percentage of Cropland in Soybeans	Number of Cattle	Number of Hogs
Till Plains Province											
Northwest Loess Hills	389,140	(157,602)	26.0	29,160	(11,810)	2.0	420,110	(170,145)	28.0	424,290	424,290
Grand River Region	289,010	(117,049)	12.0	27,200	(11,106)	1.0	755,160	(305,840)	32.0	576,220	531,450
West-Central Loess Hills	259,020	(104,904)	22.0	39,680	(16,071)	3.0	322,650	(130,674)	27.0	264,330	385,160
Chariton River Hills	106,390	(43,088)	12.0	13,090	(5,302)	2.0	236,390	(95,738)	28.0	393,900	186,400
Wyaconda Hills	157,050	(63,606)	18.0	9,790	(3,965)	1.0	315,810	(127,903)	37.0	180,090	195,360
Audrain Prairies	198,860	(80,539)	13.0	33,830	(13,702)	2.0	629,060	(254,770)	42.0	307,280	503,800
Mississippi River Hills	159,800	(64,719)	19.0	41,380	(16,759)	5.0	287,950	(116,620)	34.0	162,780	389,610
Western Plains Province											
Osage Plains	131,370	(53,205)	9.0	68,380	(27,694)	5.0	253,899	(102,829)	17.0	414,440	323,430
Cherokee Plains	47,410	(19,201)	8.0	72,870	(29,513)	12.0	220,470	(89,291)	36.0	245,280	125,340
Ozark Province											
Springfield Plain	15,165	(6,142)	1.0	60,750	(24,604)	4.0	112,790	(45,680)	9.0	661,080	168,420
White River Hills	770	(312)	0.1	2,200	(891)	0.4	1,125	(456)	0.2	320,390	91,350
Central Plateau	5,465	(2,213)	0.1	9,625	(3,899)		35,720	(14,467)	0.8	551,980	177,670
Osage-Gasconade Hills	16,840	(6,821)	3.0	10,270	(4,160)	2.0	23,795	(9,637)	4.0	261,550	137,480
Northern Ozark Border	78,240	(31,688)	9.0	43,080	(17,448)	5.0	106,935	(43,309)	12.0	291,510	318,820
Courtois Hills	4,875	(1,974)	0.1	4,385	(1,776)	0.5	29,190	(11,822)	0.8	133,912	75,170
St. Francois Mountains	6,742	(2,731)	2.9	2,235	(906)	1.0	2,335	(946)	1.0	73,110	34,010
Eastern Ozark Border	62,680	(25,386)	12.0	38,040	(15,407)	7.0	95,830	(38,812)	17.0	149,230	214,990
Southeast Lowlands Province											
Southeastern Ridge and Basin	53,170	(21,534)	11.0	63,490	(25,714)	13.0	143,450	(58,098)	4.0	38,510	40,430
Southeastern Alluvial Basin	109,820	(44,478)	8.0	204,590	(82,859)	14.0	1,033,700	(418,649)	10.0	36,080	37,090
Urban Regions											
St. Louis Region	27,420	(11,106)	13.0	21,840	(8,846)	10.0	72,460	(29,347)	35.0	34,060	41,600
Kansas City Region	36,830	(14,917)	12.0	14,920	(6,043)	5.0	51,990	(21,056)	16.0	80,460	57,150

Source: Missouri Crop and Livestock Reporting Service. Missouri Farm Facts, 1980. Missouri Department of Agriculture, Jefferson City, 1980.

APPENDIX C

Area and Population of Missouri's Geographic Regions

	Area Miles^2	(km^2)	Population	Population Density per Mile^2	(km^2)
Till Plains Province					
Northwestern Loess Hills	3,397	(8,798)	217,692	64	(25)
Grand River Region	5,729	(14,838)	106,747	19	(7)
West-Central Loess Hills	2,923	(7,570)	98,573	34	(13)
Chariton River Hills	2,766	(7,164)	100,468	36	(14)
Wyaconda Hills	2,201	(5,700)	42,252	19	(7)
Audrain Prairies	4,014	(10,396)	140,658	36	(14)
Mississippi River Hills	2,320	(6,008)	116,385	50	(19)
Western Plains Province					
Osage Plains	3,764	(9,748)	151,379	40	(16)
Cherokee Plains	2,578	(6,677)	55,121	21	(8)
Ozark Province					
Springfield Plain	5,093	(13,190)	387,639	76	(29)
White River Hills	3,520	(9,117)	87,347	24	(9)
Central Plateau	6,743	(17,466)	161,161	23	(9)
Osage-Gasconade Hills	3,718	(9,629)	112,043	30	(11)
Northern Ozark Border	4,204	(10,888)	271,130	64	(24)
Courtois Hills	4,670	(12,095)	82,764	17	(6)
St. Francois Mountains	1,872	(4,848)	72,378	38	(15)
Eastern Ozark Border	2,113	(5,472)	114,860	54	(21)
Southeast Lowlands Province					
Southeastern Ridge and Basin	1,280	(3,315)	68,450	53	(20)
Southeastern Alluvial Basin			135,459		
Urban Regions					
St. Louis Region	1,424	(3,688)	1,621,152	1,138	(441)
Kansas City Region	1,188	(3,076)	729,841	614	(237)
Total	68,995	(178,697)	4,908,288	71	(27)

Source: U.S. Department of Commerce, Bureau of the Census. Census of Population, 1980. Vol. 1, Chapter A, pt. 27, "Missouri." Washington, D.C.: Government Printing Office, 1982.

248

Appendix D

Area and Population of Missouri's Counties, 1980

County	Area Mi^2	(km^2)	Population Total	Population Density Mi^2	(km^2)
Adair	572	(1481)	24,894	44	(17)
Andrew	436	(1129)	14,027	32	(12)
Atchison	549	(1421)	8,606	16	(6)
Audrain	692	(1792)	26,391	38	(15)
Barry	763	(2027)	24,362	31	(12)
Barton	594	(1538)	11,259	19	(7)
Bates	841	(2178)	15,896	18	(7)
Benton	735	(1903)	12,195	17	(6)
Bollinger	621	(1608)	10,325	17	(6)
Boone	685	(1774)	100,240	146	(57)
Buchanan	404	(1046)	87,720	217	(84)
Butler	715	(1851)	37,637	53	(20)
Caldwell	430	(1113)	8,672	20	(8)
Callaway	835	(2162)	32,404	39	(15)
Camden	640	(1657)	18,394	29	(11)
Cape Girardeau	574	(1486)	58,745	102	(40)
Carroll	697	(1805)	12,116	17	(7)
Carter	506	(1310)	5,429	11	(4)
Cass	698	(1807)	50,982	73	(28)
Cedar	490	(1269)	11,894	24	(9)
Chariton	754	(1952)	10,454	14	(5)
Christian	567	(1468)	22,401	40	(15)
Clark	506	(1310)	8,458	17	(6)
Clay	412	(1067)	136,196	331	(127)
Clinton	420	(1087)	15,823	38	(15)
Cole	384	(994)	56,561	147	(57)
Cooper	566	(1465)	14,585	26	(10)
Crawford	760	(1968)	18,176	24	(9)
Dade	504	(1305)	7,365	15	(6)
Dallas	537	(1390)	12,104	23	(9)
Daviess	563	(1458)	8,932	16	(6)
De Kalb	423	(1095)	8,185	19	(7)
Dent	756	(1958)	14,538	19	(7)
Douglas	809	(2095)	11,586	14	(6)
Dunklin	543	(1406)	36,244	67	(26)
Franklin	934	(2419)	71,158	76	(30)
Gasconade	519	(1344)	13,076	25	(10)
Gentry	488	(1263)	7,806	16	(6)
Greene	677	(1753)	183,653	271	(105)
Grundy	435	(1126)	11,951	27	(11)
Harrison	720	(1864)	9,880	14	(5)
Henry	734	(1901)	19,684	27	(10)
Hickory	377	(976)	6,375	17	(7)
Holt	458	(1186)	6,915	15	(6)
Howard	472	(1222)	9,965	21	(8)
Howell	920	(2382)	28,805	31	(12)
Iron	554	(1434)	11,068	20	(8)
Jackson	603	(1561)	627,967	1042	(402)
Jasper	642	(1662)	86,879	135	(52)
Jefferson	668	(1730)	145,924	218	(84)
Johnson	826	(2139)	38,995	47	(18)
Knox	512	(1326)	5,530	11	(4)

County	Area Mi^2	(km^2)	Population Total	Population Density Mi^2	(km^2)
Laclede	770	(1994)	24,347	32	(12)
Lafayette	632	(1636)	29,913	47	(18)
Lawrence	619	(1603)	28,917	47	(18)
Lewis	508	(1315)	10,898	21	(8)
Lincoln	625	(1618)	22,147	35	(14)
Linn	622	(1610)	15,557	25	(10)
Livingston	530	(1372)	15,806	30	(12)
McDonald	540	(1398)	14,913	28	(11)
Macon	798	(2066)	16,443	21	(8)
Madison	496	(1284)	10,726	22	(8)
Maries	525	(1359)	7,541	14	(6)
Marion	438	(1134)	28,611	65	(25)
Mercer	455	(1178)	4,696	10	(4)
Miller	600	(1554)	18,550	31	(12)
Mississippi	415	(1331)	15,664	30	(12)
Moniteau	419	(1085)	12,183	29	(11)
Monroe	669	(1732)	9,699	15	(6)
Montgomery	534	(1383)	11,500	22	(8)
Morgan	592	(1533)	13,755	23	(9)
New Madrid	679	(1758)	22,852	34	(13)
Newton	629	(1629)	40,437	64	(25)
Nodaway	877	(2271)	22,293	25	(10)
Oregon	784	(2030)	10,232	13	(5)
Osage	608	(1574)	11,981	20	(8)
Ozark	732	(1895)	7,965	11	(4)
Pemiscot	493	(1276)	25,032	51	(20)
Perry	471	(1219)	16,783	36	(14)
Pettis	679	(1758)	36,482	54	(21)
Phelps	677	(1753)	33,725	50	(19)
Pike	681	(1763)	17,493	26	(10)
Platte	427	(1105)	46,207	108	(42)
Polk	637	(1649)	18,806	30	(11)
Pulaski	551	(1427)	42,029	76	(29)
Putnam	518	(1341)	6,118	12	(5)
Ralls	478	(1238)	8,874	19	(7)
Randolph	473	(1225)	25,413	54	(21)
Ray	573	(1484)	21,434	37	(14)
Reynolds	817	(2116)	7,231	9	(3)
Ripley	639	(1655)	12,452	19	(8)
St. Charles	551	(1427)	143,659	261	(101)
St. Clair	697	(1805)	8,617	12	(5)
St. Francois	457	(1183)	42,630	93	(36)
St. Louis	499	(1292)	967,428	1939	(749)
St. Louis City	61	(157)	450,790	7,390	(2871)
Ste. Genevieve	499	(1292)	15,151	30	(12)
Saline	757	(1960)	24,916	33	(13)
Schuyler	306	(792)	4,964	16	(6)
Scotland	441	(1142)	5,436	12	(5)
Scott	421	(1090)	39,582	94	(36)
Shannon	999	(2587)	7,895	8	(3)
Shelby	501	(1297)	7,900	16	(6)
Stoddard	823	(2131)	28,959	35	(14)
Stone	449	(1162)	15,604	35	(13)
Sullivan	654	(1693)	7,478	11	(4)

(Continued)

County	Area Mi^2	(km^2)	Population Total	Population Density Mi^2	(km^2)
Taney	615	(1592)	20,464	33	(13)
Texas	1183	(3063)	21,067	18	(7)
Vernon	838	(2170)	19,798	24	(9)
Warren	426	(1103)	14,817	35	(13)
Washington	760	(1968)	18,017	24	(9)
Wayne	766	(1983)	11,338	15	(6)
Webster	590	(1528)	20,458	35	(13)
Worth	267	(691)	2,995	11	(4)
Wright	684	(1771)	16,139	24	(9)

Source: U.S. Department of Commerce, Bureau of the Census. Census of Population, 1980. Vol. 1, Chapter A, pt. 27, "Missouri." Washington, D.C.: Government Printing Office, 1982.

INDEX